Applications and Innovations in Intelligent Systems IX

Springer
London
Berlin
Heidelberg
New York
Barcelona
Hong Kong
Milan
Paris
Santa Clara
Singapore
Tokyo

Ann Macintosh, Mike Moulton
and Alun Preece (Eds)

Applications and Innovations in Intelligent Systems IX

Proceedings of ES2001, the Twenty-first SGES International Conference on Knowledge Based Systems and Applied Artificial Intelligence, Cambridge, December 2001

Springer

Ann Macintosh, BSc, CEng
International Teledemocracy Centre, Napier University, Edinburgh, UK

Mike Moulton, BSc
Department of Accounting and Management Science, Portsmouth Business School, University of Portsmouth, Portsmouth, UK

Alun Preece, BSc, PhD
Department of Computer Science, University of Aberdeen, Aberdeen, UK

British Library Cataloguing in Publication Data.
Applications and innovations in intelligent systems IX :
    proceedings of ES2001, the twenty-first SGES International
    Conference on Knowledge Based System and Applied
    Artificial Intelligence, Cambridge, December, 2001
    1.Expert systems (Computer science) - Congresses
    2.Intelligent control systems - Congresses
    I.Macintosh, Ann II.Moulton, Michael III.Preece, Alun
    1968- IV.British Computer Society. Specialist Group on
    Expert Systems V.SGES International Conference on Knowledge
    Based Systems and Applied Artificial Intelligence (21st :
    2001 : Cambridge, England)
    006.3'3
    ISBN 1852335300

Library of Congress Cataloging-in-Publication Data
A catalog record for this book is available from the Library of Congress.

ISBN 1-85233-530-0 Springer-Verlag London Berlin Heidelberg
a member of BertelsmannSpringer Science+Business Media GmbH
http://www.springer.co.uk

Typesetting: Camera ready by contributors
Printed and bound at the Athenæum Press Ltd., Gateshead, Tyne and Wear
34/3830-543210 Printed on acid-free paper SPIN 10842802

APPLICATION PROGRAMME CHAIRMAN'S INTRODUCTION

Ann Macintosh
Napier University, UK

The papers in this volume are the refereed application papers presented at ES2001, the Twenty-first SGES International Conference on Knowledge Based Systems and Applied Artificial Intelligence, held in Cambridge in December 2001. The scope of the application papers has expanded over recent years to cover not just innovative applications using traditional knowledge based systems, but also to include applications demonstrating the whole range of AI technologies. These papers continue to illustrate the maturity of AI as a commercially viable technology to solve real world problems.

The papers were subject to refereeing by at least two expert referees. All papers that were in any way controversial were discussed in depth by the Application Programme Committee. For the ES2001 Application Stream, a paper is acceptable even if it describes a system that has not yet been installed, provided the application is original and the paper discusses the kind of things that would help others needing to solve a similar problem. Papers have been selected to highlight critical areas of success - and failure - and to present the benefits and lessons learnt to other developers.

This volume contains sixteen papers describing deployed or emerging applications in a range of diverse areas: business and commerce, engineering, manufacturing, knowledge and information management, and music.

This year the best refereed application paper is "Finite Element Mesh Design Expert System" by B. Dolšak, University of Maribor, Slovenia. The Finite Element Method is one of the most successful numerical methods used by engineers to analyse stresses and deformations in physical structures. However the design of the appropriate geometric mesh model is a very difficult and time consuming task. The system described in this paper, called FEMDES, is a consultative rule-based system to support the mesh design. The knowledge base comprises some 1900 rules and was built using machine learning techniques.

This is the ninth volume in the *Applications and Innovations* series. The Technical Stream papers from ES2001 are published as a companion volume under the title *Research and Development in Intelligent Systems XVIII*.

The conference was organised by SGES, the British Computer Society Specialist Group on Knowledge Based Systems and Applied Artificial Intelligence. On behalf of the conference organising committee I should like to thank all those who contributed to the organisation of this year's technical programme, in particular the programme committee members, the referees and our administrators Linsay Turbert and Lynn Harrison.

Ann Macintosh
Application Programme Chairman, ES2001

ACKNOWLEDGEMENTS

ES2001 CONFERENCE COMMITTEE

Dr. Alun Preece, University of Aberdeen *(Conference Chairman)*
Dr Robert Milne, Intelligent Applications Ltd *(Deputy Conference Chairman, Finance and Publicity)*
Richard Ellis, Stratum Management Ltd *(Deputy Conference Chairman, Exhibition)*
Prof. Adrian Hopgood, Nottingham Trent University *(Tutorial Organiser)*
Ann Macintosh, Napier University *(Application Programme Chair)*
Mike Moulton, University of Portsmouth *(Deputy Application Programme Chair)*
Professor Max Bramer, University of Portsmouth *(Technical Programme Chair)*
Dr Frans Coenen, University of Liverpool *(Deputy Technical Programme Chair)*

APPLICATION PROGRAMME COMMITTEE

Ann Macintosh, Napier University *(Chair)*
Mike Moulton, University of Portsmouth *(Deputy Chair)*
Richard Ellis, Stratum Management Ltd
Rob Milne, Intelligent Applications Ltd
Richard Wheeler

APPLICATION PROGRAMME REFEREES

Andreas Abecker (DFKI)
Stuart Aitken (University of Edinburgh)
Paul Chung (Loughborough University)
Richard Ellis (Stratum Management Ltd)
John L. Gordon (Applied Knowledge Research Institute)
Robert de Hoog (University of Amsterdam)
John Kingston (University of Edinburgh)
Alan Montgomery
Alun Preece (University of Aberdeen)
Ulrich Reimer (Swiss Life)
Peter Ross (Napier University)
Paul Slater

CONTENTS

SESSION 4: KNOWLEDGE AND INFORMATION MANAGEMENT

SESSION 5: INTELLIGENT SYSTEMS

BEST APPLICATION PAPER

Finite Element Mesh Design Expert System

Bojan Dolšak

Faculty of Mechanical Engineering, University of Maribor, Slovenia
dolsak@uni-mb.si

Abstract: The paper presents a consultative rule-based expert system for finite element mesh design. The aim of the expert system presented is to propose the appropriate type of the finite elements and determine the resolution values for the finite element mesh to be used for the analysis. The extensive knowledge base, comprising about 1900 rules, was built mainly by the use of machine learning techniques. Several examples will confirm that an expert system shell written in Prolog enables efficient use of the knowledge base and adequate communication between the system and the user. The system has the ability to explain the inference process. Thus, it can also be used as a teaching tool for inexperienced users – students. The results of the experimental use of the system are encouraging and can be used as guidelines for further developments and improvements of the system.

1.   Introduction

The Finite Element Method (FEM) is the most successful numerical method used extensively by engineers to analyse stresses and deformations in physical structures [1]. In FEM, such structures have to be represented as finite element meshes. Defining an appropriate geometric mesh model that ensures low approximation errors and avoids unnecessary computational overheads is a very difficult and time-consuming task. It is the major bottleneck in the FEM analysis process. In practice, finite element mesh design is still based mostly on the user's experience. Despite extensive research activities in this field of application, no satisfactory general method exists for automatic construction of the appropriate finite element model.

Usually a few different meshes need to be created until the right one is found. The trouble is that each mesh has to be analysed, since the next mesh is generated with respect to the results derived from the previous one. Considering that one FEM analysis can take from a few minutes to several hours and even days of computer time, there obviously exists a great motivation to design "optimal" finite element mesh models more efficiently – in the first step or at least with minimum trials.

As the alternative to the conventional "trial-and-fail" approach to this problem, we will present the application of the Finite Element Mesh Design Expert System named FEMDES [2]. The system was designed to help the user to define the appropriate finite element mesh model easier, faster, and more experience independent.

The system can also help the user to gain some knowledge and experience about finite element mesh design by answering the questions "Why?" and "How?" asked by the user. In continuation of this paper, we will present the architecture of the system and some examples to show the actual performance of the system in different situations.

2.   The Architecture of the System

Figure 1 shows the architecture of the FEMDES, as it should be integrated with the existing FEM software.

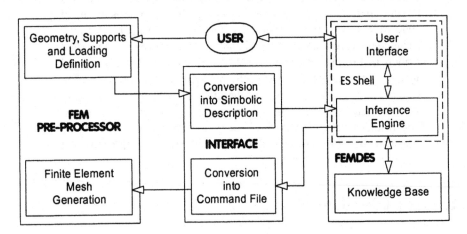

Figure 1. FEMDES integrated with the commercial FEM pre-processor.

In any case, the user has to define the problem (geometry, loads, supports). The data about the problem need to be converted from the FEM pre-processor format into the symbolic qualitative description to be used by the ES. FEMDES task is to propose the appropriate types of finite elements and determine the mesh resolution values. A command file for the mesh generator can be constructed according to the results obtained by the ES.

2.1   The Knowledge Base

FEM has been applied extensively for the last 30 years. Still, there is no clear and satisfactory formalisation of the mesh design know-how. Finite element design is still a mixture of art and experience, which is hard to describe explicitly. However, many published reports exist in terms of the problem definition, an adequate finite element mesh (chosen after several trials) and the results of the analysis. These reports were used as a source of training examples for Machine Learning (ML). Problem definitions and the appropriate finite element models from the reports were presented to the Inductive Logic Programming (ILP) system CLAUDIEN [3] to construct the rules for finite element mesh design by generalising the given examples.

Ten real-life mesh models that have been analysed in the past were used as a source of training examples. Each mesh model was represented as a collection of edges. The edges were labelled and described in terms of geometric form, loads, and supports. Some topological relations between the edges were also presented to the learning algorithm. Figure 2 shows an example of the structure with some labelled edges and part of corresponding description in Prolog syntax.

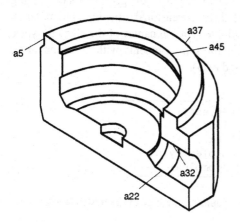

```
% Type of the edge
short(a22).
not_important(a32).
half_circuit(a37).

% Supports
fixed(a22).
two_side_fixed(a37).

% Loadings
cont_loaded(a22).
not_loaded(a37).

% Topological relations
neighbour(a5,a37).
opposite(a22,a32).
equal(a37,a45).
```

Figure 2. A structure with labelled edges and a sample of corresponding description.

The mesh data set was probably the first real-world relational data set, and became one of the most widely used training set for experimenting with ILP systems. A typical procedure of applying ML tools has been carried out [4]. This includes experimenting with several ML tools to explore the domain and the data, improving the data set according to the shortcomings exposed by the initial experiments, detection of desirable domain-specific properties of ML tools, and accordingly, the choice of a tool satisfying these properties for further improved application.

Since the training set was based on real-life mesh models, it had not been considered as perfect. Some noise was therefore expected and allowed. Thus, not all the rules in the knowledge base are equally accurate. The accuracy being considered as acceptable for the knowledge base was limited to 90%. Figure 3 presents the example of the classification rule with 100% accuracy (perc_cov(1)).

```
rule(340,[perc_cov(1),body(4),cpu(19375.2)],
    (mesh(Edge1,7) :-
        usual(Edge1),
        neighbour(Edge1,Edge2),
        quarter_circuit(Edge2),
        two_side_fixed(Edge2),
        cont_loaded(Edge2))).
```

Figure 3. The example of the classification rule.

The rule presented in Figure 3 specifies seven finite elements for the "usual" edges, which have continuously loaded and both sided fixed neighbour with the quarter circuit geometric form.

Some additional rules were added into the knowledge base after the learning process. The rules for determining the appropriate type of the finite elements were also built manually. They specify the primary and secondary type of the elements to be used, considering the space dimension, complexity of the geometry, and loading case, as well as the thickness in case of three-dimensional structure. The notation used in FEM system BERSAFE [5] is adopted for the names of the element types. Figure 4 shows the example of the rule for solid elements with a second order approximation function (elements ez60 and ez45).

```
finite_element(ez60,ez45) :-
     space_dimension(3),
     thickness(thick),
     ( geometry_complexity(high) ;
     loading_case(complex) ).
```

Figure 4. The example of the rule for proposing the type of the finite elements.

The resulting knowledge base, used in FEMDES, comprises 1873 rules and 31 facts written in Prolog syntax. All the rules in the knowledge base were ordered to optimise the effectiveness and accuracy of the system. Because of the top-down search strategy implemented in Prolog, which was used as a programming language for the ES shell, the most reliable rules were placed on top of the knowledge base. The overall evaluation [4] shows the conditions within domain are well represented by the rules in the knowledge base.

2.2 Expert System Shell

From the beginning of the ES applications, several commercial tools have been developed for building ES [6]. These tools contain a domain independent inference engine, an empty knowledge base, and a user-friendly interface. With the use of these tools, development of the ES can be concentrated on the knowledge representation, while complex inference engine strategies can be neglected. However, the choice of the suitable knowledge representation scheme and inference reasoning technique is very important ingredient to the success of an ES. The available tools should therefore be used carefully.

For the FEMDES, we have built our own program to gain the most efficient correlation between the knowledge and the program part of the system. The ES shell is also written in Prolog. It makes feasible the proper use of the knowledge base for finite element mesh design (inference engine) as well as the communication between the user and the system (user interface). Very important and useful feature of the user interface is its capability to explain the inference process, by answering the questions "Why?" and "How?".

The ES shell consists of 120 rules and 13 facts, which are used to define 47 procedures – 9 for inference engine, 29 for user interface, and 9 assistant procedures mainly for operations on lists. We did not use "non-standard" procedures from the libraries to ensure the system can be easily adapted to different versions of Prolog.

A complete source code of the ES shell, together with the explanations of the algorithms performed by the program, can be found in [2].

2.3   System Requirements

Quintus Prolog (Quintus Computer Systems, Inc.) installation on the mainframe computer VAX 4000-600 was used in development phase. Yet, the ES can also be run on personal computer with Arity Prolog (Arity Corporation). The overall memory space required to run the system is about 600 KB, depending on the complexity of the problem. The running time is also quite reasonable. In our most extensive experiment, 37 CPU seconds were spent on VAX 4000-600 to determine finite element mesh parameters for the structure with 96 edges. The communication between the user and the system was reduced to minimum in that particular case.

The user has to prepare the input data file before running the system. The structure that is going to be analysed needs to be described exactly on the same way as the training examples were presented to the learning algorithm in the knowledge acquisition phase. It could be done automatically by using the geometric model of the structure. Guidelines for automatic transformation from numeric form to symbolic qualitative description are presented in [2]. Yet, at present the FEMDES is not integrated with any commercial FEM pre-processor. Thus, problem description currently needs to be made manually. It takes some time to do that, especially for the structures that are more complex. However, following a few simple algorithms the task does not require special knowledge and experience.

3.   The Application of the System

To run the system the user needs to consult it into Prolog environment. An automatic start-up is then performed by the system itself. The system is introduced and the user is asked to specify the name of the input data file. After the FEMDES is acquainted with the data, the user has three basic options (Figure 5).

```
[ type | elements | mesh | exit | help ] (mesh)  --> help

     type - determine the appropriate type of finite elements
 elements - determine the resolution values for finite element mesh
     mesh - begin the complete inference process (default)
     exit - terminate the inference process
     help - this explanation

[ type | elements | mesh | exit | help ] (mesh)  -->
```

Figure 5. Basic options explained after the user input "help".

The type of finite elements to be used for the analysis is determined considering dimension of the structure, complexity of the geometry, complexity of the loading case, and thickness of the walls of the structure. An example of the communication between the system and the user, while specifying one of the basic characteristics of the analysis, is presented in Figure 6. The user input is again typed in bold.

```
What kind of loading case is going to be considered in the analysis?
[ complex | simple | why | help ] (complex)  --> why

Complex loading case demands the use of complex finite elements.

What kind of loading case is going to be considered in the analysis?
[ complex | simple | help ] (complex)  --> help

   complex - complex loading case such as pressure (default)
   simple - simple loading case such as single point load
     help - this explanation

[ complex | simple | help ] (complex)  --> simple
```

Figure 6. Specifying the complexity of the loading case.

The system always proposes two different shaped compatible finite elements - primarily and secondary element type (Figure 7).

```
BERSAFE element type "ez60" is proposed to be used as primary
   and "ez45" as secondary element type.
[ how| change | continue | exit | help ] (continue)  --> how

   =========== Begin of the inference explanation ==========

It was told that:
   a dimension of structure to be idealised is "3"
      the geometry complexity is "high",
         loading case is "simple"
            and thickness is "thick".

Upon these parameters it was concluded that:
   BERSAFE element type "ez60" should be used as primary
      and "ez45" as secondary element type.

   =========== End of the inference explanation ===========

[ change | continue | exit | help ] (continue)  --> change

Specify the type of finite elements (small letters please):
      Primary element (ez60) -->
   Secondary element (ez45) --> ez24

"ez60" was specified as primary and
"ez24" as secondary element type.

WARNING: Specified elements are not compatible!

[ change | continue | exit | help ] (continue)  --> change
```

Figure 7. Proposed element type, inference explanation and user modification.

The secondary element type is meant to be used in case the number of the nodes in particular direction/area of the finite element mesh needs to be increased or reduced. According to his or her personal knowledge and experience, the user can chose the other element types than those proposed by the system. In the example presented in Figure 7, it was done after the system explanation how the element types were determined. Figure 7 also shows the warning appearing in case the finite element types specified by the user are not compatible.

A process of specifying a density of the finite element mesh in terms of the number of finite elements on each edge of the structure is much more complicated. Most of the rules in the knowledge base serve to that purpose. There is not enough space in this paper to present and comment quite extensive algorithm followed through performing this task. A detail explanation can be found in [2]. Let us just notice that despite a declarative nature of Prolog we had to pay the attention to procedural meaning of the program as well to prevent the endless loops in many recursive calls and to make the system as effective as possible.

Again, at any time, the user can ask the system what are the possible actions (help) and how the number of finite elements for certain edge of the structure was determined (Figure 8).

```
2 finite elements are proposed for edge "a22".

[ how | change | next | complete | exit | help ] (next)  --> help

         how - explain the inference process
      change - user amendment to the result of inference process
        next - proceed the inference process (default)
    complete - complete the inference process without further user input
        exit - terminate the inference process
        help - this explanation

[ how | change | next | complete | exit | help ] (next)  --> how

    ============ Begin of the inference explanation ===========

According to rule no. 60 (Acc=1) the edge "a22", which is:
    short and
        has opposite edge "a32", which is
            not important
should have 2 finite elements.

    ============ End of the inference explanation ============

[ change | next | complete | exit | help ] (next)  -->
```

Figure 8. Proposed number of elements, possible actions and inference explanation.

The accuracy of the rule(s) used to determine the number of finite elements, which is given in the first line of explanation for each rule participated in the classification process, can be very helpful, especially if the user is not sure about the proposed number.

Inference process presented in Figure 8 is quite simple. Only one rule from the knowledge base was used to determine the number of finite elements for the actual edge of the structure. In many cases the inference process is much more complex, as for example in Figure 9, where two rules were used to determine an interval of four classes, and two more rules to chose one single class out of the proposed interval.

The following classes are proposed for edge "a31": [1,2,3,4]

1 finite element is chosen for that edge.

[how | change | next | complete | exit | help] (next) --> **how**

  =========== Begin of the inference explanation ===========

According to recursive rule
    the edges "a31" and "a9" should have the same number of elements,
      since they are "equal".

According to rule no. 1652 (Acc=1) for the edge "a9", which is:
    fixed and
        cont_loaded and
            has neighbour edge "a47", which is:
                half_circuit
the following classes are proposed: [1,2,3,4].

Edge "a9" is opposite to edge "a3".

According to rule no. 1522 (Acc=0.916667) the edge "a3", which is:
    fixed and
        not_loaded and
            has neighbour edge "a34", which is:
                long
        and has neighbour edge "a34", which is:
                one_side_fixed and
                  one_side_loaded
should have 1 finite element.

Because edge "a9" is "short"
  and edge "a3" is "usual"
      edge "a9" should have 1 finite element less than edge "a3".

The nearest value to 0 was chosen from the list of proposed classes:

Thus 1 finite element is proposed for edge "a9".

1 finite element is therefore proposed for the edge "a31" too.

  ============= End of the inference explanation =============

[change | next | complete | exit | help] (next) -->

Figure 9. An explanation of the complex inference process.

Following the inference explanation presented in Figure 9, it can be seen many rules compare the actual edge with some other edges of the structure that are in geometric relation with this edge. If such an edge has already been classified, the number of finite elements is not determined again, since the results of the inference process are added as the facts to the program during the execution.

Because of that, the working database grows insignificantly. Yet, the effectiveness of the system is much better. The number chosen by the user is stored in case the user has modified the number of finite elements proposed by the system.

The amendments to the results of the inference process (change) are also allowed. Although it is not necessary, the usual way in such a case would be to ask the system about the inference explanation first. As it can be seen in Figure 10, the system warns the user against the changes that seem to be wrong.

```
The following classes are proposed for edge "a6": [1,2]

1 finite element is chosen for that edge.

[ how | change | next | complete | exit | help ] (next) --> change

Specify the number of finite elements for edge "a6" --> 3

3 finite elements have been specified for edge "a6".

WARNING: The specified class is not in the proposed list!
        [1,2]

[ change | next | complete | exit | help ] (next) -->
```

Figure 10. The user is warned if choosing the class, which is not in the proposed list.

The user has to leave Prolog environment before running the system again to clear the working database of all the facts that have been added to the program during the last execution. At the end, the results are written into output file specified by the user. A command file for the mesh generator can be developed upon these results. However, they can also be proceeded to the FEM pre-processor manually.

4.   Illustrative Example

The following example presents the results obtained by the FEMDES, which was employed to specify the mesh resolution values for a completely new cylindrical structure that was not included in the training set. Comparing with the reference design (Figure 11c), the performed classification accuracy was 86.67%. There were only four misclassified edges (encircled in the Figure 11a). For all quarter circuit edges, the FEMDES proposed one finite element more than in the reference design, yet this was qualified as an allowable deviation according to the construction of our training set.

With respect to the results of the FEMDES, the FEM pre-processor built almost the same finite element mesh (Figure 11b) as that designed manually (Figure 11c). Partitioning of the part into smaller sub-volumes with a maximum of six surfaces was done to satisfy the requirements of the mapped meshing procedure. This example also shows that classification accuracy may be misleading as a measure of success in this domain. The reason is that the mesh generator will automatically correct some "errors".

In this case, it actually happened. The mapped meshing technique assumes an equal number of finite elements on the opposite sides of the surfaces. The FEM pre-processor put 14 finite elements on the edges for which the FEMDES specified 11 finite elements, since the total number of finite elements on the opposite side is also 14.

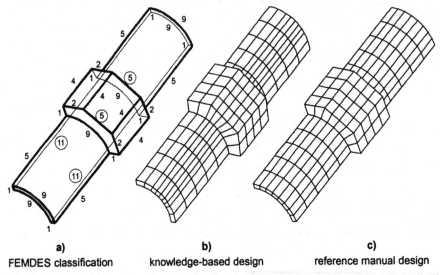

a)	b)	c)
FEMDES classification	knowledge-based design	reference manual design

Figure 11. Example – mesh design for cylindrical structure.

5. Conclusions

The paper addresses an important application of ES technology in design. One of the major bottlenecks in the process of engineering analysis using the FEM – a design of the finite element mesh model – is a subject of improvement. Currently, defining the appropriate geometric mesh model is a very difficult and time-consuming task based mainly on the user's experience.

According to our practical experience with FEM systems, it would be very difficult to extract the knowledge about finite element mesh design from the human expert. Thus, a development of the knowledge base was performed mostly by using the ML techniques. It was found a very efficient approach to this matter. The extensive knowledge base comprising some 1900 rules was built. The architecture based on production rules allows relatively simple method for its enhancement if necessary.

To simplify the learning problem, the training set used for development of the knowledge base was designed with the aim of being representative of a particular type of structures. The limitations that were taken into account are:

- All structures were cylindrical
- Only forces and pressure were considered as loads
- Highly local mesh refinement was not required

However, the FEMDES can also be applied as a general tool for determining the mesh resolution values for the real-life three-dimensional structures outside the scope of these limitations too. The results of the ES have to be adjusted subsequently according to the specific requirements of the particular analysis. Furthermore, they can always serve as a basis for an initial finite element mesh, which is subject to further adaptations considering the results of the numerical analyses. It is very important to choose a good initial mesh and minimise the number of iterative steps, leading to an appropriate mesh model. Thus, the presented ES can be very helpful to inexperienced users, especially by using the ability to explain the inference process.

The system is still not properly integrated with the existing FEM system. The data flow is therefore much more complicated as it should be. The user has to prepare the input data file for the FEMDES manually. The task does not require a lot of knowledge and experience, yet it is quite obstructive. The user also needs to pay the attention to avoid errors during manual data input. After consulting the input data, the system is robust enough to response properly in case of any user "mistakes" while communicates with the system.

Irrespective some problems that are a consequence of a current lack of proper integration between the FEMDES and conventional FEM system, the presented ES can be considered as simple for use and user friendly. Both, the time and memory space requirements of the system, are modest and do not represent any significant problem within the frame of nowadays computer hardware.

We have first presented our vision of an integrated knowledge-based system for intelligent support to finite element analysis process at the world congress on FEM in Monte Carlo in 1993 [7]. A development of the proposed system is divided into three steps, each dealing with a separate module:

- Intelligent module for guiding inexperienced users through the analysis
- Intelligent module for finite element mesh design and
- Intelligent module for post–processing the results of the analysis

The scheme, based on independent modules, enables a step-by-step development of the knowledge-based sub-systems and their direct implementation in practice. Actually, some of the FEM packages already have modules for guiding inexperienced users. Yet, their efficiency and applicability are still rather limited.

In Laboratory for Technical Software at the Faculty of Mechanical Engineering, University of Maribor, we have started to realise our vision with development of the second module – intelligent system for finite element mesh design, which is presented in this paper. The academic version of the FEMDES is in experimental usage at our faculty, mostly for the students of mechanical engineering design.

Currently, we are developing the third intelligent module for post-processing the results of the finite element analysis. We are not acquainted with any existent intelligent system in this field that might represent the basis for further development. According to our experience gained so far, the artificial intelligence application again makes sense and could be very helpful.

Acknowledgements

A research work presented was financially supported by the Ministry of Science and Technology, Republic of Slovenia and by the European Community within the action for co-operation in science and technology with Central and Eastern European countries (PECO92) - ILPNET, contract no. CIPA3510OCT920044. We are expressing our gratitude to the researchers from several ILPNET nodes that have been involved in a number of ML experiments to the finite element mesh design problem for making their learning algorithms available for that purpose. We would further like to acknowledge Professor Ivan Bratko and his AI group at Jožef Stefan Institute in Ljubljana for very fruitful co-operation. Special thanks also to Professor Trevor K. Hellen from Imperial College of Science, Technology and Medicine, London, for his suggestions, comments, and expert evaluation of the ES.

References

[1]   Zienkiewicz, O.C. & Taylor, R.L. (1988). The Finite Element Method: Basic Formulation and Linear Problems. Vol.1, McGraw-Hill Book Company, London.

[2]   Dolšak, B. (1996). A Contribution to Intelligent Mesh Design for FEM Analyses. PhD Thesis (in Slovene with English Abstract), Faculty of Mechanical Engineering, University of Maribor, Slovenia.

[3]   De Raedt, L. & Bruynooghe, M. (1993). A Theory of Clausal Discovery. Proceedings of Thirteen International Joint Conference on Artificial Intelligence, San Mateo, CA, USA, Morgan Kaufmann, pp. 1058–1063.

[4]   Dolšak, B., Bratko, I. & Jezernik, A. (1998). Application of Machine Learning in Finite Element Computation. Machine Learning, Data Mining and Knowledge Discovery: Methods and Applications (Edited by Michalski, R.R., Bratko, I. & Kubat, M.), John Wiley & Sons, pp. 147–171.

[5]   Hellen, T.K. (1970). BERSAFE: A Computer System for Stress Analysis by Finite Elements. Stress Analysis Group of Institution of Physics and the Physics Society, Guildford, Surrey, UK.

[6]   Gilmore, J.L. & Pulaski, K. (1985). A Survey of Expert System Tools. Proceedings of the IEEE Second Conference on Artificial Intelligent Application, Miami Beach, Florida, pp. 498–502.

[7]   Jezernik, A. & Dolšak, B. (1993) Expert Systems for FEM. FEM – Today and the Future, Proceedings of the Seventh World Congress on Finite Element Methods (Edited by Robinson, J.) – Monte Carlo, pp. 150–153.

SESSION 1:

BUSINESS AND COMMERCE APPLICATIONS

Residential Property Price Time Series Forecasting with Neural Networks

I. D. Wilson, S. D. Paris, J. A. Ware and D. H. Jenkins

School of Technology, University of Glamorgan,
Pontypridd, Mid Glamorgan, CF37 1DL, United Kingdom.
idwilson@glam.ac.uk
http://www.glam.ac.uk/research/

Abstract

The residential property market accounts for a substantial proportion of UK economic activity. Professional valuers estimate property values based on current bid prices (open market values). However, there is no reliable forecasting service for residential values with current bid prices being taken as the best indicator of future price movement. This approach has failed to predict the periodic market crises or to produce estimates of long-term sustainable value (a recent European Directive could be leading mortgage lenders towards the use of sustainable valuations in preference to the open market value). In this paper, we present artificial neural networks, trained using national housing transaction time-series data, which forecasts future trends within the housing market.

1   Introduction

Today's mortgage valuation process is not able to perform a socially useful role, with property valuation wholly dictated by current market forces (the open market value). This is because lenders, who manage this process, have been able to off-load the risk on to consumers and insurance companies. Major changes in the housing market can have a significant impact on the economy as a whole. The fall in UK house prices between '89 and '92 (which fell by about 25%) was a period during which the savings rate almost doubled (from just over 6% to around 12%), GDP stagnated and business confidence declined [1]. Many individuals were left in a situation of negative equity, where they had paid (and were usually still paying) more for their homes than they could realise by selling. This had a significant social cost in terms of increased repossessions and reduced labour mobility. This experience has led to a recent European Directive, which may lead mortgage lenders toward the use of sustainable value in preference to open market value. Therefore, it can be seen that the development of models that provide a sustainable valuation for properties would be of great usefulness to the consumer.

The consumer would be able to make informed decisions based upon pricing models that give a clearer indication of the real, sustainable, value of property. Accurate valuations would forestall negative equity and facilitate movement between jobs in today's mobile labour market.

The aim is that, by drawing upon economic, social and residential property transaction data at the national, regional and sub-regional level, appropriate valuation functions can be identified. The results of this preliminary, national, stage of this EPSRC funded project are presented in this paper.

First, the reader is presented with a background to traditional, linear, and non-linear approaches to forecasting. Next, an overview for the data is provided, along with an examination of the methodology that underpins the experimental work undertaken. Finally, conclusions are drawn and the plans for future work are explained.

2   Traditional time series forecasting

Forecasting is the rational prediction of future events on the basis of related past and current information. Time series forecasting is a challenging problem that has long attracted the attention of investors and academics alike. The process is comparable with modeling, where the outcome of an unknown variable is generated from known or controllable variables. A combination of statistical analysis and informed judgement can approximate the relationships between the known and unknown variables. When complete information about relationships is available, then a reliance upon the statistical data is invariably more reliable since it reflects patterns in the data in an unbiased way. [2]

Most time series consist of members that are serially dependent in the sense that one can estimate a coefficient or a set of coefficients that describe continuous members of the series from specific, time-lagged (previous) members. This process of *autoregression* can be summarised in the equation:

$$y_t = \xi + \phi_1 y_{(t-1)} + \phi_2 y_{(t-2)} + \phi_3 y_{(t-3)} + \ldots + \varepsilon \qquad (1)$$

Where y represents the values of the series at point t, ξ is a constant, ϕ_1, ϕ_2 and ϕ_3 are the linear regression coefficients, and a random error component is denoted by ε. In other words, each observation is made up of a random error component and a linear combination of prior observations.

Independent from the autoregressive process, each member in the series can also be affected by the past error ε, which cannot be accounted for by the autoregressive component, that is:

$$y_t = \mu + \varepsilon_t - \phi_1 \varepsilon_{(t-1)} - \phi_2 \varepsilon_{(t-2)} - \phi_3 \varepsilon_{(t-3)} - \ldots \qquad (2)$$

Where y represents the value of the series at point t, μ is a constant and ϕ_1, ϕ_2 and ϕ_3 are the moving average model parameters. In words, each observation is made up of a random error component ε and a linear combination of prior random errors.

Once the next value in the sequence has been predicted, this can be substituted into the equation to make further predictions. However, the practical success of models of this type are limited by their linearity, their ravenous data requirements, and because one needs to be reasonably skilled to obtain a good forecast.

3 Non-linear time series forecasting

Non-linear models, including Artificial Neural Networks (ANN) are potentially better than regression models. Indeed, it has been shown that an ANN using logistic functions can model any functional relationship, linear and non-linear. [3] It would be expected that such models are better than regression since regression is essentially a linear technique used in a non-linear problem domain.

However, although non-linear systems inherently demonstrate more potential than linear systems, implementation of such is problematic. This arises from the fact that non-linear systems will attempt to fit all data encountered, including any noise present. Therefore, processing must be stopped once all useful information has been internalized but before any noise within the data is absorbed.

Independent validation allows the training algorithm to extract what information it can from the data before identifying a point beyond which it may be mislead by noisy or ill-conditioned data. Ill-conditioning usually arises when similar, or linearly dependent, input data are associated with very different output data.

Here, the data set is split into two parts, the training set and the test set. The test set is only used for independent validation; it is not used for training, but only for independently assessing the quality of the mapping being obtained from the training set. If the quality of the training set is good, then the error in predicting the outputs from the independent test set will fall during training. This process continues until there is no measurable improvement, indeed, the error will increase providing an indication that the model may have begun to assimilate noise within the training set and a useful heuristic for ending the modelling process.

The fall in the measure of error happens before the rise because there is a strong tendency for the best fit to the underlying model to be located close to the unbiased starting point. Therefore, the best fit to the underlying model is located at the point where the validation set measure of error is minimised.

Unfortunately, partitioning the data set in this way is, itself, problematic when the data set is small. For large data sets, this is not a problem, but most property data sets cover long periods, punctuated by a relatively small number of statistical measures. Here, partitioning the data set into two parts might take valuable data points away from the training set and consequently impede the ANN's ability to extrapolate a reliable model from the time series. An alternative approach, where the data is not partitioned and training is instead terminated at a pre-determined measure of error would be advantageous.

One such measure, the Gamma (or Near Neighbour) test can provide an estimate for the best Mean Squared Error (MSError) that can be achieved by a continuous or smooth (bounded first partial derivatives) data model. [4] This simple technique promises to provide a means for simplifying the design process for constructing a smooth data model such as an ANN.

4   The Gamma Test

The Gamma (near neighbour) test is a data analysis algorithm that estimates the Mean Squared Error (MSE) that can be achieved by a model constructed using this data. This test can be used to simplify the process of constructing a smooth data model, such as an ANN. An overview of the technique is provided here.

If a time series can be assumed to hide an underlying smooth model

$$y = f(v) + r \qquad (3)$$

where y is a scalar output and v is an input vector, restricted to a close bounded set $v \subseteq R^m$, and r represents noise, then the Gamma test can provide a data-derived estimate for the variance of r given that:

- the training and testing data are different sample sets;
- the training set inputs are non-sparse in input-space;
- each output is determined from the inputs by a deterministic process which is the same for both training and test sets;
- each output is subjected to statistical noise with finite variance whose distribution may be different for different outputs, but which is the same in both training and test sets for corresponding outputs [*ibid.*]

Given this, small variations in v, written Δv, and y, written Δy, should be constant between points in the time series that are close together. The gradient, $\Delta y/\Delta v$, between neighbours is more or less constant. Therefore, for each small successive section of the time series, if Δv is decreased to zero then Δy should also tend to zero provided there is no noise within the data. [5] With property prices, although Δv tends to zero, Δy does not because of the noise within the data, with the Gamma test providing an estimate for this noise.

The test is applied to each point within the time series, in turn. The distance between it and the nearest neighbour in terms of the input vector v, and the corresponding output scalar value y is found, and the process is repeated for n nearest neighbours. The corresponding, squared, v and y, distances are plotted on a graph and a linear regression line is then fitted to the points. This, linear regression line provides two useful measures, namely:

- the intercept of the line on the y-squared axis when Δv is zero, which gives the MSE, or Gamma value; and
- the gradient of the line, which provides an indication of the complexity of the model under analysis. Where, the steeper the line the more complex the relationship between y and v.

These measures provide a basis for constructing and training an ANN, with the training process being stopped once the MSE reaches the Gamma value. For a fuller discussion of the Gamma test algorithm, the reader is directed to the work of Stefánsson *et al.* [4]

5   Literature Review

This section presents a background to the property market, and provides an overview of previous work related to determining residential property prices.

The property market can be viewed at three levels:
- National (i.e., UK)
- Regional / sub-national (e.g., South East, Wales)
- Urban / sub-market

Theoretical market models indicate that the main variables expected to influence house prices at both the national and regional levels are [6]:
- incomes
- interest rates (real or nominal)
- the general level of prices
- household wealth
- demographic variables
- the tax structure
- financial liberalisation
- the housing stock

However, because measures of some of these variables are not readily available at the regional level, models of regional house prices are typically much s'mpler than their national counterparts. [*Ibid.*] The Merrill Lynch forecasting model [7] uses just four variables:
- Real House Price (log of house price index divided by RPI)
- Real incomes (log of real disposable incomes at constant prices)
- Retail prices (log of RPI)
- Mortgage interest rate (tax-adjusted interest rate)

UK national and regional level models have developed primarily from the modelling of the market at the macroeconomic level. These models have not been integrated with modelling at the urban level.

At the sub-market level, property valuation has centred on arriving at current prices for individual properties rather than predicting a time series. The traditional method for valuing residential property is Direct Capital Comparison. [8] Here, valuers select comparable properties sold in the open market and make "an allowance in money terms" [7] for any differences between the subject property and the comparable properties. This subjective method relies heavily upon the experience of the valuer. This paper builds upon the work of other researchers, grouped here into the following classes:
- General, related, models [6, 10, 11];
- Hedonic (a measure of general, overall opinion) regression analysis models [12, 13, 14];
- Artificial intelligence [15, 16], including ANNs [17, 18, 19].

6   Forecasting using Artificial Neural Networks

Despite the many satisfactory characteristics of an ANN, building a neural network for a particular forecasting problem is a nontrivial task. Modelling issues that affect the performance of an ANN must be considered carefully. First, an appropriate architecture, that is, the number of layers, the number of nodes in each layer, and the number of arcs that interconnect with the nodes must be determined. Other network design decisions include the choice of activation function for the processing nodes, the training algorithm, data normalisation methods, training data, and performance measures. [20]

In this section, an overview of the fully-connected-feed-forward back-propagation ANN implemented is provided with special attention being given to how training data was presented and how performance was measured.

6.1   The network architecture

Our ANN is composed of an input layer, which corresponds to the length of the input vector, an output layer, which provides the forecast values, and two layers of hidden nodes. It has been shown that a single hidden layer is sufficient for an ANN to approximate any complex non-linear function with any desired accuracy. [21] However, recent findings have shown that two hidden layers can result in a more compact architecture that achieves a higher efficiency than single hidden layer networks. [22, 23, 24]

6.1.1   The number of nodes in the hidden layers

It is important that the network has generalised across the time series and not simply fitted the inputs to their corresponding outputs. Therefore, the number of hidden nodes in each layer was determined by trial and error, with large numbers of nodes in the hidden layers being incrementally pruned to a minimum whilst still producing relatively good forecasting capabilities. The gradient statistic provided by the Gamma test [4] provides a heuristic for estimating the complexity of the underlying model, and hence the number of nodes that will be required, but no significant results can be reported here.

6.1.2   The number of nodes in the input layer

The number of nodes in the input layer corresponds to the length of the *window*, or the number of lagged observations used to discover the underlying pattern in a time series. This is the most critical decision variable for a forecasting problem, since the vector contains important information about complex (linear and/or non-linear) structure in the data. However, there is no widely accepted systematic way to determine the optimum length for the input vector. [20] Given this, varying length vectors were used during our experiments with the best *window* length being selected. The Gamma test may provide a meaningful approach to determining a near optimum length for the input vector [4], and a detailed analysis of this will form a significant part of our continued research.

6.1.3   The number of nodes in the output layer

For the time series forecasting problem described in this paper, the number of output nodes corresponds to the forecasting horizon. Here, two types of forecasting were considered, namely: one-step-ahead, which requires only one output node, and multi-step-ahead. Experiments with these two approaches to making multi-step forecasts, the iterative and direct methods, were made. The iterative method requires only a single output node, with forecast values being substituted into the input vector to make further predictions. The, second, direct method provides for multiple output nodes that correspond to the forecasting horizon, with this approach generating the best predictions.

6.2   Activation function

The transfer, or activation, function determines the relationship between inputs and outputs of a node and a network. In general, the transfer function introduces a degree of non-linearity into the ANN and, in theory, any differential function can qualify as a transfer function. However, in practice, only a small number of bounded, monotonically increasing and differential functions are used. It has been suggested [25] that sigmoid (logistic) transfer functions, such as the sigmoid function:

$$f(x) = (1 + \exp(-x))^{-1} \qquad (4)$$

provide better results and a more robust learning when dealing with average behaviour, with hyperbolic tangent function (tanh):

$$f(x) = (\exp(x) - \exp(-x))/((\exp(x) + \exp(-x))) \quad (5)$$

providing better results if the problem involves learning about deviations from the average, such as the forecasting problem. Experimentation with both the logistic and tanh functions led the authors to adopt the tanh function.

6.3   Data normalisation

Non-linear transfer functions will squash the possible output from a node into, typically, (0,1) or (-1,1). Given the range of the property time series being predicted, data normalisation was required before the training process could begin. Here, linear transformation [22] was applied to the time series values, with an upper limit of 1 and lower limit of -1 so as to coincide with the theoretical boundaries of the transfer function.

$$[a,b]: x' = (b - a)(x - x_{min})/((x_{min} - x_{max}) + a \qquad (6)$$

Of the methods for input normalisation reported in literature [26], the external method (all the training data is normalised into a specific range) was selected since it is the most appropriate procedure for a time series forecasting problem.

6.4 Performance measure

Although there can be many performance indicators associated with the construction of an ANN the decisive measure of performance is the prediction accuracy it can achieve beyond the training data. No one universally accepted measure of accuracy is available, with a number of different measures being frequently presented in literature. [27]

$$\sqrt{\sum (et)^2 / N} \qquad (7)$$

The performance measure shown above, adopted by the authors, is the Root Mean Squared Error (RMSE) function. The RMSE provides a measure of the difference between the actual (desired) and predicted value, where e_t is the individual forecast error and N is the number of error terms.

6.5 Partitioning of the time series

Typically, training and test data sets are used during the ANN creation process. In this paper, the training set was used to construct the ANN's underlying model of the time series and the test set was used to measure the accuracy of this model. A third set, called the validation set, was used to determine when the training process should be stopped (the validated training procedure). [28] As was mentioned earlier, this paper presents two approaches to timing when the training procedure should be stopped.

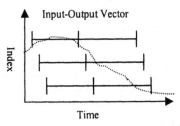

Figure 1 Moving Window

First, the normalised data set was converted into input/output vectors, using an overlapping *moving window* (shown in Figure 1). Next, the set of vectors was partitioned into a training set and a test set. The M-competition convention of retaining the last eight quarterly points for testing, mapped to input/output vectors, was adopted. [29] The remaining vectors were partitioned into a validation set (20%) and training set (80%) for where the validation set was used to indicate when training should end. This validation set was created by removing every fifth vector from the test set. Partitioning the test set in this way provides a meaningful validation set drawn from across the whole range of values present. Where the Gamma test statistic was used to stop the training procedure, there was no need to partition the vectors since the whole training set is presented during training.

7 Experimental work

The investigation consisted of three parts. ANN forecasting models were constructed using the validated training procedure (the Validation model). Similarly, ANN forecasting modes were constructed using the Gamma test statistic model (the Gamma model). Comparisons between the best results from each approach were then made.

7.1 Data source

Takens' Theorem suggests that all influences on a time series are coded into the single time series. [30] Therefore, a single indicator (the housing price index provided by the Nationwide Building Society, shown in Figure 2) was selected to model the projected movements in property prices.

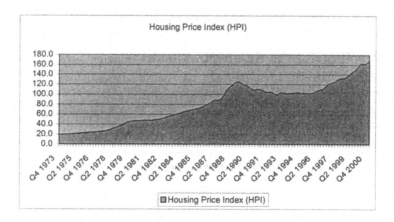

Figure 2 Nationwide Building Society Housing Price Index

The time series is modelled by presenting a *moving window* of five input and eight output values to the ANN. Here, the ANN learns the relationships between x past quarters and the next y quarters. Experimental results are outlined below.

7.2 Results using the Validation model

Here, the weights within the ANN are adjusted using the training portion of the training/validation set. However, the RMSE, which is used to determine when the training process stops, isn't calculated across training set. Instead, the validation set (see Section 6.5) is presented to the ANN at regular intervals with the resultant RMSE across this data set being used to determine how well the ANN has modelled the time series. This iterative training process continues until the RMSE generated by the validation set shows no improvement (see Section 3).

Upon completion of the training procedure outlined above, the test set was presented to the ANN, the best of which producing predictions with a 3.9% error whose trend line falls below the actual trend (see Figure 3).

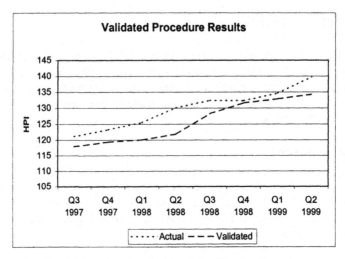

Figure 3 Results using the Validation Training Procedure

7.3 Results using the Gamma test model

Here, the weights within the ANN are adjusted using the whole of the training set. This iterative training process continues until the RMSE generated by the validation set shows no improvement (see Section 3 and 4).

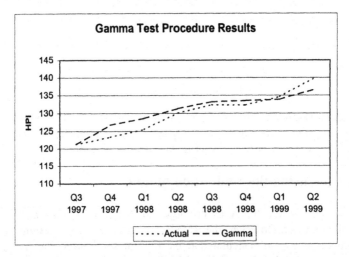

Figure 4 Results using the Gamma Test Procedure

Upon completion of the training procedure, the test set was presented to the ANN, with the best of which producing predictions with a 1.8% error and a trend line that more closely approximates to the actual (see Figure 4).

7.4   Discussion of results

Time series forecasting depends upon patterns in the past that determine, to a greater or lesser extent, the future course of the time series. These patterns encapsulate the market forces so that when it is internalised within an ANN, the resultant model contains some knowledge of the market. This knowledge is then used to forecast the series ahead of the training data.

The Validation method of training the ANN approximates to the trend line of the actual data, but falls somewhat below it. However, the Gamma test method has produced a model that produces quite accurate forecasts that more closely approximate to the actual trend. This is, perhaps, no surprise given that the whole of the training set is used to train the ANN.

8   Conclusion

The work has shown that promising forecasting models can be produced using an ANN that provide a meaningful measure to facilitate the consumers short-term (two-year) decision making process. Given that the models constructed using the outlined Gamma test procedure outperformed the validated approach, this work has shown that the Gamma test provides a significant measure of the robustness of an underlying continuous or smooth model. The experience of the authors strongly suggests that the Gamma test is of practical utility in area of time series modelling.

9   Future Work

Given these promising, initial, experiences with the Gamma test, it is the authors intention to explore whether related documented measures [4], based upon the Gamma test, show equal promise. In addition, work will be extended to include modular networks that map trends within related economic measures such as the Retail Price Index, unemployment rate and interest rate to the Housing Price Index. Ultimately, it is the authors' intention to produce long-term (five-year) forecasts for regional, sub-regional and local property markets.

References

[1] Miles D. Housing, Financial Markets and the Wider Economy, Wiley, 1994
[2] Hoptroff R G. The Principles and Practice of Time Series Forecasting and Business Modelling Using Neural Nets. Neural Computing & Applications 1993; 59-66
[3] Bishop C M. Neural networks for pattern recognition. Christopher M. Bishop, Oxford, Clarendon Press, 1995
[4] Stefánsson A, Konĉar N, Jones A J. A Note of the Gamma Test. Neural Computing and Applications 1997; 5:131-133
[5] Connellan O, James H. Time Series Forecasting of Property Market Indices. The Cutting Edge, 2000
[6] Meen G, Andrew M. Modelling Regional House Prices: A Review of the Literature. University of Reading for the Department of the Environment, Transport and the Regions, 1998

28

[7] Miles D, Andrew S. Merrill Lynch Model of the UK housing market. Merrill Lynch, Pierce, Fenner and Smith Limited, 1997

[8] Jenkins D H. Residential Valuation Theory and Practice. Chandos Publishing, 2000

[9] Millington A F. An Introduction to Property Valuation. Estates Gazette, 1994

[10] Ball M, Grilli M. UK Commercial Property Investment: Time-Series Characteristics and Modelling Strategies. Journal of Property Research 1997; 14:4:279-296

[11] Barkham R J, Geltner D M. Price Discovery and Efficiency in the UK Housing Market. Journal of Housing Economics 1996;5:1:41-63

[12] Antwi A. Multiple Regression in Property Analysis. Estates Gazette Interactive, 1995

[13] Adair A S, Berry J N, McGreal W S. Hedonic Modelling, Housing Sub-markets and Residential Valuation. Journal of Property Research 1996; 13:67-83

[14] Lam ET-K, Modern Regression Models and Neural Networks for Residential Property Valuation. The Cutting Edge, 1996

[15] McCluskey W, Anand S. The Application of Intelligent Hybrid Techniques for the Mass Appraisal of Residential Properties. Journal of Property Investment and Finance 1999; 17:3:218-238

[16] Wang S. An Adaptive Approach to Market Development Forecasting. Neural Computing and Applications 1999; 8:1:3-8

[17] McGreal S, Adair A, McBurney D, Patterson D. Neural Networks: The Predication of Residential Values. Journal of Property Valuation and Investment 1998; 16:1:57-70

[18] Vemuri V R, Rogers R D. Artificial Neural Networks Forecasting Time Series. IEEE Computer Society Press, California, 1994

[19] Worzala E, Lenk M, Silva A. An Exploration of Neural Networks and its Application to Real Estate Valuation. The Journal of Real Estate Research 1995; 10:2:185-201

[20] Zhang G, Patuwo B E, Hu M Y. Forecasting with Artificial neural networks: The state of the art. International Journal of Forecasting 1998; 14:35-62

[21] Hornik K. Approximation capabilities of multi-layer feed-forward networks. Neural Networks 1991; 4:251-257

[22] Srinivasan D, Liew A C, Chang C S. A neural network short-term load forecaster. Electric Power Systems Research 1994; 28:227-234

[23] Zhang X. Time series analysis and prediction by neural networks. Optimization Methods and Software 1994; 4:151-170

[24] Chester D L. Why two hidden layers are better than one? In: Proceedings of the International Joint Conference on Neural Networks 1990, pp 1265-1268

[25] Klimasauskas C. Applying neural networks. Part 3: Training a neural network. PC AI 1991; 5:3:20-24

[26] Azoff E M. Neural Network Time Series Forecasting of Financial Markets. John Wiley and Sons, Chichester, 1994.

[27] Makridakis S, Wheelwright S C, McGee V E. Forecasting: Methods and Applications, 2nd ed. John Wiley, New York, 1983.

[28] Weigend A S, Huberman B A, Rumelhart D E. Predicting sunspots and exchange rates with connectionist networks. In: Casdagli M, Eubank S (ed), Nonlinear Modeling and Forecasting. Addison-Wesley, Redwood City, CA, 1992, pp 395-432

[29] Foster W R, Collopy F, Ungar L H. Neural network forecasting of short, noisy time series. Computers and Chemical Engineering 1992; 16:4:293-297

[30] Takens F. Lecture Notes in Mathematics 898. Springer-Verlag, Berlin, 1981

Supporting the actors in an electronic market place

John Debenham

Faculty of Information Technology, University of Technology, Sydney
debenham@it.uts.edu.au

Abstract. An electronic market has been constructed in an on-going collaborative research project between a university and a software house. The way in which actors (buyers, sellers and others) use the market will be influenced by the information available to them, including information drawn from outside the immediate market environment. In this experiment, data mining and filtering techniques are used to distil both individual signals drawn from the markets and signals from the Internet into meaningful advice for the actors. The goal of this experiment is first to learn how actors will use the advice available to them, and second how the market will evolve through entrepreneurial intervention. In this electronic market a multiagent process management system is used to manage all market transactions including those that drive the market evolutionary process.

1. Introduction

The project described here addresses the problem of identifying timely information for e-markets with their rapid, pervasive and massive flows of data. This information is distilled from individual signals in the markets themselves and from signals observed on the unreliable, information-overloaded Internet. Distributed, concurrent, time-constrained data mining methods are managed using business process management technology to extract timely, reliable information from this unreliable environment. The long term goal of this project is to derive fundamental insight into how e-markets evolve. The perturbation of market equilibrium through entrepreneurial action is the essence of market evolution. Entrepreneurship relies both on intuition and information discovery. The term 'entrepreneur' is used here in its technical sense [1]. This long term goal includes the provision of timely information to support the market evolutionary process.

A subset of this project is substantially complete; it is called the *basic system* and is described in Sec. 2. The goal of this subset is to identify timely information for traders in an e-market. The traders are the buyers and sellers. This basic system does not address the question of market evolution. The basic system is constructed in two parts:

- the e-market
- the actors' assistant

The e-market has been constructed by Bullant Australasia Pty Ltd—an Australian software house with a strong interest in business-to-business (B2B) e-business [www.bullant.com]. The e-market is part of their on-going research effort in this area. It has been constructed using Bullant's proprietary software development tools. The e-market was designed by the author. The actors' assistant is being constructed in the

Fig 1. The four actor classes in the basic e-market system

Faculty of Information Technology at the University of Technology, Sydney. It is funded by two Australian Research Council Grants; one awarded to the author, and one awarded to Dr Simeon Simoff.

One feature of the whole project is that every transaction is treated as a business process and is managed by a process management system as described in Sec. 3. In other words, the process management system makes the whole thing work. In the basic system these transactions include simple market transactions such as "buy" and "sell" as well as transactions that assist the actors in buying and selling. For example, "get me information on the financial state of the Sydney Steel Co. by 4.00pm". The process management system is based on a robust multiagent architecture. The use of multiagent systems is justified first by the distributed nature of e-business, and second by the critical nature of the transactions involved. This second reason means that the system should be able to manage a transaction (eg: buy ten tons of steel by next Tuesday at the best available price) reliably in an essentially unreliable environment. The environment may be unreliable due to the unreliability of the network and components in it, or due to the unreliability of players—for example, a seller may simply renege on a deal.

The overall goal of this project is to investigate the evolution of e-markets. The investigation of e-market evolution will commence at the end of 2001. The overall design framework is already complete and a brief description of it is given in Sec. 4.

2.   The basic system

The basic system consists of the e-market and the actors' assistant. The goal of the basic system is to identify timely information for traders in the e-market. Trading in the e-market either takes place through the 'e-exchange' or through a 'solution provider'. The *e-exchange* is an open exchange where goods and services are offered on a fixed price basis or by some competitive mechanism. The *solution providers* assist in the negotiation of contracts and facilitate the development of business relationships between buyers and sellers. So the actor classes in the basic system are buyer, seller, e-exchange and solution provider. The four actor classes are shown in Fig. 1. Before describing the system itself a justification is given of this choice of four actor classes.

2.1   Actor classes in the basic system

For some while there has been optimism in the role of agents in electronic commerce. "During this next-generation of agent-mediated electronic commerce,..... Agents will strategically form and reform coalitions to bid on contracts and leverage economies of scale...... It is in this third-generation of agent-mediated electronic commerce where companies will be at their most agile and markets will approach perfect efficiency." [2].

There is a wealth of material, developed principally by micro-economists, on the behaviour of rational economic agents. The value of that work in describing the behaviour of human agents is limited in part by the inability of humans to necessarily behave in an (economically) rational way, particularly when their (computational) resources are limited. That work provides a firm foundation for describing the behaviour of rational, intelligent software agents whose resource bounds are known, but more work has to be done [3]. Further, new market' mechanisms that may be particularly well-suited to markets populated by software agents is now an established area of research [4] [5]. Most electronic business to date has centred on on-line exchanges in which a single issue, usually price, is negotiated through the application of traditional auction-based market mechanisms. Systems for multi-issue negotiation are also being developed [6], also IBM's Silkroad project [7]. The efficient management of multi-issue negotiation towards a possible solution when new issues may be introduced as the negotiation progresses remains a complex problem [8].

Given the optimism in the future of agents in electronic commerce and the body of theoretical work describing the behaviour of rational agents, it is perhaps surprising that the basic structure of the emerging e-business world is far from clear. The majority of Internet e-exchanges are floundering, and it appears that few will survive [9]. There are indications that exchanges may even charge a negative commission to gain business and so too market intelligence [op. cit.]. For example, the Knight Trading Group currently pays on-line brokers for their orders. The rationale for negative commissions is discussed in Sec. 4. One reason for the recent failure of e-exchanges is that the process of competitive bidding to obtain the lowest possible price is not compatible with the development of buyer-seller relations. The preoccupation with a single issue, namely price, can overshadow other attributes such as quality, reliability, availability and customisation. A second reason for the failure Internet e-exchanges is that they deliver little benefit to the seller—few suppliers want to engage in a ruthless bidding war [op. cit.]. The future of electronic commerce must include the negotiation of complex transactions and the development of long-term relationships between buyer and seller as well as the e-exchanges. Support for these complex transactions and relationships is provided here by *solution providers*.

A considerable amount of work has been published on the comparative virtues of open market e-exchanges and solution providers that facilitate direct negotiation. For example, [10] argues that for privately informed traders the 'weak' trader types will systematically migrate from direct negotiations to competitive open markets. Also, for example, see [11] who compare the virtues of auctions and negotiation. Those results are derived in a supply/demand-bounded world into which signals may flow. These signals may be received by one or more of the agents in that world, and so may cause those agents to revise their valuation of the matter at hand. No attempt is made to accommodate measures of the intrinsic validity of those signals, measures of the significance of those signals to the matter at hand, or measures of interdependencies between those signals. That is, those models ignore the general knowledge that is required to make good business decisions. That general knowledge may be drawn from outside the context of the market place. So those results do not necessarily mean that e-exchanges will be preferred over negotiated contracts in the real world. For example, the negotiation of a long term contract for some commodity may be based on an individual's 'hunch' that future political instability in a foreign country will (partly) cause the price of that commodity to rise.

The issue addressed here is limited to single issue negotiation either in an e-exchange or through a solution provider. This problem is not trivial. For example, if a company has a regular requirement for so-many tons of steel a month then will it be better off for the next 24 months *either* making offers in an e-exchange on a monthly basis *or* negotiating a 24-month contract?

2.2   The e-market

The construction of experimental e-markets is an active area of research. For example, [12] describes work done at IBM's Institute for Advanced Commerce. The basic e-market described here has been designed in the context of the complete system described briefly in Sec. 4. There are two functional components in the *basic e-market*: the e-exchange and a solution provider. The *solution provider* is 'minimal' and simply provides a conduit between buyer and seller through which long term contracts are negotiated. The *solution provider* in its present form does not give third-party support to the negotiation process.

An e-exchange is created for a fixed duration. An *e-exchange* is a virtual space in which a variety of market-type *activities* can take place at specified times. The time is determined by the e-exchange *clock*. Each activity is advertised on a notice *board* which shows the start and stop time for that activity as well as what the activity is and the *regulations* that apply to players who wish to participate in it. A human player works though a PC (or similar) by interacting with a *user agent* which communicates with a *proxy agent* or a solution provider situated in the e-market. The inter-agent communication is discussed in Sec 3. The user agents may be 'dumb', or 'smart' being programmed by the user to make decisions. Each activity has an *activity manager* that ensures that the regulations of that activity are complied with.

When an e-exchange is created, a specification is made of the e-exchange *rules*. These rules will state who is permitted to enter the e-exchange and the roles that they are permitted to play in the e-exchange. These rules are enforced by an *e-exchange manager*. For example, can any player create a sale activity (which could be some sort of auction), or, can any player enter the e-exchange by offering some service, such as advice on what to buy, or by offering 'package deals' of goods derived from different suppliers? A high-level view of the e-market is shown in Fig. 2.

The activities in the basic e-market are limited to opportunities to buy and sell goods. The regulations for this limited class of activities are called *market mechanisms* [5]. The subject of a negotiation is a *good*, buyers make *bids*, sellers make *asks*. Designing market mechanisms is an active area of research. For example, see optimal auctions [4]. One important feature of a mechanism is the 'optimal' strategy that a player should use, and whether that strategy is "truth revealing" [11]. Mechanisms can be for single-unit (ie a single good) or multi-unit (ie a number of identical goods). Any single-unit mechanism may be extended to a multi-unit mechanism by using it to establish a price for a good, permitting the 'winner' to take as many goods as required at that price (and maybe then permitting other buyers to take further goods at that price),

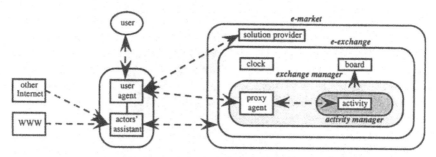

Fig. 2. High-level model of the e-market and user

then putting the remaining goods up for sale to determine another price, and so on, until the process terminates.

A market mechanism is specified by the player who creates an activity and is displayed on the notice board. The market mechanism will determine:

- what is the *starting time* and *closing time* of the activity.
- what is the *subject* of the activity; eg. if the activity is to sell goods then what are the goods for sale.
- the *commission*, if any, payable on any successful transaction—this may be negative, may be a flat fee and/or a percentage of the value of the trade.
- the *reserve price*, if any, below which the good is not for sale—this is usually specified by the seller.
- what *market information* is available—eg. some auctions are 'open cry' and some are 'sealed bid'.
- under what circumstances can a player participate? For example, can a player 'sell/buy short'. For example, is a player required to make a *deposit* or pay an *entry fee*?
- if a player can 'sell/buy short' then what penalty applies if they are unable to deliver.
- what a player has to do to participate—for example, in an auction a buyer has to submit a bid, in which case what does a bid consist of?
- how many bids/asks can a player submit?
- having submitted a bid/ask can a player withdraw or modify that bid/ask?
- what has to happen for somebody to 'win'?
- if at least one person 'wins' then: When does the activity clear? How are the goods distributed amongst the 'winners'? Including, for example, what happens if there are two equal bids/asks in a sealed-bid multi-unit auction. What is the price for the goods as distributed amongst the 'winners'? What happens to the unfilled bid(s) of the winner(s), and, if it is a double auction, the ask(s) of the seller(s)?

To enable the activity manager to do its job, each proxy agent reveals in confidence the assets that the proxy agent possesses to the activity manager. The activity manager may 'ear mark' some amount of a buying proxy agent's money if the market mechanism requires that that amount must be set aside to support a bid, or if a buyer's deposit is required. Each player may withdraw assets from the proxy agent and so from the

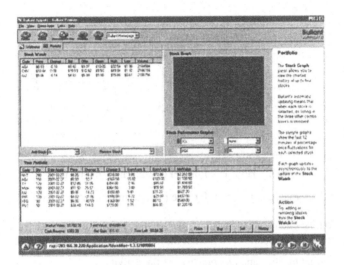

Fig. 3. User's screen for an e-exchange that is hooked to the Sydney Stock Exchange.

e-market. Fig. 3 shows a user's screen for an e-exchange that is hooked to the Sydney Stock Exchange.

2.3   The actors' assistant

In 'real' problems, a decision to use an e-exchange or a solution provider will be made on the basis of general knowledge that is external to the e-market place. Having decided to use either an e-exchange or a solution provider, the negotiation strategy used will also depend on general knowledge. Such general knowledge will typically be broadly based and beyond the capacity of modern AI systems whilst remaining within reasonable cost bounds.

E-markets reside on the Internet alongside the vast resources of the World Wide Web. In the experiments described here, the general knowledge available is restricted to that which can be gleaned from the e-markets themselves and that which can be extracted from the Internet in general—including the World Wide Web. The actors' assistant is a workbench that provides a suite of tools to *assist* a buyer or seller in the e-market. [Sec. 4 describes how the actors' assistant will assist other market actors as well.] The actors' assistant does *not* attempt to replace buyers and sellers. For example, there is no attempt to automate 'speculation' in any sense. Web-mining tools assist the players in the market to make informed decisions. One of the issues in operating in an e-market place is coping with the rapidly-changing signals in it. These signals include: product and assortment attributes (if the site offers multiple products), promotions shown, visit attributes (sequences within the site, counts, click-streams) and business agent attributes. Combinations of these signals may be vital information to an actor. A new generation of data analysis and supporting techniques—collectively labelled as *data mining* methods—are now applied to stock market analysis, predictions and other financial and market analysis applications [13]. The application of data mining methods in e-business to date has predominantly been within the B2C framework, where data is mined at an on-line business site, resulting in the derivation of various behavioural metrics of site visitors and customers.

The basic steps in providing assistance to actors in this project are:
- identifying potentially relevant signals;
- evaluating the reliability of those signals;
- estimating the significance of those signals to the matter at hand;
- combining a (possibly large) number of signals into coherent advice, and
- providing digestible explanations for the advice given.

For example, the identification of potentially relevant signals includes scanning news feeds. In the first pass the text is stripped of any HTML or other formatting commends—this is *preprocessing*. Then keyword matches are performed by *scanners*. Provided the number of 'hits' has not been too large, these two steps alone produce useful information. For example, in response to a query "find anything you can on Sydney Steel in the international press during the past 24 hours' is represented simply as:

"...takeover bid for Sydney Steel" (New York Times)
"Sydney Steel board announce..." (CNN)

Here the search phrase is Sydney Steel, and the references quoted give n (=2 here) significant additional words in the sentence in which the search phrase was found. The underlining in these examples are clickable and take the user to the source material. Or, if the source material has been pre-fetched, to a small window containing the immediate surrounding text. This is not 'rocket science' but it does show that useful information may be presented simply by employing existing news bots through a common interface. Bots that have been built into the system include: News Hub [www.newshub.com], NewsTrawler [www.newstrawler.com] and CompanySleuth [www.companysleuth.com]. Following the prepossessing and scanning steps, an *assessment* is made of the overall reliability of the source. At present this is simply a measure of the overall reputation that the source has for accuracy. In addition, *watchers* detect changes to material on the Web. Here URLyWarning [www.urlywarning.com] and other watcher bots are used to identify pages in which designated information *may* have changed; they may be used to trigger a detailed search of other pages.

The estimation of the significance of a signal to a matter at hand is complicated by the fact that one person may place more faith in the relevance of a particular signal than others. So this estimation can only be performed on a personal basis. This work does *not*, for example, attempt to use a signal to predict whether the US dollar will rise against the UK pound. What it *does* attempt to do is to predict the value that an actor will place on a signal [14]. So the feedback here is provided by the user in the form of a rating of the material used. A five point scale runs from 'totally useless' to 'very useful'. Having identified the signals that a user has faith in, "classical" data mining methods [15] are then applied to combine these signals into succinct advice again using a five point scale. This feedback is used to 'tweak' the weights in Bayesian networks and as feedback to neural networks [16]. Bayesian networks are preferred when some confidence can be placed in a set of initial values for the weights. The system is able to raise an alarm automatically and quickly when a pre-specified compound event occurs such as: four members of the board of our principal supplier "Good Co" have resigned, the share price has dropped unexpectedly and there are rumours that our previous supplier "Bad Co" is taking over "Good Co".

The actors' assistant integrates two different approaches in data mining — the data driven and the hypothesis-driven approach. In the data-driven approach the assistant is just "absorbing" the information discovered by the scanners. It only specifies broad parameters to constrain the material scanned. For example, in the text analysis of the news files a text miner observes the frequencies of word occurrences and co-occurrences that appear to be relevant to a keyword such as 'steel prices'. The result of this process is an initial representative vocabulary for that news file. In the hypothesis-driven approach, the actors' assistant specifies precisely what it is looking for, for example, it formulates a hypothesis that a fall in the price of steel is likely within a month. The combination of data-driven and hypothesis driven approaches aims to provide a mechanism for meeting tight time constraints. Managing and synchronising the actors' assistant is handled by process management plans in the user agents. For example, a request is made for the best information on the Sydney Steel Co to be delivered by 4.00pm. This request triggers a business process. Things can go wrong with this process, for example a server may be down, in which case the process management plans activate less-preferred but nevertheless useful ways of obtaining the required information by the required time.

3. Managing e-market transactions with a multiagent system

A multiagent business process management system manages *all* e-market transactions and so it makes the e-market operate.

3.1 The process management problem

Fig 2. may give the false impression that all the process management system does is to support communication between the user agents and their corresponding proxy agents. All transactions are managed as business processes, including a simple 'buy order', and a complex request for information placed with an actor's assistant. For example, a simple 'buy order' placed by a user agent may cause its proxy agent to place a bid in an activity which may then provoke interaction with a number of user agents who are trying to sell the appropriate goods, and so on. Alternatively, a user agent may seek out other agents through a solution provider. In either case, any buy or sell order will be partly responsible for triggering a reaction along the entire supply (or value) chain. Building e-business process management systems is business process reengineering on a massive scale, it often named *industry process reengineering* [17]. This can lead to considerable problems unless there is an agreed basis for transacting business. The majority of market transactions are constrained by time ("I need it before Tuesday"), or more complex constraints ("I only need the engine if I also have a chassis and as long as the total cost is less than..). The majority of transactions are *critical* in that they must be dealt with and can't be forgotten or mislaid. Or at least it is an awful nuisance if they are. So this means that a system for managing them is required that can handle complex constraints and that attempts to prevent process failure.

E-market processes will typically be *goal-directed* in the sense that it may be known *what* goals have to be achieved, but not necessarily *how* to achieve those goals today. A goal-directed process may be modelled as a (possibly conditional) sequence of goals. Alternatively a process may be *emergent* in the sense that the person who triggers the process may not have any particular goal in mind and may be on a 'fishing expedition' [18]—this is particularly common in the entrepreneurial processes described briefly in Sec. 4. There has been little work on the management of emergent processes [19]. There a multiagent process management system is described that is based on a three-layer, BDI, hybrid architecture. That system 'works with' the user as emergent processes unfold. It also manages goal-directed processes in a fairly conventional way using single-entry quadruple-exit plans that give almost-failure-proof operation. Those plans can represent constraints of the type referred to above, and so it is a candidate for managing the operation of the system described in Sec. 2, and elaborated in Sec. 4.

One tension in e-business is that the transactions tend to be critical and the environment in which they are being processed is inherently unreliable. On one level sellers and buyers may renege on a deal, or may take an unpredictable amount of time to come to a conclusion. On another level the whole e-business environment, including the computer systems on it and the Internet itself, can not be relied on to perform on time, and, on occasions, may not operate at all. So this means that the system which manages the transactions must be able to adapt intelligently as the performance characteristics of the various parts of its environment are more or less satisfactory and more or less predictable. A more subtle complicating factor is that whereas much valuable information may be available free of charge on the World Wide Web it is not necessarily current. For example, the Sydney Stock Exchange publishes its quoted prices free of charge but with a time delay of several minutes—current information costs money. So, while working in an unreliable environment, the system for managing processes should balance time and cost tradeoffs in sub-processes whilst attempting to keep the whole process on time and within budget, and whilst delivering results of an acceptable standard.

3.2   The multiagent system

Multiagent technology is an attractive basis for industry process re-engineering [20] [21]. A multiagent system consists of autonomous components that negotiate with one another. The scalability issue of industry process reengineering is "solved"—in theory—by establishing a common understanding for inter-agent communication and interaction. Standard XML-based ontologies will enable data to be communicated freely [22] but much work has yet to be done on standards for communicating expertise [23]. Results in ontological analysis and engineering [24] [23] is a potential source for formal communication languages which supports information exchange between the actors in an e-market place. Systems such as CommerceNet's Eco [www.commerce.net] and Rosettanet [www.rosettanet.org] are attempting to establish common languages and frameworks for business transactions and negotiations. Specifying an agent interaction

38

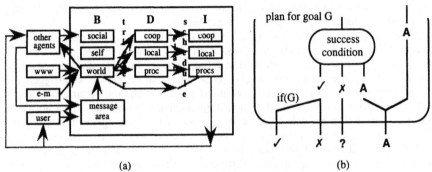

(a)   (b)

Fig 4. (a) conceptual architecture, (b) the four plan exits

protocol is complex as it in effect specifies the common understanding of the basis on which the whole system will operate.

A variety of architectures have been described for autonomous agents. A fundamental distinction is the extent to which an architecture exhibits deliberative (feed forward, planning) reasoning and reactive (feed back) reasoning. If an agent architecture combines these two forms of reasoning it is a *hybrid architecture*. One well reported class of hybrid architectures is the three-layer, BDI agent architectures. One member of this class is the INTERRAP architecture [25], which has its origins in the work of [26]. A multiagent system to manage "goal-driven" processes is described in [19]. In that system each human user is assisted by an agent which is based on a generic three-layer, BDI hybrid agent architecture similar to the INTERRAP architecture. That system has been extended to support emergent processes and so to support and the full range of industry processes. That conceptual architecture is adapted slightly for use here; see Fig 4(a). Each agent receives messages from other agents (and, if it is a personal agent, from its user) in its message area. The world beliefs are derived from reading messages, observing the e-market and from the World Wide Web (as accessed by an actor's assistant).

Deliberative reasoning is effected by the non-deterministic procedure: "on the basis of current *beliefs*—identify the current *options*, on the basis of current options and existing commitments—select the current commitments (called the agent's *goals* or *desires*), for each newly-committed goal choose a *plan* for that goal, from the selected plans choose a consistent set of things to do next (called the agent's *intentions*)". A *plan* for a goal is a conditional sequence of sub-goals that may include iterative or recursive structures. If the current options do not include a current commitment then that commitment is dropped. In outline, the reactive reasoning mechanism employs triggers that observe the agent's beliefs and are 'hot wired' back to the procedural intentions. If those triggers fire then they take precedence over the agent's deliberative reasoning. The environment is intrinsically unreliable. In particular plans can not necessarily be relied upon to achieve their goal. So at the end of every plan there is a *success condition* which tests whether that plan's goal has been achieved; see Fig 4(b). That success condition is itself a procedure which can succeed (✓), fail (✗) or be aborted (**A**). So this leads to each plan having four possible exits: success (✓), failure (✗), aborted (**A**) and unknown (**?**). In practice these four exists do not necessarily have to lead to different sub-goals, and so the growth in the size of plan with depth is not quite as bad as could be expected.

KQML (Knowledge Query and Manipulation Language) is used for inter-agent communication [27]. Each process agent has a *message area*. If agent A wishes to tell something to agent B then it does so by posting a message to agent B's message area. Each agent has a *message manager* whose role is to look after that agent's message area. Each message contains an instruction for the message manager. Two such instructions are:

- post message and remove on condition—the sender is asking the receiving agent's message manager to display the message in the receiving agent's message area *until* the stated condition is satisfied, and
- remove message—the sender is asking the receiving agent's message manager to remove an existing message from the receiving agent's message area.

The system operates in an environment whose performance and reliability are unreliable and unpredictable. Further, choices may have to be made that balance reliability with cost. To apply the deliberative reasoning procedure requires a mechanism for *identifying* options, for *selecting* goals, for *choosing* plans and for *scheduling* intentions. A plan may perform well or badly. The process management system takes account of the "process knowledge" and the "performance knowledge". *Process knowledge* is the wisdom that has been accumulated, particularly that which is relevant to the process instance at hand. *Performance knowledge* is knowledge of how effective agents, people, systems, methods and plans are at achieving various things. A plan's *performance* is defined in terms of: the likelihood that the plan will succeed, the expected cost and time to execute the plan, the expected value added to the process by the plan, or some combination of these measures. If each agent knows how well the choices that it has made have performed in the past then it can be expected to make decisions reasonably well as long as plan performance remains reasonably stable. One mechanism for achieving this form of adaptivity is reinforcement learning. An alternative approach based on probability is described in [19]. In addition, an agent may know things about the system environment, and may have some idea of the *reason why* one choice lead to failure. An agent's belief in these reasons may result from communication with other agents. Such beliefs may be used to revise the "historical" estimates to give an *informed* estimate of plan performance that takes into account the *reasons why* a plan behaved the way that it did [op. cit.].

4. Future work: investigating e-market evolution

E-markets, with their rapid, extensive, pervasive and visible flows of information provide an ideal context in which (a) to study market evolution in a context that is undergoing rapid evolution and innovation, and (b) to build systems that assist entrepreneurial intervention in actual market situations. The term 'entrepreneur' is used here in its technical sense [1]. Entrepreneurial transactions are typically more complex than the basic e-market transactions described in Sec. 2. Work on this part of the project will commence in the latter half of 2001, and the outline design is complete.

One entrepreneurial transaction is a request for information. For example, "look for Sydney-based manufacturing companies with a high asset backing that have been subject of at least one failed takeover bid in the past two years". Such a request triggers an instance of an *information process* in the user agent that will invoke information discovery and data mining methods, and perhaps hand-crafted analytical tools, in that agent's actors' assistant. These methods and tools are applied to either the e-market data or to Internet data. So there are four basic problems here. First, determining where to access the individual signals. Second, assessing some measure of confidence in the validity of those signals. Third combining those signals—which may be invalid and which may have been observed at different times and different places—into reliable advice. Fourth to do all this within tight time and cost constraints. Another entrepreneurial transaction is *entrepreneurial intervention* itself. For example, "I am offering the following unique combination of products and services with a novel payment structure.....". Such a transaction also triggers a business process that sets up the required structures within the e-market.

In the full e-market system, additional actor classes are introduced to support market evolution. *E-speculators* take short term positions in the e-exchange. This introduces the possibility of negative commission charges for others using an e-exchange. Sell-side *asset exchanges* exchange or share assets between sellers. *Content aggregators*, who act as forward aggregators, coordinate and package goods and services from various sellers. *Specialist originators*, who act as reverse aggregators, coordinate and package orders for goods and services from various buyers. The specialist originators, content aggregators and e-speculators represent their presence in the e-exchange by creating activities. This finally gives justification to the use of the term 'activity' to describe what happens in the e-exchange rather than 'sale' which might be more appropriate to the limited range of transactions in the basic system described in Sec. 2. The eight actor classes are illustrated in Fig. 5. They are a super-set of the actor classes in the basic system.

The full system will be used to study market evolution. E-markets are a fruitful arena for hunting entrepreneurial opportunities—witness the proliferation of new market forms and players [28], [9] and the characterisation of the new network economy as an "opportunity factory". The rich flows of information in and around e-markets can be tapped to facilitate the discovery of potentially profitable opportunities and thereby stimulate the innovation and evolution process.

There are valuable studies on the cognitive processes and factors driving alertness to opportunities [29]. There is also a wealth of established work in economic theory, that provides a basis for work in e-markets, including: the theory of auctions, theory of bargaining, and theory of contracts. [8] presents mechanisms for negotiation between computational agents. That work describes tactics for the manipulation of the utility of deals, trade-off mechanisms that manipulate the value, rather than the overall utility, of an offer, and manipulation mechanisms that add and remove issues from the negotiation set. Much has to be done before this established body of work may form a practical basis for an investigation into electronic market evolution [3]. Little is known on how entrepreneurs will operate in electronic market places, although the capacity of the vast amount of information that will reside in those market places, and on the Internet generally, to assist the market evolution process is self-evident. The long term aim of this project is to understand the e-market evolutionary process.

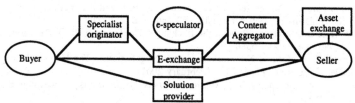

Fig 5. The eight actor classes in the full e-market system

5. Conclusion

One of the innovations in this project is the development of a coherent environment for e-market places, a comprehensive set of actor classes and the use of a powerful multiagent process management system to make the whole thing work. The use of a powerful business process management system to drive all the electronic market transactions unifies the whole market operation. The development of computational models of the basic market transactions, deploying those models in the e-market place, and including them as part of the building blocks for creating a complete e-market place provides a practical instrument for continued research and development in electronic markets.

Acknowledgment

The work described herein was completed whilst the author was a visitor at the CSIRO Joint Research Centre for Advanced Systems Engineering, Macquarie University, Sydney. The contribution to the work by the members of that Centre is gratefully acknowledged.

References

[1]   Israel M. Kirzner Entrepreneurial Discovery and the Competitive Market Process: An Austrian Approach" Journal of Economic Literature XXXV (March) 1997 60-85.

[2]   R. Guttman, A. Moukas, and P. Maes. Agent-mediated Electronic Commerce: A Survey. Knowledge Engineering Review, June 1998.

[3]   Moshe Tennenholtz. Electronic Commerce: From Economic and Game-Theoretic Models to Working Protocols. Invited paper. Proceedings Sixteenth International Joint Conference on Artificial Intelligence, IJCAI'99, Stockholm, Sweden.

[4]   Milgrom, P. Auction Theory for Privatization. Cambridge Univ Press (2001).

[5]   Bichler, M. The Future of E-Commerce: Multi-Dimensional Market Mechanisms. Cambridge University Press (2001).

[6]   Sandholm, T. Agents in Electronic Commerce: Component Technologies for Automated Negotiation and Coalition Formation. Autonomous Agents and Multi-Agent Systems, 3(1), 73-96.

[7]   Ströbel, M. Design of Roles and Protocols for Electronic Negotiations. Electronic Commerce Research Journal, Special Issue on Market Design 2001.

[8]   Peyman Faratin. Automated Service Negotiation Between Autonomous Computational
        Agents. PhD dissertation, University of London (Dec 2000).
[9]   R. Wise & D. Morrison. Beyond the Exchange; The Future of B2B. Harvard Business
        review Nov-Dec 2000, pp86-96.
[10]   Neeman, Z. & Vulkan, N. Markets Versus Negotiations. The Hebrew University of
        Jerusalem Discussion Paper 239. (February 2001).
[11]   Bulow, J. & Klemperer, P. Auctions Versus Negotiations. American Economic
        Review, 1996.
[12]   Kumar, M. & Feldman, S.I. Business Negotiations on the Internet. Proceedings
        INET'98 Internet Summit, Geneva, July 21-24, 1998.
[13]   B. Kovalerchuk & E. Vityaev. Data Mining in Finance: Advances in Relational and
        Hybrid Methods. Kluwer, 2000.
[14]   J. Han, L.V.S. Lakshmanan & R.T. Ng. Constraint-based multidimensional data
        mining. IEEE Computer, 8, 46-50, 1999.
[15]   Han, J. & Kamber, M. Data Mining: Concepts and Techniques. Morgan Kaufmann
        (2000).
[16]   Chen, Z. Computational Intelligence for Decision Support. CRC Press, Boca Raton,
        2000.
[17]   Feldman, S. Technology Trends and Drivers and a Vision of the Future of e-business.
        Proceedings 4th International Enterprise Distributed Object Computing Conference,
        September 25-28, 2000, Makuhari, Japan.
[18]   Fischer, L. (Ed). Workflow Handbook 2001. Future Strategies, 2000.
[19]   Debenham, J.K.. Supporting knowledge-driven processes in a multiagent process
        management system. Proceedings Twentieth International Conference on Knowledge
        Based Systems and Applied Artificial Intelligence, ES'2000: Research and
        Development in Intelligent Systems XVII, Cambridge UK, December 2000, pp273-
        286.
[20]   Jain, A.K., Aparicio, M. and Singh, M.P. "Agents for Process Coherence in Virtual
        Enterprises" in Communications of the ACM, Volume 42, No 3, March 1999, pp62—
        69.
[21]   Jennings, N.R., Faratin, P., Norman, T.J., O'Brien, P. & Odgers, B. Autonomous
        Agents for Business Process Management. Int. Journal of Applied Artificial
        Intelligence 14 (2) 145—189, 2000.
[22]   Robert Skinstad, R. "Business process integration through XML". In proceedings
        XML Europe 2000, Paris, 12-16 June 2000.
[23]   Guarino N., Masolo C., and Vetere G., OntoSeek: Content-Based Access to the Web,
        IEEE Intelligent Systems 14(3), May/June 1999, pp. 70-80
[24]   Uschold, M. and Gruninger, M.: 1996, Ontologies: principles, methods and
        applications. Knowledge Engineering Review, 11(2), 1996.
[25]   Müller, J.P. "The Design of Intelligent Agents" Springer-Verlag, 1996.
[26]   Rao, A.S. and Georgeff, M.P. "BDI Agents: From Theory to Practice", in proceedings
        First International Conference on Multi-Agent Systems (ICMAS-95), San Francisco,
        USA, pp 312—319.
[27]   Finin, F. Labrou, Y., and Mayfield, J. "KQML as an agent communication language."
        In Jeff Bradshaw (Ed.) Software Agents. MIT Press (1997).
[28]   Kaplan, Steven and Sawhney, Mohanbir. E-Hubs: The New B2B Marketplace. Harvard
        Business Review 78 May-June 2000 97-103.
[29]   Shane, Scott. Prior knowledge and the discovery of entrepreneurial opportunities.
        Organization Science 11 (July-August), 2000, 448-469.

SMART Software for Decision Makers

KDD Experience

Dr. Giles Oatley, Prof. John MacIntyre, Dr. Brian Ewart & Ernest Mugambi

Centre for Adaptive Systems (cas.sunderland.ac.uk) University of Sunderland

Abstract

SMART Software for Decision Makers (SSDM) was a Department of Trade and Industry (DTI) initiative running during the period 1998-2000. The Centre for Adaptive Systems at the University of Sunderland was appointed by the DTI to run one of the two Demonstrator Clubs in the UK. The purpose of these clubs was to facilitate technology transfer between academia and industry, in the areas of fault diagnosis and prediction, intelligent control systems, and knowledge discovery in databases (KDD).

Sunderland SSDM Club decided to use the various industrial members problems and data to build a number of "mini-demonstrators". In the KDD cluster, three demonstrator applications were developed, accompanied by supporting material and a series of seminars, which illustrated the various stages in the KDD process to all club members.

This paper describes three KDD application demonstrators, developed with data from a manufacturing company, with consultants in business clustering, and from data from a local police force, to investigate the phenomena of repeat victimization.

The work involved data preprocessing, data transformation, data mining, and the development of visual tools for interpretation. With both the business clustering and police data much of the time was spent in data preparation, and so tools were developed so that the members could conduct their own data mining and interpretation experiments, lessening the need for the extraction of domain knowledge from the members.

Keywords: Data preparation, data visualization, data mining, data interpretation, Needlemann-Wunsch algorithm, kernel-based, string matching

1. Introduction

The Centre for Adaptive Systems at the University of Sunderland is a focussed research group affording industry the opportunity to achieve real benefits from advanced computing techniques in areas that include (among others) condition monitoring, intelligent control, and knowledge discovery in databases. The Centre was appointed by the Department of Trade and Industry (DTI) to run one of the SMART Software for Decision Makers (SSDM) demonstrator clubs precisely to transfer this technological expertise to industry.

Three separate demonstrator applications were developed in the following areas: (i) detection of duplications in a parts database- this work was solely directed at data pre-processing; (ii) investigation of business clusters - this work included data pre-processing, transformation and interpretation; and, (iii) investigation of repeat victimisation in a crimes database - this work included data pre-processing, transformation, data mining and interpretation.

Because of the time scale involved for the SSDM project, approximately three months was dedicated to each of the demonstrator systems. It is known that determining the business objective or question is the key to the data mining process [1]. While each company had an objective, obtaining the relevant domain knowledge to support this was not possible due to the time scale, and so SSDM focussed on the development of visualisation tools (see, for instance: [2, 3, 4]) that the various companies could take away and further experiment with. This is in accord with the observation that data mining can and should be packaged in such a way that the business professionals can participate directly in the data mining process [5].

This paper describes KDD technology transfer between the Centre for Adaptive Systems and three very different companies. The manufacturing company required help with data cleaning, the business clustering consultants required help with data cleaning, data transformation and data visualization, and the police force were interested in the phenomena of repeat victimization. In two of the projects visualization tools were developed was so that the business professionals could participate directly in the data mining process [5].

2. Parts code reconciliation

2.1 Introduction

This work was for a large company with 50-70 factories world-wide, each factory involved in the production of, or selling/ buying of, tens of thousands of parts. They approached SSDM when moving to a single platform data-warehouse for the whole company, and were interested in the benefits of data mining their resource. However, a more pressing concern than data mining was the cleaning of their data, and so SSDM chose to help with data reconciliation. The factory that SSDM mainly worked with had about 217000 part number descriptions, containing many duplicate ways of referring to similar parts under different names and codes. The same part occurred many times because it had been supplied from different manufacturers, or was re-engineered by the company. There was too much data to manually check it without an automated method to help this process. An example of the duplication of parts can be seen in Table 1 (this data has had the specific part name anonymised).

Part Code	Duplication
PART_NAME.62002RS	6200-2RS/30X9SKF
PART_NAME.FAG6008RS	6008-2RS40/68X15
PART_NAME.608-2Z,ABM250	608-2Z8/22X7

Table 1. Examples of part duplication.

2.2 Technology choice

There were various candidates for use of technology in this problem, including recurrent neural networks [6, 7], because of their demonstrated use in text classification problems. This type of neural network does not just treat text as a "bag of words" (or characters) but also takes ordering into account. Also, the problem could be resolved by either Hidden Markov Models [8], suffix trees [9], or by learning regular expressions from string data [9, 10].

However the vast amount of string matching literature in the field of biological sequencing proved the most useful [9, 11, 12, 13, 14, 15]. The particular algorithm chosen was the *Needleman-Wunsch algorithm* [16].

The Needleman-Wunsch algorithm is a general algorithm for sequence comparison, and gives a maximum match (the best 'global' alignment of any two sequences) between two sequences of characters, indicating the largest number of characters of one sequence that can be matched with another, allowing for all possible deletions (missing characters). As an example consider the two strings ("MPRCLCQRJNCBA" and "PBRCKCRNJCJA") shown in Figure 2. The lines within each string indicate gaps, and the lines between the two strings indicate matching characters. According to the algorithm this (Figure 2) is the maximal match for these two strings.

The Needleman-Wunsch algorithm represents both sequences in a 2-dimensional array and involves an iterative matrix method of calculation. All possible alignments (comparisons) are represented by pathways through this array. This algorithm is implemented by means of the 'dynamic programming' rationale. It is applicable when a large search space can be structured into a succession of stages, such that the initial stage contains trivial solutions to sub-problems, each partial solution in a later stage can be calculated by recurring on only a fixed number of partial solutions in an earlier stage, the final stage contains the overall solution.

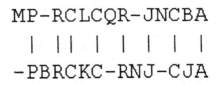

Figure 2. Resultant maximal string matching.

In order to use this algorithm for the purposes of our project, the richly represented matching information was converted into a numerical measure of similarity. The similarity was determined as follows:

Similarity = X + Y/3   (1.)

Where:

X = total occurrences of two or more adjacent matching characters

Y = total occurrences of matching characters not in X

And so for the strings "MPRCLCQRJNCB" and "PBRCKCRNJCJ", X = 2 (the adjacent matching characters; R-R, C-C), and, Y=6 (the remaining matching characters; P-P, C-C, R-R, J-J, C-C, A-A), giving a similarity of 4 (see previous Figure 2).

In this way the similarity is weighted towards the occurrence of adjacent matching characters, though the single matching characters are also considered. It is clear that the original Needlemann-Wunsch string matching format can be augmented with much domain knowledge at this stage, however even this very simplistic method of post-processing the format was found to produce good initial results. The algorithm was coded to match two datasets together, and assign the similarity scoring. Because of the size of the dataset, only similarities of 6 and over were considered, otherwise there were too many matches for a user to consider.

Unfortunately a good evaluation to estimating the accuracy of this method would require something like a traditional Information Retrieval measure of *recall and precision* [17]. This was not possible because of the time scale of the work. Also, because of the confidential nature of the data all that can be reported is that this technique revealed many previously unknown duplications, and has assisted the company in their data cleansing.

While the implemented algorithm worked sufficiently well to find duplications, interesting further work would involve tailoring the string matching algorithm so that it is more domain specific, which would require input from the company, for instance, look-up tables containing manufacturers codes. Also, it would be interesting to compare the Needleman-Wunsch algorithm against alternative string matching algorithms, for example the Smith-Waterman algorithm [15], which is a relative of the Needleman-Wunsch algorithm. The Smith-Waterman algorithm looks potentially more useful for this particular problem as instead of looking at each sequence in its entirety this compares segments of all possible lengths ('local' alignments) and chooses whichever maximize the similarity measure, and for every cell the algorithm calculates *all* possible paths leading to it. These paths can be of any length and can contain insertions and deletions.

3. Detecting business clusters

3.1 Introduction

There are various reasons for interest in business clustering. The government would like to spot cluster decline – for instance, why did the Northeast 'ship-building cluster' vanish. Businesses may be interested in finding the most advantageous place to relocate to. While early economics theory maintained that "monopoly is the key to economic success", recent findings suggest that companies that cluster together stimulate economic efficiency. Examples of the latter are that 80% of hosiery manufacturing is in Leicestershire (and most of that is in Leicester city), that auctioneering in London is very localized and very successful, and that Italian clothes are very successful because all the textiles processes are very close together. The main aim of this work was to develop a visual clustering program that used alternative technology to k-means clustering [18] and hierarchical clustering [19], which the company were already familiar with.

3.2 Data preprocessing

The data supplied to SSDM included approximately 15,300 records of Computer Manufacturing Services across the UK (see Figure 3). The data included such fields as the sales figures for 1998 and 1995, the pre-tax profit and net worth of the company for the same years. The data supplied contained many missing values, and values that had possibly been input incorrectly. While some experiments were later carried out on cut-down datasets that had no missing values, methods were developed to estimate missing values, and identify possible inaccuracies in the data.

Figure 3. Computer business companies across the UK.

In order to predict missing values statistical models of the data were built using the features that were determined to contain most of the variance in the data (the principal components), namely "NETWORTH", "PRE-TAX PROFIT", "SALES", and "NUMBER OF EMPLOYEES". A problem was the highly distorted distribution of the variables, with each showing a skewed central distribution with some very large positive (and sometimes negative) extremes. The negative extremes were excluded from "NETWORTH" and "PRE-TAX PROFIT", and a log transformation was performed on the data. This produced a set of strongly correlated variables. Linear models were developed on the transformed data, creating a simple model relating the four variables. This was used for predicting missing values (and detecting anomalous cases or 'outliers') with some degree of precision. Neural models (non-linear) were not found to improve significantly upon the linear models because of the strong linear correlations between the transformed data, and the fact that only four variables were used. Neural models would possibly perform better if more variables were used in model building, or if the relationships between the variables were more complex. Using these models the missing values were 'plugged'.

The next stage of pre-preprocessing involved the augmentation of the dataset with graphical coordinates, as it had been established through consultation with the company that the best kind of tool for this problem would involve a visual interpretation of the data. A bought-in look-up table was used to transform the (mostly available) postcodes into coordinates. Approximately 1000 records had approximate coordinates assigned as the postcodes did not appear in the table, and the coordinates were estimated using the average for that postcode 'stem' (e.g. the stem 'SR6' for the unfound postcode 'SR6 0DD').

3.3 Interpretation

A software tool was produced for the company that graphically plotted the data points on an image of the UK. The approach taken was to use a kernel-based approximation for the probability density function [20, 21, 22, 23]. The kernel function used was Gaussian (bell-shaped). Given that sufficient training points were available, this yielded a sufficiently good approximation to the true probability density function. Also included into the function were the values for all of the (deemed) important fields, for instance "NETWORTH" and "PRE-TAX PROFIT". Each of these values had an associated weight that could be manipulated through the tool. Also available for manipulation was the smoothing factor. This meant that the company could investigate the relationship of these factors by changing their associated weights and viewing the changing graphical output.

However, a problem encountered immediately was that the London data completely swamped the other data, resulting in a huge cluster over London, and no other clusters being seen. In order to counter this a 'bias-factor' was incorporated into the calculations. If there are more computer companies in London, then there should also be an equivalently larger amount of all types of companies in London. We obtained data describing all companies per postcode region, and incorporated this into the function as the following bias factor:

number_of_computer_companies_per_postcode_region

/ number_of_all_companies_per_postcode_region

Unfortunately this had no effect, indicating that there are proportionally more computer companies in London than anywhere else. A rather drastic next step was taken, so that initial experiments could be carried out, which was to ignore the London data. Figures 4, 5, 6 show clustering about various named cities, after the London data has been removed.

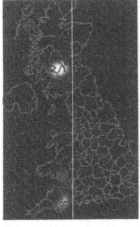
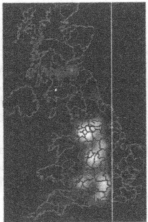
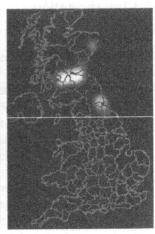

Figure 4. Clusters left of line (top to bottom): Glasgow, Cardiff, Plymouth-Exeter.

Figure 5. Clusters left of line (top to bottom): Aberdeen, Glasgow-Edinburgh, Newcastle-Sunderland-Middlesbrough, Manchester, Birmingham-Nottingham, Swindon-Bristol, Reading.

Figure 6. Clusters above line (top to bottom): Glasgow-Edinburgh, Newcastle-Sunderland-Middlesbrough.

Changing the smoothing factor in the calculation means that it is possible to sharpen or blur the presentation of the data points, in order to better investigate clusters, (see Figures 7 & 8).

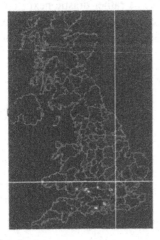
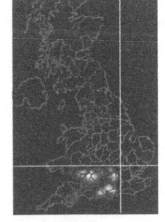

Figure 7. Sharp data presentation.

Figure 8. Blurred data presentation.

The company was left with the tool in order that they could investigate business clustering, though through the experiments it became clear that the definition of business clusters based solely on location and performance is perhaps too limiting.

It is important to consider what exactly is the definition of a cluster. To what degree does spatial proximity indicate a cluster? How 'deep' is a cluster – if computer software companies are to be considered, how far into hardware companies (if at all) should be considered? Business clusters are based also on social relationships, and networks of people are not really data susceptible, and so how is this knowledge to be modeled? These were questions left with the company.

4. Detecting Repeat Victimization

4.1 Introduction

The concept of revictimisation [24, 25, 26], first noted by Sparks [27], is the observation that people and/or places which have suffered a crime once, are disproportionately likely to be a victim of crime again. For example, the risk of being burgled again was highest within 28 days following the first burglary, and reduced to normal levels after approximately six months [28]. Furthermore, Ewart, Inglis and Wilbert [29] demonstrated that the time interval decreased between successive burglary revictimisations at a property. The significance of revictimisation to policing strategies is only just being recognized and Pease [24, p.32] concludes that, "the best analysis requires the simultaneous consideration of victimsation, place and perpetrator information". This section details work with a local police force, to investigate the potential uses of computer modeling and data mining. The work focussed on trying to determine whether someone is likely to be susceptible to repeat victimization or not, to also investigate the time course issues, and see when the possibility of being a repeat victim diminishes. These issues clearly have ramifications towards management of police resources.

4.2 Data

SSDM was supplied with 10021 records, which was a three-month time slice of data, from a crimes database. The fields of the data are listed in Table 2. The data was anonymised by putting a unique number in place of the persons' name. For the purposes of this paper all presented data is further anonymised by mixing up the field values between records, including the RASCODE and WARD geographical fields. A sample of the data can be seen in Table 3, and a 'repeat victim' can be seen, as the reference number 10 occurs three times. It should also be noted that the 'ethnicity' for this person was noted in only two of these records. The value '999' indicates a missing value. The data provided had many other obvious inaccuracies.

FIELD	EXPLANATION
REF	The person reference number
DATE_ADD	Date added to database
AGE	Age of person when added to database
ETHNIC	1. White 2. Black 3. Asian 4. Other
OCCUPATION	Occupation
HOCLASS	Home Office Category of Crime
RASCODE	Police beat area
REP_VIC	Whether person has been a victim of a repeat crime – 1. No 2. Yes
WARD	Local Authority ward boundaries
SEX	Sex of the victim

Table 2. Crime data descriptive fields.

REF	DATE_ADD	AGE	ETHNIC	OCCUPATION	HOCLASS	RASCODE	REP_VIC	WARD	SEX
1	31-Aug-1999	51	1	HOUSEWIFE	30/1	M201A01	2	COATHAM	2
2	19-Jul-1999	30	1	PROPRIETOR	49/10	L301P01	2	WESTBOURNE	1
3	04-Jul-1999	40	1	PLATER	44	L204A01	2	ORMESBY	1
4	19-Jul-1999	38	1	999	126	L206A02	2	GRANGETOWN	2
5	17-Aug-1999	68	1	RETIRED	40	M112A01	2	GRANGE	2
6	17-Jul-1999	34	1	HOUSEWIFE	28/1	S203A01	2	KADER	1
10	11-Aug-1999	39	999	PIZZA CHEF	48/1	L201P01	2	SOUTH BANK	2
10	09-Sep-1999	39	1	PIZZA CHEF	48/1	L201P01	2	THORNTREE	2
10	10-Sep-1999	39	1	PIZZA CHEF	56/2	M204P04	999	BECKFIELD	2
11	20-Jul-1999	35	4	UNEMPLOYED	58/3	M106P07	2	AYRESOME	1

Table 3. Example crime data. The 'OCCUPATION' field is free text and is a rich source of information. The 'RASCODE' and 'WARD' are geographic. The 'HOCLASS' is the crime type, the code referring to a specific type of crime, for instance, HOCODE's 28, 29, 30, 31, are all types of burglary.

Upon examination there were inaccuracies in the REP_VIC field (reference numbers that occur more than once - clearly repeat victims - often have a value indicating they are 'not a repeat victim'), and so a new field was added. If a person occurred more than once in the data set they were considered a repeat victim (938 records), else they were not (9083 records).

OCCUCODE	DESCRIPTION
I	Professional occupations
II	Managerial and technical occupations
IIIM	Skilled manual occupations
IIIN	Skilled non-manual occupations
IV	Partly-skilled occupations
V	Unskilled occupations
VI	Armed forces
& UNEMPLOYED, RETIRED, DISABLED, SCHOOLBOY, STUDENT	

Table 4. Occupation and description. 'Social Classes based on Occupation' fields (I, II, IIIM, IIIN, IV, V, VI) appended with additional fields that did not fit into this classification.

The data was initially transformed in two ways – the 'DATE_ADD' field was changed to a single numerical value base-lined to the earliest date. Also the 'HOCLASS' field was reduced to the main category to which the specific crime relates (e.g. '28' - Burglary in a dwelling, and '29' - Aggravated burglary in a dwelling, are both now just 'Burglary') – this variable is now called 'NEWHO' (i.e. 'new HO class'). The next step was how to use the rich source of information in the free-text 'OCCUPATION' field. Meetings with a criminologist at University of Sunderland concluded with the use of an amended version of the 1990 Standard Occupational Classification (SOC; [30]) - see Table 4. This new variable was called 'OCCUCODE'. The amendments were made because much of the data could not be fitted into the SOC divisions. The full data set, ordered according to frequency of occurrence of 'OCCUPATION' type, revealed that 'UNEMPLOYED', 'RETIRED', 'DISABLED', 'SCHOOLBOY', and 'STUDENT' all appear high up in this list, and that removing these would reduce the data set by 80%. A cut off was decided upon, subject to revision in later experiments, of inclusion of occupations that occurred more than 15 times. Table 5 shows the classification of the 'OCCUPATIONS' into the SOC divisions. The 'RAS_CODE', the police beat details, were not used in this project. The 'WARD' was cleaned by cross-reference to a (relatively) clean file detailing the four areas within which each of these wards fell.

OCCUPATION (SOC)	FREQ	OCCUPATION (SOC)	FREQ	OCCUPATION (SOC)	FREQ
UNEMPLOYED	1438	LABOURER (IV)	49	ACCOUNTANT (I)	23
<MISSING VALUES>	1161	PROCESS WORKER (IV)	49	COOK (IIIM)	23
RETIRED	1145	DRIVER (IIIM)	47	PROCESS OPERATOR (IIIM)	22
HOUSEWIFE (V)	749	CIVIL SERVANT (IIIN)	47	PLUMBER (IIIM)	22
STUDENT	549	FACTORY WORKER (IV)	44	SCAFFOLDER (IIIM)	22

SHOP ASSISTANT (IV)	152	BUILDER (IIIM)	42	DIRECTOR (I)	21
PROPRIETOR (IIIN)	134	BARMAID (IV)	41	POSTMAN (IIIM)	21
TEACHER (II)	92	SECRETARY (IIIN)	39	RECEPTIONIST (IIIN)	21
NURSE (II)	90	MACHINIST (IIIM)	38	SECURITY OFFICER (IIIM)	21
CARE ASSISTANT (IIIN)	84	HAIRDRESSER (IIIM)	38	SECURITY GUARD (IIIM)	20
CLEANER (V)	80	POLICE OFFICER (IIIN)	37	STAFF NURSE (II)	19
JOINER (IIIM)	77	SUPERVISOR (IIIN)	37	BRICKLAYER (IIIM)	18
MANAGER (II)	74	SCHOOLBOY	36	LANDLORD (IIIN)	18
SALES ASSISTANT (IIIN)	73	FITTER (IIIM)	33	PRODUCTION WORKER (IIIM)	18
ELECTRICIAN (IIIM)	73	TECHNICIAN (II)	32	GENERAL LABOURER (IIIM)	18
ENGINEER (IIIM)	73	COMPANY DIRECTOR (I)	28	PLATER (IIIM)	18
TAXI DRIVER (IIIM)	68	LECTURER (I)	27	DOCTOR (I)	18
CLERK (IIIN)	61	SOCIAL WORKER (II)	27	STUDENT NURSE (II)	18
SELF EMPLOYED (IIIM)	60	WELDER (IIIM)	26	SHOP OWNER (IIIN)	18
HGV DRIVER (IIIM)	55	FIREMAN (IIIM)	26		
DISABLED	52	MECHANIC (IIIM)	26		

Table 5. Occupation and frequency. Frequency of occurrence of OCCUPATIONS in the full data set, where frequency is greater than 15

4.3 Initial Experiments

A cleaned and transformed dataset included both single victims and repeat victims. Various statistical approaches were adopted to investigate whether or not repeat victimization is indeed a phenomena based upon certain characteristics of an individual, or whether it is equally likely to occur to any individual regardless of their characteristics. It has been reported in the literature that the former case is true [24]. The chi-squared tests employed did not take into account the different wards, but covered the whole county in question. A major problem faced, however, was the lack of information concerning the amount of people in the various 'social classes', and the results of these tests (very weakly) concluded that repeat victimization is dependent on social class ('OCCUCODE'), and that it is more likely to occur in the social classes 'threeM', 'threeN' and 'five'. It is very weakly concluded because of the 'ad hoc' nature of calculating the total members per social class, the lack of correct value for the total population, and the inclusion of extra values for social class (e.g. 'RETIRED', 'UNEMPLOYED')

Following on from these experiments various neural network models [31] were created using the Trajan package [32] on this dataset. Unfortunately even the best network (multi-layered perceptron with 5 hidden units) performed poorly. Sensitivity analysis of features in these networks revealed that 'OCCUCODE', 'NEWHO' and 'AGE' can be considered the most important features. No geographic features were used in these network experiments.

4.4 Predicting the NEXT CRIME and NEXT TIME (of victimization)

In these experiments the 'WARD' variable has been generalized to one of four larger categories. From the repeat victims in the dataset, a new dataset was produced, as in Figure 10. It can be seen that there are three records with reference number 10 in the top dataset, and only two records in the new dataset. For the first occurrence of reference 10, it is known that the next crime is 'Robbery' (from the second occurrence of reference 10), and that this took place 29 days (71-42) later. The new 'TIME' value is generalized to the value 'fifteentothirty'. The same procedure is carried out for the second occurrence of reference 10, by looking at the next crime and time values. Nothing can be done with the third occurrence of reference 10, as the next crime and time are unknown.

The best neural network models trained on this data for predicting 'NEXT CRIME' achieved very average performance, and it was impossible to find a neural network model for predicting 'NEXT TIME' without either obvious over-training, or extremely poor performance. It is unfortunate that there was no time to use a dataset where the 'NEXT TIME' value was not generalized into categories, but remained as an integer, as previous studies have shown the significance of time intervals [28, 29].

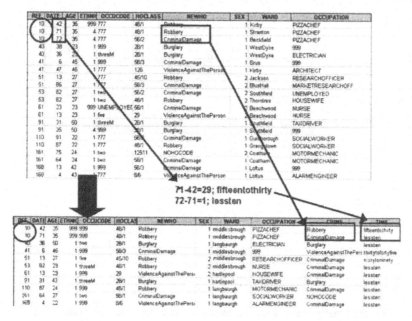

Figure 10. Creation of 'NEXT CRIME' and 'NEXT TIME' datasets.

4.5 Data visualization

This section briefly covers the aspects of the developed software tool for the company to conduct their own data mining experiments. The bar chart feature of the tool shown in Figure 2 shows each person as a separate bar. The y-axis is time, and ranges from 0 to 90 days. The start of the red part of the bar indicates the point in this 90-day period when the first crime occurred against the person. The start of the blue part of the bar indicates when the next crime occurred, and so on. By clicking on any of these bars, the detail of the person is displayed in the open box below. For instance, Figure 11 shows that record (person) 132 started with a crime of 'ViolenceAgainstThePerson' (Crime0), then the first repeat crime (CrimeR1) was 'CriminalDamage', followed by 'ViolenceAgainstThePerson' (CrimeR2) and 'Burglary' (CrimeR3). The areas where each of these crimes occurred are also detailed. By pressing the 'Process' button, the data is filtered according to the choices made in the drop-down boxes (filters). These filters include all values for the attributes, for instance 'ETHNIC' has the selections of {1, 2, 3, 4, 'All'}. The pie charts feature shown in Figure 12 show this same data presented in a different format.

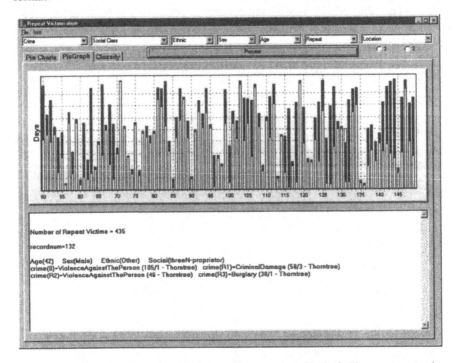

Figure 11. Bar chart presentation. Each bar represents an individual. The y-axis extends from 0 to 90 days. The start of the colored portions of the bar indicate the first crime, and successive borders between colored parts of the bar are further crimes.

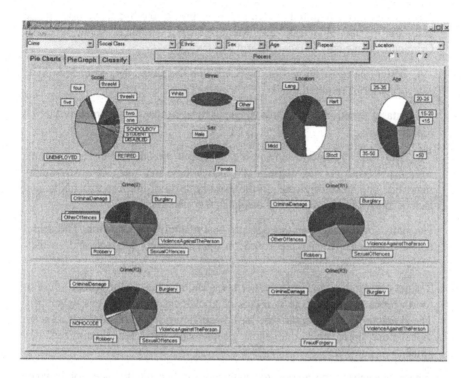

Figure 12. Pie chart presentation. The data is 'unfiltered' and so shows the breakdown according to all features, e.g. the data points were mainly white, approximately half male, and the first repeat crime (crimeR1) was evenly distributed between {Burglary|CriminalDamage|Robbery|ViolenceAgainstThePerson}.

A third feature of the tool incorporates the various neural network classifiers. The characteristics of a person can be entered by means of drop-down boxes ('First Crime', 'OCCUPATION', 'ETHNICITY', 'SEX', AGE', 'LOCATION'), and it is reported whether the person is likely to be a repeat victim, what the next crime is likely to be, and how far in the future this will occur. Because of the poor performance of these models, this feature was flagged as being 'highly dubious'.

4.6 Summary and future work

Future work should use transformation into geographical coordinates for a graphical view of this data, and incorporation of demographic data and police intelligence information. At the very least each area can be labeled with a certain "CRIME LEVEL" (e.g. high/medium/low crime levels).

The following limitations of this work should be noted:

- A better analysis is required related to the features of the 'repeat victims' in the data, before the HOCODE is generalized. For instance, some types of CriminalDamage may in fact be Burglary attempts.

- A better categorization for OCCUPATION than the amended SOC categorization is required.

- The dataset is only 90 days, and single victims in this dataset may in fact be repeat victims.

- The data was very noisy, and in order to 'clean' this data many assumptions were made (with varying degrees of justification), and much data was simply removed. The noise originates in the main because of the free text fields, and lack of motivation on the part of the data entry personnel.

- The statistics derived from this data are best treated with suspicion. The neural network models likewise are based on heavily biased datasets, and so their usefulness is compromised.

- It is not certain that the first repeat crime is as important as the second, third or fourth repeat crimes. There is a lack of knowledge in the models developed. The characteristics of people who have been victimized four times would seem to be more 'interesting' than those people who have been victimized only twice.

- The data needs to be augmented with more police intelligence, for instance details of known drug suppliers, prostitutes, political activists etc.

Further problems arise due to the collection of the data, for instance there may be multiple people living in a house, however only the person who answers the door will have their name recorded as having been victimized (for instance "burglary"). It could be that this person was not actually the victim, or that a different person is interviewed on separate occasions.

An important point that the police took on board was the recommendation to design new data input forms (for instance by drop-down boxes offering a fixed selection of categories), so that the data is stored more reliably, and in a format that can be explored more successfully. Certainly the neural network models would be improved a great deal with better data. The police force was also very happy with the developed tool, allowing them to see the 'history' of individual victims. They were unable to do this in their previous data format.

Also, a very useful direction for future work would be to develop a *case-based or instance-based classifier* [33, 34] to predict future crimes and time intervals of crimes. This technology is more able to take into account the whole series of crimes in the matching process, and is amenable to the inclusion of police intelligence and other forms of domain knowledge.

5. Conclusions

By means of data and problems supplied by SSDM Club members, and presentation of results in seminars, SSDM was able to illustrate the KDD process and the use of a wide range of algorithms. All of the data presented to SSDM required a lot of preprocessing and preparation. The time scale involved meant that while simple experiments could be carried out, the inclusion (or extraction) of sufficient domain knowledge meant that software tools were developed for the individual companies to conduct their own data mining experiments.

The demonstrator applications included the novel use of a bio-sequencing algorithm for identification of duplicate codes in a large database, as a data cleaning process, the development of a software tool for visualizing business clusters, and a repeat victimization application which demonstrated the KDD stages of data preparation, data transformation, data mining, and data visualization.

Acknowledgments

The University of Sunderland is grateful to the DTI for the grant "Smart Software for Decision Makers" which made this work possible.

References

1. Fayyad, U. M, Stolorz, P. Data Mining And KDD: Promises and Challenges. Future Generation Computer Systems 13 (1997) 99-115, 1997.

2. Visible Decisions. [Online]. Available: http://www.pinetreecapital.com/pine0-2-13.html [2001, January 17].

3. SpotFire. [Online]. Available: http://www.spotfire.com/ [2001, January 17].

4. Metaphor Mixer. [Online]. Available: http://www.inworldvr.com/partners/maxus/mixer.html [2001, January 17].

5. Montgomery, A. Data Mining: Computer Support Discovering and Deploying Best Practice In Business and Public Service. Expert Update, Knowledge Based System and Applied Artificial Intelligence SGES, Autumn 1999, vol2, No 3,ISSN 1465-4091.

6. Wermter, S., Arevian, G., & Panchev, C. Recurrent neural network learning for text-routing. In: Proceedings of the International Conference on Artificial Neural Networks, Edinburgh, UK, September 1999.

7. Wermter, S., Arevian, G., & Panchev, C. Hybrid neural plausibility networks for news agents. In: Proceedings of the National Conference on Artificial Intelligence, Orlando, USA, July 1999.

8. Baldi, P., & Brunak, S. Bioinformatics: machine learning approach MIT press, Chs. 7 & 8, 1998.

9. Gusfield, D. Algorithms on strings, trees and sequences, Cambridge: Cambridge University Press, 1997.

10. Brazma, A., Jonassen, I., Eidhammer,I. & Gilbert,D. Approaches to the automatic discovery of patterns in biosequences, Journal of Computational Biology (1998), Vol (5), Issue (2), pp. 279-305, 1998.

11. Durbin, R., Eddy, S.R., Krogh, A., & Mitchison, G. Biological sequence analysis: probabilistic models of proteins and nucleic acids, Cambridge: Cambridge University Press, 1998.

12. Pearson, W.R. CABIOS (1997) 13(4): 325-332

13. Waterman, M. Introduction to Computational Biology, Chapman & Hall, 1995.

14. Pearson, W.R., & Lipman, D.J. Proc. Natl. Acad Sci. USA (1988) 85: 2444-2448

15. Smith, T. F., Waterman, M. S. J. Mol. Biol. (1981) 147:195-197

16. Needleman, S.B., & Wunsch, C.D. J. Mol. Biol. (1970) 48:443-453

17. Van Rijsbergen, C.J. Information Retrieval. London: Butterworths, 1975.

18. Bradley, P. S., Usama M., & Fayyad. Refining Initial Points for K-Means Clustering. In: Proc. 15th International Conf. on Machine Learning, 1998.

19. Hartigan, J. A. Clustering Algorithms. New York: Wiley, 1975.

20. Hunter A. Feature Selection Using Probabilistic Neural Networks. In: Neural Computing & Applications (2000) 9:124-132, Springer-Verlag, London.

21. Patterson, D.W. Artificial Neural Networks: Theory and Applications, Prentice Hall (Sd), ISBN: 0132953536, 1998.

22. Bishop. Neural Networks for Pattern Recognition, Clarendon Press, Oxford, 1995.

23. Speckt D.,F. Probabilistic Neural Networks. Neural networks 1990; 3(1):109-118.

24. Pease, K. Repeat Victimisation: Taking Stock. Police Research Group. Crime Detection and Prevention Series, Paper 90. London, Crown Copyright, 1998.

25. Trickett, A., Osborn, D., Seymour, J., & Pease, K. What is Different About High Crime Areas? British Journal of Criminology, 32, 1, 81-89, 1992.

26. Tilley, N., Webb, J. & Gregson, M. Vulnerability to burglary in an inner-city area: Some preliminary findings. Issues in Criminological and Legal Psychology, 2, 17, 112-119, 1991.

27. Sparks, R.H. Multiple victimisation, evidence theory and future research. Journal of Criminal Law and Criminology, 72, 762-778, 1981.

28. Polvi, N., Looman, T., Humphries, C., & Pease, K. The Time Course of Repeat Burglary Victimization. British Journal of Criminology, 31, 4, 411-414, 1991.

29. Ewart B.W., Inglis P., Wilbert , M.N. & Hill, I. An analysis of time intervals of victimisation. Forensic Update, 50, pp 4-9, 1997.

30. Elias, P. Social Class and the Standard Occupational Classification, In: D. Rose (1995), A Report on Phase 1 of the ESRC Review of Social Classifications. Swindon: ESRC, 1995.

31. Craven, M.W., & Shavlik J.W. Using Neural Networks For Data Mining. Future Generation Computer Systems 13, 211-229, 1997.

32. Trajan. Homepage of Trajan Software [Online]. Available: http://www.trajan-software.demon.co.uk [2001, February 5].

33. Lenz, M., Bartsch-Spörl, B., Burkhard, H-D., & Wess, S. Case-Based Reasoning Technology: From Foundations to Applications. Springer-Verlag Berlin, Heidelberg, ISBN 3-540-64572-1, 1998.

34. Gebhardt, F., Voss, A., Grather, W., & Schmidt-Belz, B. Reasoning with complex cases, Kluwer Academic Publishers, 1997.

SESSION 2:

ENGINEERING APPLICATIONS 1

Expert System for Design Optimisation Using Results of Finite Element Analysis

Marina Novak

Faculty of Mechanical Engineering, University of Maribor
Maribor, Slovenia

Abstract: Design optimisation has a very important role in modern technology. In practice, the results of finite element analysis are often the basic parameters for the optimising process. If the structure does not satisfy given criteria, certain optimisation steps, such as redesign, use of other materials, etc., have to be taken. However, the existing software for finite element analysis still fails to provide advice about any optimisation steps based on the results of the analysis. Thus, redesign steps still depend mostly on the user's knowledge and experience. In this paper, we present our vision of an expert system for advising the designer which redesign steps should be taken into account in particular cases. The system is still in the development phase. The knowledge acquisition process is described in detail. It is anticipated that the system will be used not only for optimising new products in practice, but also in design education, where the students are typical representatives of inexperienced designers.

1.   Introduction

The design process is a complex task that has a significant influence on the competitiveness of future products on the market. Nowadays, designers work under the high pressure of high-tech technology. The market demands from them their new products with high quality in the shortest possible time scale. They should use all modern methods and tools to be successful. For a long time, the use of computers has been crucial in the design process. Their use in a wide assortment of systems, such as Computer Aided Design (CAD) and other CAx systems, is very valuable to the design process. Those designers who use computers with success can be more precise, and manage more complex problems. Thus, they become more effective and produce products of higher quality. CAD applications are often used in the design process in tasks such as modelling, kinematical simulation, structural analysis and drawing of documentation. The CAD software is quite complex and offers to the user an extensive assortment of services, which can easily become confusing. Modellers offer a visualisation of the designer's ideas and provide verification of the kinematics and collision. Programs for engineering analyses provide better understanding of how the structure will behave during its exploitation.

Modern tools are quite user friendly. They often guide the designer through the process, but they do not help the designer in the more creative parts of the design process, such as generation of possible design decisions and solutions, or in those aspects that involve complex reasoning about design.

Design optimisation also has a very important role in modern technology. The Finite Element Method (FEM) [1] is the most frequently used numerical method to analyse stresses and deformations in physical structures, and is usually a part of a CAD system. In practice, the results of finite element analysis are often basic parameters for the optimising process. If the structure does not satisfy given criteria, certain optimisation steps, such as redesign, use of other materials, etc., have to be taken. A decision about what should be done directly depends on the correct interpretation of the analysis results and on design knowledge and experience. However, the existing software for finite element analyses still fails to provide advice about optimisation steps based on the analysis results. Thus, design optimisation still depends heavily on the individual's experience.

In this paper, we present our vision of an expert system (ES) for advising the designer which redesigns steps need to be taken into account in certain cases. At present, some FEM packages already contain certain intelligent modules for guiding inexperienced users through the analysis process. Supported by sophisticated computer graphics technology, they also offer good visual representation. Even this, however, is not efficient enough for someone who also needs instructions about suitable redesign steps, procedures from design knowledge, and experience.

2.   Expert System for Redesign

An optimal design performed at the first attempt is rare in engineering. Design is an iterative process. How many iterations/cycles are needed directly depends on the quality of the initial design and redesign actions. The selection of the correct redesign action is a result of knowledge of the principles of mechanics, structures and materials technology. User experience also has a great influence on successessful redesign actions. Encoding this knowledge and experience, and creating rules for selecting a correct action, would give an opportunity for developing an intelligent advisory system for redesign.

The development of the proposed ES for redesign support needs to be implemented in several steps [2]. First of all, the theoretical and practical knowledge about the design and redesign actions should be investigated and collected. After that, the appropriate formalism for the acquired knowledge representation should be defined. The commonly used formalisms for encoding knowledge are production rules, which are quite similar to the actual rules used in the design process. The collected rules will construct the knowledge base of the ES. Our next step will be encoding the rules, most likely in Prolog syntax [3], and building the prototype of the ES. The ES shell should enable user-friendly input of data about the problem itself, including the results of the FEM analysis. The output would be suggestions about redesign, some help, and advice.

Figure 1 shows the basic architecture of the proposed ES for redesign support.

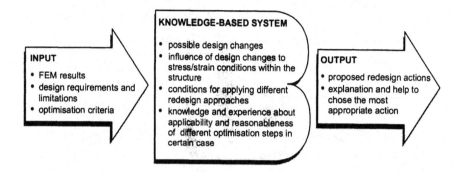

Figure 1. Knowledge-based system for redesign support.

3.   Design Knowledge

The main task of the designer is to find a technical solution to satisfy human needs and demands. The designer attempts to optimise the solution with given material, technological and economic constraints. Design is a creative activity, which requires basic knowledge such as mathematics, physics, chemistry, mechanics, thermodynamics and hydrodynamics, as well as knowledge about electrical engineering, production engineering, materials technology, and design theory. Also required is the relevant practical knowledge, skill, and experience in special fields. Following this, redesign involves a great amount of different knowledge. The literature concerning collected and documented knowledge and experience of redesign is scarce. Extensive knowledge is accumulated by experts who have worked on design problems over many years. However, it is pertinent to comment that many experts have quite different opinions, and they also admit to many exceptions to their own rules.

Generally, there are several redesign steps involved in design improvement. The selection of each redesign step depends on the requirements, possibilities and intentions. Figure 2 presents an example of the proposed initial design and some possibilities for optimisation redesign.

4.   Knowledge Acquisition

The knowledge acquisition and formation of the knowledge base for the proposed ES is our main task at the moment. We would like to extract as many rules as possible concerning the redesign, then write them down in the form of production rules [4]. In our case, we are performing the knowledge acquisition in three ways:

- Study of the literature
- Examination of old FEM analyses, and
- Interviewing experts

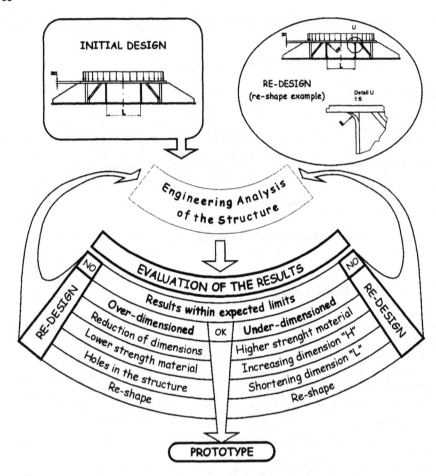

Figure 2. Initial design and some possible further design actions.

It is quite difficult to find much in the literature about redesign. This implies that the study of it is not popular. However, rules can also be extracted from some well-known equations, as for example from the equation for bending stresses [5]:

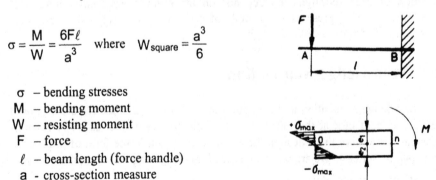

$$\sigma = \frac{M}{W} = \frac{6F\ell}{a^3} \quad \text{where} \quad W_{square} = \frac{a^3}{6}$$

- σ – bending stresses
- M – bending moment
- W – resisting moment
- F – force
- ℓ – beam length (force handle)
- a - cross-section measure

Figure 3. Bending stresses calculation for the beam with square cross-section.

According to the equation on the previous page, the bending stress can be decreased by applying the following redesign rule:

IF bending stresses are too high
AND example of one side (console) or two sides fixed "beam"
THEN
- Increase the radius at the fixing point
- Reduce the force handle length to reduce the bending moment
- Change the beam cross-section to increase the resisting moment (increase dimension in a force line)
- Reduce the force (distribute loads in several points)

The examination of previously conducted engineering analyses and redesigns is more valuable. Many problems and corresponding redesign rules can be discovered. Figure 4 shows an example how stress concentrations can be reduced by changing the wall thickness (stiffness). These kinds of problems are quite common in design practice.

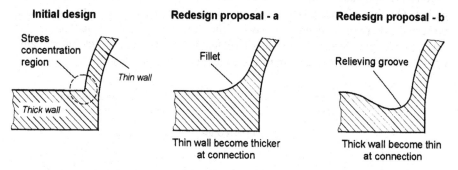

Figure 4. Design problem – stress concentrations because of a different wall thickness.

Considering Figure 4, the following redesign rule can be defined:

IF stresses are too high
AND connection of thick and thin plate (wall) at different planes
THEN
- Make or increase the fillet radius at connection point
- Make a relieving groove to change the thickness progressively
- Make the thickness uniform - preserve strength

A lot of practical knowledge can also be acquired by interviewing human experts. However, interviews and examination of the existing redesigns with experts can be very time-consuming. In our case, we have established a team of several domestic and foreign experts who are prepared to help us build up such a knowledge base. We have started to interview them and study the old analyses and redesign elaborates in the company AVL-AST in Maribor, Slovenia. Under certain conditions, which are mostly subject to preserving confidentiality, the people working in this company were willing to act as a medium for transfer of knowledge and experience gained from many extensive analyses of crucial parts of internal combustion engines, performed for several car companies all over the world.

Considering the results of the finite element analyses, critical places in the structure were defined and expert recommendations, as design changes to overcome potential problems, were given. Since the analyses were made for other companies, design recommendations were given without taking into account all the technological and functional restraints. Instead, as many sensible redesign actions as possible were recommended. After that, the engine designers chose the most appropriate optimisation measures, considering all limitations. Such an approach is more sensible from the knowledge acquisition point of view, since all possible redesign actions were considered, even when some of them would not be applicable in the actual case. Usually, the effect of the final optimising measures were re-examined by additional finite element analyses.

During the knowledge acquisition process in the company AVL-AST, several analyses of some crucial parts of internal combustion engines conducted previously were discussed. The engine head, cylinder block, and the gasket between them were analysed. The results of the finite element analyses were beyond the allowable limits at several places in the engine head and also in the gasket. On the left hand side in Figure 5, an example of the initial design is presented, where the temperature between the valve seats (critical place) on the gas side of the engine head's fire deck is too high. On the right hand side in the same figure, a design recommendation to solve the problem is presented.

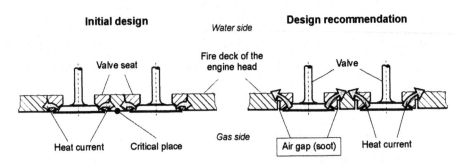

Figure 5. Redirection of the heat current by changing the geometry of the valve seats.

The design recommendation presented in Figure 5 is not the only possible solution to improve the design in such a case. After a detailed discussion with the expert, we extracted a more general redesign rule that can be applied to solve similar problems dealing with the heat transfer:

IF temperature is too high
AND area is small and narrow
THEN
- Use higher thermal conductible material
- Use material with higher strength at high temperature
- Add material – make wider area or add vertical cooling rib
- Move the heat contact area out of the critical region, (e.g. with a gap)
- Redirect the heat current

The knowledge presented here is written in the form of production rules, which is the most commonly used formalism for encoding knowledge in ES, as mentioned before. The rules have the form:

IF problem
AND limits
THEN
    Redesign action 1
    Redesign action 2
    ...
    Redesign action n

Each rule presents a list of recommended redesign actions that should be taken into consideration while dealing with a certain problem constrained by some limitations. The rules are generalized, and do not refer solely to the examples that were used during the knowledge acquisition process. They can be used every time the problem and limits match with those in the head of the rule. In such a case, the application of the appropriate rule would result in a list of recommended redesign actions for dealing with the given problem. A user/designer, with his or her own knowledge and experience, should chose and apply one or more redesign actions that are possible, reasonable and most effective, for their particular case.

This method of knowledge acquisition is time-consuming, and the scope of results is small and limited by the availability of experts. The collected rules will construct the knowledge base of the ES for redesign support. Through expert evaluation, we plan to discuss and examine these rules with human experts, again in comparison with some previously conducted examples. It is expected that we will discover some new rules in the process.

5. Conclusion

The decision to develop the ES for redesign support is the result of experience acquired through the design education process [6], and previous development of an intelligent system for finite element mesh design [7], [8]. The aim of our future research work is to develop an intelligent system, which will be able to support the user through the design process, especially at the design verification and redesign phase. The system should help and guide the user through engineering analyses and suggest the appropriate redesign actions in the case of an under-dimensioned physical structure. The system should also report about over-dimensioned places in the structure and suggest possible redesign actions for optimisation.

In this paper, we presented the nature of design knowledge and the knowledge acquisition process leading to the ES for advising the designer as to which redesign steps should be taken into account in each case. At the moment, we are still developing the knowledge base for the ES.

It is anticipated, that the presented ES will be used not only for optimising new products in practice, but also in design education.

The students are typical representatives of inexperienced designers. Thus, the use of the presented ES should be very useful in the design education process. Here, the important feature of the knowledge based system – the ability to explain the inference process by answering questions "How?" and "Why?" – will be especially welcome, and should enable the students to acquire some new knowledge. It may help them to learn more about basic principles of design processes, and to avoid the many wrong conclusions and mistakes which appear frequently due to their lack of experience. We believe the expert system application can help to prepare the students for their future engineering profession, when their work will be exposed to the rigours of the competitive market place, where optimal solutions are more and more indispensible.

References

[1]   Zienkiewicz, O.C. & Taylor, R.L. (1988). The Finite Element Method: Basic Formulation and Linear Problems. Vol.1, McGraw-Hill Book Company, London.

[2]   Merritt, D. (1989). Building Expert Systems in Prolog. Springer-Verlag.

[3]   Bratko, I. (1990). Prolog: Programming for Artificial Intelligence. Second Edition, Addison-Wesley.

[4]   Miles, J. & Moore, C. (1994) Practical Knowledge-Based Systems in Conceptual Design, Springer-Verlag.

[5]   Dorf, R.C. (1996). The Engineering Handbook. CRC Press, Inc.

[6]   Novak, M., Dolšak, B. & Jezernik, A. (2000). Expert Supporting System for Teaching Design. Proceedings of the 6th International Design Conference - DESIGN'00 (Edited by Marjanović, D.), pp. 477–482.

[7]   Dolšak, B. & Jezernik, A. (1998). A Rule-Based Expert System for Finite Element Mesh Design. Proceedings of the 5th International Design Conference - DESIGN'98 (Edited by Marjanović, D.), pp. 287–292.

[8]   Dolšak, B., Bratko, I. & Jezernik, A. (1998). Application of Machine Learning in Finite Element Computation. Machine Learning, Data Mining and Knowledge Discovery: Methods and Applications (Edited by Michalski, R.R., Bratko, I. & Kubat, M.), John Wiley & Sons, pp. 147–171.

Automatic Generation of Design Improvements by Applying Knowledge Based Engineering to the Post-processing of Finite Element Analysis

Craig B Chapman[1], Martyn Pinfold, Warwick Manufacturing Group, School of Engineering, University of Warwick, Coventry, UK

Abstract: An integral part of the design cycle for many engineering components is the analysis of them using finite element (FE) techniques. The components are prepared for the specific requirements of the FE process and analysed. The resulting analysis information is then studied and decisions made to the suitability of the initial design with regards to its engineering specification, this verification stage may lead to a new validation stage where design changes are made to address the concerns of the engineering team. Due to the inherent limitations in the current methods of describing and handling a complete representation of component product models by geometric focussed CAD systems engineers do not automatically integrate the FE post-processing validation stage into their design process. This paper describes the methods being used and the information required for the application of an automotive engine mount bracket using a Knowledge Based Engineering (KBE) environment to automate the results interpretation phase of the design/analysis cycle and to directly validate the initial design model by altering the 3D product model until a satisfactory result is obtained.

1. Introduction: The Design/Analysis Problem

The need to consider a number of different alternatives at an early stage in design has been well established. Virtually all design projects include the need for some form of analysis often using finite element (FE) techniques. The analysis process may be broken down into three distinct phases, pre-processing (model creation), analysis and post-processing (results interpretation). As Jones et al [1] state the geometric model created in a CAD system can be incoherent and ambiguous and "may require significant cleaning and modification in preparation for meshing and analysis". To avoid these problems analysts may create their own simplified models from scratch [1,2] leading to model duplication with subsequent time and cost implications. Consequently these extra models have no associativity with the original CAD models. After an analysis the analysts use their experience to

---

[1] Correspondence should be emailed to Craig B Chapman, at c.b.chapman@warwick.ac.uk

interpret the results and make suggestions to the design engineering team, who if necessary, then apply an agreed change strategy to the analysis model or to the original CAD model. The analysis – modify loop is entered into again until a satisfactory result is obtained.

1.1 Traditional Design / Analysis Tools

In a traditional CAD environment the design stage is de-coupled from the analysis stage. As Sahu and Grosse [3] point out a 'concurrent engineering computational environment should have the ability to interpret the results from numerical analyses, and then use these inferences for automating, suggesting, or facilitating design modification.' They go on to state that 'what is needed, therefore, is a mechanism to extract meaningful qualitative design information from simulation results and to couple this information to a design modification system'. They add that few attempts have been made at this and the few systems that have been developed 'do not have the capability to interpret numerical simulation results'. Present CAD systems do not consider in their modelling strategies the very different requirements of the analysis process and therefore are only used to 'dump' a geometric model as a starting point for the analysis modelling process.

Present FEA systems require specialist skills to obtain meaningful results that will validate the behaviour of the product under review and are traditionally used to predict why a product failed in a late pre-manufacture testing process. We are seeing a move within the analysis vendor community to address this problem by breaking away from traditional working methods and providing tools that can be used by the engineers at the initial design process. These tools are a step in the correct direction but still fail to allow design analysis automation as they still rely on the geometric model as a starting point for the process, have no inference capabilities and only provide a limited set of user functionality compared to dedicated FEA systems. The steps are becoming easier to create a meaningful analysis model, but still remain a highly interactive and specialist process.

1.2 Automating the design/analysis loop

From the literature [4,5,6] it can be seen that there are many examples of automation in the design analysis loop by the incorporation of Knowledge Base or Expert systems. Whilst these systems have been primarily aimed at the pre-processing stage, i.e. the mesh creation, they are usually undertaken within two separate systems leading to subsequent model associativity and transfer problems. The US Air Force Research Laboratory has published examples of integrating analysis software requirements into the design environment, significantly reducing the time to create the FE models [7,8]. Recent EPSRC sponsored work has demonstrated the opportunities for using KBE techniques to automate this pre-processing stage by the use of a single unified model for both the design and analysis representations [9,10]. The importance for this proposed research project is that the model created is automatically simplified whilst maintaining associativity with the original design model description and the subsequent generated geometry.

This, however only solves part of the problem, that of pre-processing. The post-processing interpretation of results has not yet been fully addressed. A typical example of the use of knowledge based approach is Haghighi and Kang [11] who create an FE mesh undertake the analysis and study the results using error estimation techniques, adapting the FE mesh based on these results and updating the analysis. Thus the system is optimising the FE mesh rather than the design of the component.

1.3 Objectives

To automate, that is to capture the knowledge used within our target domain and replace the time consuming repetitive tasks, that at present demand human involvement, we must overcome the current limitations discussed with our current CAD FEA tools and represent our product design model more fully. The design engineers will initialise the design/analysis process by specifying the requirements of the product and then allowing the computer to create a product model that satisfies the initial specification. To do this we must:

- Create a demonstrator application that assists in the understanding of the stages involved in automating the feedback of FE analysis results directly into the original design model.

To understand the application, we shall look at KBE, stepping through the development used and then the design of the application.

2. Knowledge Based Engineering

KBE represents an evolutionary step in CAE and is an engineering method that represents a merging of object oriented programming, Artificial Intelligence (AI) techniques and computer aided design technologies, giving benefit to customised or variant design automation solutions. KBE systems aim to capture product and process information in such a way as to allow businesses to model engineering design processes, and then use the model to automate all or part of the process. The emphasis is on providing, informational complete product representations, captured in a product model. The product model represents the engineering intent behind the product design, storing the how, why and what of a design. The product model is an internal computer representation of the product design process and can contain information on both the product and processes that go to create the part.

Attributes can describe geometry, functional constraints, material type and processes such as the methods required to analyse, manufacture and cost a part. The KBE product model can also use information outside its product model environment such as databases and external company programs. The ultimate goal of the KBE system is to capture the best design practices and engineering expertise into a corporate knowledge base. KBE methodology provides an open framework for formally capturing and defining the process of design creation within a system that can infer and then act on this information. Toyota believes that KBE computational tools for design have the potential to revolutionise the way products are developed and are investing two billion dollars to achieve their goal [12].

3. Application development

There have been many development methodologies suggested for the KBS domain, such as KADS [13]. These methodologies have been aimed at assisting the developer define and model the problem in question, but do not address the specific needs for the development of a KBE application [14]. Successful commercial KBE developments have not followed these routes, as the methodologies are felt not to be flexible enough to model the dynamic design engineering environment. Work carried out by the MOKA Consortium (Methodology & software Tools Oriented to Knowledge Based Engineering Applications) recognises the deficiency in dynamic methodologies specific to the KBE domain [15] and aims to provide the KBE community with a working implementation / development methodology. The flexible nature of KBE tools does not dictate a particular implementation or development approach. However many applications follow a similar pattern, that of a normal design-engineering problem. The only difference being, the use of a KBES language to implement the desired solution and due to their object-oriented nature, the use of Rapid Application Development (RAD) programming techniques. The process of incremental development accomplishes implementation.

The first step is to state the problem. Full definition is not required as the prototype model is often used to "bring out" full and open discussions between all personnel involved in the product life cycle. The projects initial specification and project requirements were gathered by using standard concurrent engineering (CE) methods, consisting of initial meetings to understand the problem, focussed interviews with relevant engineering staff, the iterative creation of solutions (paper based) and open brainstorming meetings bringing about focussed agreed actions between all product-cycle concerns. Treating the project as a normal engineering problem solving exercise meant that all people involved in supplying rules and defining the system had the necessary skill sets.

After stating the problem and identifying the information required by the model, key objects were created, to form a parts library. As each of the part objects were defined they were individually tested, by creating an instance of the object. Part objects created within the KBE system form the building blocks of any model, often representing real world objects. These parts then decompose further, each stage of decomposition varying the intelligence of the objects. For example primitive objects might only know how to draw themselves, whereas higher level objects will use the knowledge base to make specific decisions regarding their shape, relationships, manufacturing process and analysis requirements. This use of object representation methods by KBE vendors is sometimes called 'smart modelling' and provides an intuitive working environment to the design engineer, who is used to thinking in terms of objects and levels of decomposition as this method is similar to the natural ways of engineering a component part. Smart models embody not only product form (geometry etc) but also process functions and a controlling framework. Knowledge in the form of rules are also encapsulated within the model.

The next step was to create an initial conceptual product model. This is not a complete representation, but acted as a first draft, a blueprint of the implementation. The conceptual product model can be thought of as a schematic of the completed system. A product model tree describes a particular design instance of a product model. This structure describes the hierarchical relationships between the various components (parts and processes) of the model. The model also determines the methods of how the objects will obtain the correct information, in order to carry out their specific tasks and as to the information they will provide to other objects. This hierarchical abstraction means the decomposition of information into levels of increasing detail [16]. The decisions made by the system to create a model will be based on the user inputs and the knowledge bases.

Using the initial part library and conceptual product model as a starting point, a subset of the overall system is defined, complete with user interfaces. The system is extended by increasing the part library, User Interface (UI) and by expanding the object class definitions. This incremental RAD development approach means that the system can be continuously evaluated and utilised, as it is always operational.

4. Application Design

To meet our objectives and to automate what is traditionally done in separate design analysis systems means the creation of a unified design/analysis modelling environment. That is an environment that has the ability to enhance the product model description with the additional information required by the FEA process and then control the FEA simulation. The post-processing of the simulation must then be fed back into the design environment, queried and automatic decisions made

78

that alter the original design model with respect to the new information provided. Figure 1 shows the current tools with their required information and generated outputs for the design/analysis feedback cycle. Figure 2 shows the new application with the FEA software only being used to run the simulation and provide the necessary results. To achieve this the application design breaks down into four necessary steps: Design, inspection, analysis and validation.

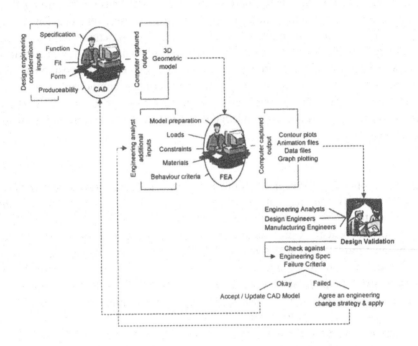

Figure 1 Current CAD/FEA usage for the design/analysis feedback cycle

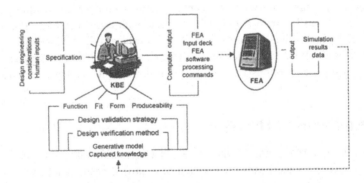

Figure 2 Automatic design/analysis feedback cycle

4.1 Design

This step allows the engineer to prepare the problem. Using KBE generative modelling techniques a default geometry model is created. KBE generative modelling for design engineering using knowledge captured from the product design cycle is well documented; examples from industry give significant cost savings over traditional CAD techniques [17,18]. Using user interfaces the models; form, fit and function properties can be altered to suit the specific case requirements. For example the user can specify a basic fabricated bracket attached at 3 positions. The KBE system will then automatically generate a bracket design (Figure 3). With this application it is critical to be able to relate the FE analysis results back to the individual features on the bracket 3D model, to do this we us the methodology of geometry attribute tagging and propagation [19]. This allows resultant geometry from a Boolean operation to refer back to the tags attached to the original geometry. For the FEA mesh creation this has two purposes, to control the refinement of the mesh on individual parts of the resultant geometry and to give the ability to query for mesh entities once the mesh has been generated. For example if the FE analysis simulation output shows that elements 1-10 are above the permissible level of von-mises stress we need to query the geometry model and find out which part relates to the node and element positions in the mesh. This information can then be used to assist in the validation strategy.

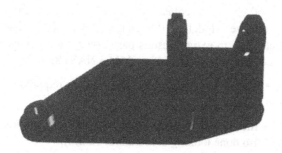

Figure 3 Generative bracket model

4.2 Inspection

At this stage we are setting up what we want to inspect from the simulation. The inspector can be broken down into two distinct stages, Pre-simulation and Post-simulation.

4.2.1 Pre-simulation

From menus the engineer can:

1. Interactively add an inspection type directly to the 3D model. For example the engineer might have an interest in the brackets face

displacement or whether the inner faces of the bracket remain parallel after analysis. This has the effect of adding a set of tags to the selected feature faces that can be queried later.

2. Use the interface to select what will be inspected from the resultant simulation output data. In the case of the bracket we are interested in Von Mises stress and deflection.

3. The engineer also has the opportunity to view the component functional specification, this specification contains rules and values that the bracket model must satisfy, for example model acceptance criteria for durability the maximum Von Mises stress must be less than 50% of the material yield strength, and for abuse load cases the maximum Von Mises stress must be less than the yield strength.

4.2.2 Post-simulation

After setting up what is to be inspected, the post-simulation phase allows the engineer to collect data required for the validation phase and to look at reports on the state of the model, i.e. if it has passed all required inspection requirements or if it has failed in some way and where these have happened on the design model. To do this it was necessary to first collect specific data from the output generated by the FE simulation and then map the relevant data back to the design model features. The method chosen to collect data was by using parsing classes. These comprehensive Adaptive Modelling Language (AML) [19] classes allow the parsing of a selected file to extract results based on pattern strings provided. For the bracket the FE output was produced in a 15MB NASTRAN file,

Figure 4 shows the type of format created. Collecting the required information was done in four stages.

1. Parse the file to collect values that exceeded our bracket specification (this was also done looking at minimum values).

2. Place the results of stage 1 in an AML table.

3. Collect the node ids from the table and parse the NASTRAN output file again using the id's to collect the associated elements.

4. Create a new AML table using the results.

We now have tables that give us specific values, nodes and element id's. The next stages of mapping back the selected nodes and elements to the associated design model features involved the use of AML query methods and the existing tags used in both the design and inspection stages. For example we can query the model to find out which features e.g. base, arms, bosses contain the elements that have a high value of stress. The use of attribute tagging and mesh querying give the necessary associativity needed for automation between the design and FEA mesh models to happen.

```
Orientation Vector   1.               1.              0.
   Nodes     1288729  1288728
Element 283991 - BAR      ( Line2 )
   Property 3            Color 124   Layer 1        AttachTo 0
    Orientation Vector  1.                1.             0.
   Nodes     1288725  1288724

MSC.Nastran for Windows Version 7.10                Thu May 10 14:49:19
2001
Model    : C:\martyn\ADAM\FE-data\craig1.MOD        Report : Node
Format   : NASTRAN Displacement

Output Set 1 - MSC/NASTRAN Case 1
                                         D I S P L A C E M E N T   V E C T O
R
      POINT ID.        T1            T2            T3            R1
R2              R3
        18421  G  -9.757627E-2  -1.249139E-1  -7.326388E-2  -2.219583E-4
1.966332E-3   -2.260190E-3
        18422  G  -2.490090E-1  -1.249139E-1  -5.839267E-2  -2.219583E-4
1.966332E-3   -2.260190E-3
      1261688  G  -1.525216E-1  -1.578795E-2   2.714073E-2   0.
0.             0.
      1261689  G  -2.272331E-2  -1.075322E-2  -3.175219E-3   0.
0.             0.
```

Figure 4 FEA NASTRAN part file output

4.2.3 Analysis

This area allows the engineer to set up all the requirements for creating a simulation. An example of the FE interfaces can be seen in Figure 5. From the list below we can see the absence of two major simulation modelling requirements, e.g. model simplification, the removal of features that using our knowledge we know will speed up the results of our analysis without hindering the structural integrity of the model and material properties. These are now taken into account at the initial component design stage. To generate itself the component model will have needed to know which material to use in order to correctly instantiate, and each feature object has simplification methods that can alter their geometrical representation when the simulation request is passed to it. Note the analyst in the FEA software environment normally does these tasks, but to automate this process we must apply these tasks to the original generative model. The requirements are as follows:

4.2.3.1 Mesh creation

Based on specialist knowledge and past experience the correct element types are selected, this is critical to create a finite element representation of our product that will behave correctly under the prescribed conditions. For the bracket we mesh using solid elements.

4.2.3.2 Loads

Based on expert knowledge load case values are assigned to the bracket. The loads have been previously determined from analysis of past mounting systems using simulation software

4.2.3.3 Constraints

Nodes around the bracket mounting holes have a rigid element connecting them to the centre of the hole that has all its degrees of freedom fixed. No fixing bushes are modelled as the load data taken from past simulation results and used as an input to the application takes into account the bushes.

4.2.3.4 Solving

Here we use the above information and mesh and run the analysis. This can be done immediately or run in batch mode overnight or at weekends depending on the complexity of the product.

4.2.3.5 Results visualisation

The final stage for the analyst in the traditional CAD/FEA process is to select various visual means to represent the data in a form that will assist in the interpretation of the FEA outputs (Figure 6). Note: this is only used for testing, for automation only the output data files are needed and the requirement of an analyst is negated.

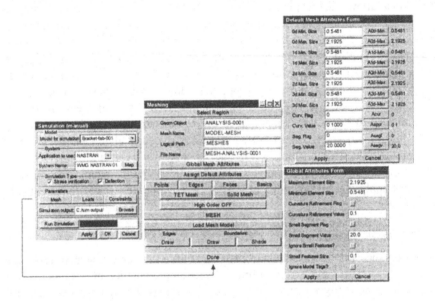

Figure 5 Example of FE interfaces for the KBE environment

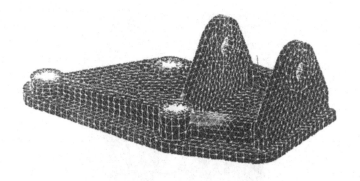

Figure 6 Visualisation of Bracket FEA result

4.2.4 Validation

At this stage we look at the inspection query report (the parsed output from the simulation) and decide how to correct our design model. We know from the inspection stage which nodes and elements relate to their corresponding feature on the 3D geometrical model and which are above or below our engineering specification for the particular bracket, the allowable changes can be set from an interactive user interface (Figure 7). Examples of two modifications for when the stresses are too high are:

1. If stresses are greater than an allowable stress limit in the bracket objects alter thickness by the specified increment in the allowable direction (for example the arms cannot move inwards as this is fixed by the torque strut width) until the stress level is satisfied or the maximum allowable increase is reached. If the limit is still too high and the allowable increase limit is reached then we go to strategy 2.

2. If stresses are still too high in the bracket objects add rib feature objects at preset positions. If not okay then go to next strategy etc.

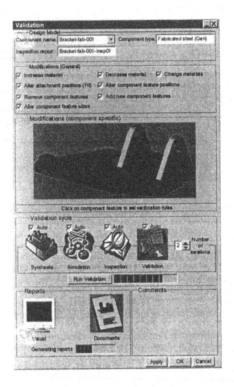

Figure 7 Example of the validation interface

5. Conclusions and further work

In this paper we have presented a demonstrator application that assists in the understanding of the stages involved in automating the feedback of FE analysis results directly into the original design model. We used off the shelf KBE technologies to implement the project. The AML system was selected as a robust tool used in many automotive design analysis projects and had the necessary integration with the project partners pre and post processing requirements of PATRAN and NASTRAN. As the project partners were geographically dispersed the system needed to be able to run locally on a PC laptop computer to assist in the RAD methods adopted. The project has been successful in that we have demonstrated the automatic feedback from the FE analysis system and this will enable the team to build on this application for a more complex system of automotive components. The engineer has to use only one system to define the problem and then the system automatically generates a design model that connects to the FE software and infers from the results of the analysis the actions needed to automatically accept or correct the 3D design model. For the application of knowledge in KBE objects see [19,20]. Experience gained on this project has highlighted some issues:

- There has to be a move away from the reliance on CAD. Geometrical modelling is not flexible enough to automate the design of a product. It is the engineering process that needs to be modelled, the geometry is only a product of that process.

- The development of this project using RAD has its advantages and also problems. The use of the system allowed the creation of 'use case' scenarios to be created that assisted the collection of further rules from experts, who remembered more information than from interviews alone when presented with the prototype system. A disadvantage is that as the engineering process is described as a set of rules and these rules are stored directly in the object parts created. While this is okay for the objectives of an academic/industrial research project it will cause problems for system updates, maintenance and to the documentation formalities needed on 'real' industrial problems. Further research into dedicated methodologies needs to be addressed. MOKA as referenced in the text is the first and at present the only attempt at such a dedicated methodology.

6. Acknowledgements

This work is being undertaken as part of a UK Government EPSRC sponsored research programme under the IMI Land Transport programme entitled "Automatic Generation of Design Improvements by Applying Knowledge Based Engineering to the Post-processing of FE Analysis". The partner companies to the University of Warwick in this programme are TWR Engineering, Luxfer Group and TechnoSoft Inc.

6.1 References

[1] Jones, M., Price, M., and Butlin, G., (1995) "Geometry management support for auto-meshing." Proc. of the 4th Int. Meshing Roundtable, Oct 1995, New Mexico, Pub. by Sandia National Laboratories, New Mexico, pp 153-164.

[2] Sheehy, M. and Grosse, I., (1997) "An object oriented blackboard based approach for automated finite element modelling and analysis of multichip modules." Engineering with Computers, Vol. 13, pp 197-210.

[3] Robertson, T., Prasad, B., and Duggirala, R., (1994) "A knowledge based engineering method to integrate metal forming process design and simulation". Proc. of the 1994 ASME database Symposium, Engineering data Management: Integrating the Engineering Enterprise, Pub. by ASME, Ed. By P. Bocks and B. Prasad, pp 41-50.

[4] Kang, E and Haghighi, K., (1995) "Intelligent finite element mesh generation" Engineering with Computers, Vol. 11 pp 70-82.

[5] Takata, O., Nakanishi, K., Horinouchi, N., Yano, H., Akashi, T., and Watanabe, T., (1996) "A knowledge based mesh generation system for forging simulation." Proc. 9th Int. Conf. on Industrial and Engineering Applications of Artificial Intelligence and

Expert Systems, Fukuoka, Japan, June 1996, Ed. By Tanaka, T., Ohsuga, S., and Ali, M., Pub. by Gordon and Breach, pp 317-326

[6] Blair, M., and Hartong, A., (2000) "Multidisciplinary design tools for affordability" American Institute of Aeronautics and Astronautics, AIAA-2000-1378.

[7] Zweber, J., Blair, M., Kamhawi, H., Bharatram, G., and Hartong, A., (1998) "Structural and manufacturing analysis of a wing using the Adaptive Modeling Language", American Institute of Aeronautics and Astronautics, AIAA-98-1758.

[8] Chapman, C., and Pinfold, M. K., (1998) "Design engineering – A need to rethink the solution using KBE." Proc. of the 18th Specialist Group on Expert Systems (SGES) Int. Conf. on Knowledge Based Systems and Applied Artificial Intelligence, December 1998, Cambridge UK. Pub. in Applications and Innovations in Expert Systems VI, Springer-Verlag, pp 112-129, ISBN 1-85233-087-2.

[9] Pinfold M. and Chapman, C., (1998) "The application of KBE techniques to the FE mesh generation of an automotive body-in-white structure". Journal of Engineering Design, To be published December 1999.

[10] Haghighi, K. and Kang, E., (1995) "A knowledge based approach to the adaptive finite element analysis." Modelling, Mesh Generation and Adaptive Numerical Methods for Partial Differential Equations, the IMA Volumes in Mathematics and its Applications Vol. 75, Pub. by Springer-Verlag, Ed. By I. Babushka et al, pp 267-276.

[11] Allen C Ward, President Ward Synthesis Inc, "Future Implications of Knowledge-based Systems Development Processes", Knowledge Based Organisation (KBO) Conference, San Diego, May 11th–13th, 1998, http:/www.KBOworld.com

[12] G N Blount, S Kneebone and M R Kingston. Selection of Knowledge-based Engineering Design Applications, Journal of Engineering Design, Volume 6, Number 1, pp 31-38. CARFAX International Periodical Publishers, 1995 - ISSN 0954-4828

[13] K Oldham, Modelling Knowledge used in the design of hosiery machines, Proceedings of the 33rd International MATADOR Conference, Dr Hayhurst (ed), Springer Verlag, July 2000, pages 93-98

[14] MOKA Consortium, MOKA - Methodology & software Tools Oriented to Knowledge Based Engineering Applications, CEC ESPRIT proposal EP25418, 1997.

[15] V Ackman, P J W Ten Hagen and T Tomiyama - A Fundamental and theoretical framework for an Intelligent CAD system - Computer-Aided Design, volume 22, number 6, July/August 1990, pp 352-367

[16] "Achieving Competitive Advantage Through Knowledge-Based Engineering – A Best Practise Guide", Paul Gay, DTI, 151 Buckingham Palace Road, London SW1W 9SS, UK, 2000.

[17] Anthony P Harper, "KBE ", engineering designer, January/February 1999, Vol 25 issues 1, published by IED UK, ISBN/ISSN 0013-7898.

[18] Adaptive Modelling Language version 3.2, TechnoSoft Inc, 4424 Carver Woods Drive, Cincinnati, Ohio 45242, USA.

[19] Chapman C B, Pinfold MK and Ingram I, "The Application of a Knowledge Based Engineering Approach to the Rapid Design and Analysis of an Automotive Structure". Advances in Engineering Software Journal 2001.

[20] Chapman C B, "Incorporation of a Process Model into a Generative Design Product Model", Proc. of the 15th Annual Technical Conference of the British Computer Society Specialist Group on Expert Systems (SGES) Int. Conf. on Knowledge Based Systems and Applied Artificial Intelligence, December 1995, Cambridge UK. Pub. in Applications and Innovations in Expert Systems III, Springer-Verlag, London, UK 1995 pp 293-307, ISBN 1 899621 03 2.

SESSION 3:

ENGINEERING, MANUFACTURING AND MUSIC APPLICATIONS

Rise again, fair knowledge

Linda S. Young , Stanley.P.Cauvain, Philip R. Davies
Campden & Chorleywood Food Research Association, Chipping Campden, UK
l.young@campden.co.uk
www.campden.co.uk

Abstract: In a Research Association rich in the technology of breadmaking, PC knowledge based systems find a synergy with the needs of its industry base. Campden and Chorleywood Food Research Association has developed a 'Bread Advisor' as a knowledge software PC tool for the baking and related industries.

This paper describes the context of the problem, the structure and implementation of the knowledge about breadmaking and the end product capable of delivery via a Web based medium or via a stand-alone CD ROM. Some lessons and experiences gained in developing knowledge based systems for the baking industry are explained and the benefits provided by this system are detailed.

1. Introduction

Knowledge can be used in many guises and to achieve many ends. In the milling and baking industries knowledge based systems have been in use for 10 years or more [1]. As the computing technology becomes ever more sophisticated it enables us to apply the knowledge in different forms and for different purposes. In a Research Association rich in the technology of breadmaking, PC knowledge based systems find a synergy with the needs of its industry base. When we developed our first knowledge tool in 1989 – a Bread Faults system – the industry asked 'What sort of PC do we need to run it on?' Now there is a PC on every desk and the expectations and questions that need addressing are far more challenging.

2. Context of the Problem

Campden & Chorleywood Food Research Association (CCFRA) has pioneered the development of knowledge tools for the baking industries for many years. Each system developed has been modest but at the same time influential within its industry sector. The mechanisms by which they have been developed have included expert system shells (both 1st and 2nd generation) [2,3,4] knowledge languages (e.g. Prolog), conventional languages (C++) and common languages such as Visual Basic. The systems have been both stand-alone and linked to control equipment. With each new system the domain knowledge took advantage of the developments in computer science and used them to provide tools within narrow bounds best suited to baking technology. All 8 systems developed apart from one were and are used commercially and are giving savings to the industry. When the first Bread Faults Expert System was started the domain was exceedingly narrow and only covered the technology of making **one type** of loaf by **one** processing method. Ideas for the use of images and other supporting information had to be relegated to the hard copy operating manual as neither the hardware or software platforms used by the target market (the baking industry) were sufficiently advanced.

With the advent of the Internet and the Windows platform the scope for knowledge systems has grown enormously and knowledge tools can start to take their rightful place [5] alongside other types of software, e.g. word processors, database software etc. Companies with foresight in the baking sector now provide PC knowledge tools for the technology requirements of the workforce. In an industry with a dwindling skills force, such PC tools are one step towards redressing the technology balance and supplementing the information and knowledge pool.

The knowledge about breadmaking has been revisited, ten years on from the first system. The baking industry is suffering more than ever from a lack of knowledgeable technologists who can bring both breadth and depth of know-how about breadmaking technology to product development and troubleshooting. The computing technology to implement many of the ideas of the knowledge engineers and experts is now available. This paper describes the 'new look' Bread Advisor – now fault diagnosis can be achieved for many generic fermented products made by the major processing methods. Experimentation by means of 'What-if' can be tried out at the PC, long before the product is made on the plant. There were two vehicles by which the system was delivered – via a Web-based extranet and via a stand-alone CD ROM.

3. The Team

The development team comprised:
1 knowledge engineer
1 principal expert plus several others for specialist detail
1 programmer

4. Objectives

The aim for the Bread Advisor was to provide a back-end application to a Web-based 'Intelligent Mediator', a Ministry of Agriculture Fisheries and Foods Link project. The core knowledge would also provide a stand-alone knowledge system available commercially to the baking industry during the Summer of 2001.

The computer knowledge-based tool should be developed to enable:

1. Bakers to modify bread quality (through the manipulation of raw materials, recipes and processing methods) and to problem solve.
2. Millers, equipment manufacturers and ingredients suppliers to service their customers and contribute to the development of new ingredients and processing

equipment.

3. Users at all skill levels to increase their individual understanding of the breadmaking process because of improved access to structured technical information (training).

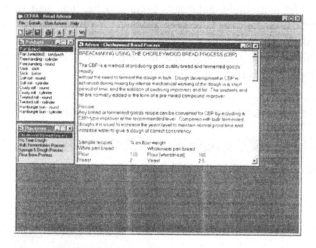

5. The Content

Figure 1 Advice Screen

The system comprises three modules - 'Advice', 'Fault Diagnosis' and 'What-if?'
An 'Advice' module provides users with important criteria that should be considered when developing a product with the specified process (Figure 1). The application takes a single input, e.g. the desired processing method. A database look-up table, containing references to the Advice text files is consulted and the information contained within the relevant files is read. This information is then fed to the user in the form of a message box.

Figure 2 Categories of faults

The second module provides users with a tool for diagnosing bread faults (optimising bread quality). The application displays a list of faults from which the user selects the ones exhibited in the faulty product, or required for a particular diagnosis. These faults are sub-divided into locations, e.g. shape, surface, crumb, aroma (Figure 2). A check is made for those faults that cannot occur together (e.g. high volume and low volume) and those where rules have been attached. If such a case is found, an error message is displayed to the user explaining that such faults cannot be selected together and further processing stops until the selection is changed. Images showing a fault in a product are available on demand (Figure 3).

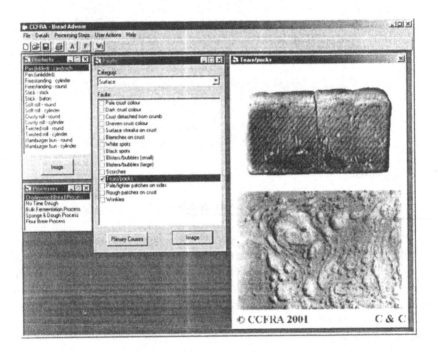

Figure 3 Faults – Tears and Pocks

Assuming that the choice of faults is satisfactory, the program then consults the database for the relevant primary causes. A diagnosis is made up of primary causes (Figure 4) and contributing factors for those primary causes (the example given in Figure 4 is for lack of gas retention). The causes and contributing factors are ranked in order of importance to the fault. Once the primary causes for a combination of fault descriptors is displayed, the user has the option of delving deeper into the contributing factors for all, or any combination of primary causes. Like the primary causes, the contributing factors are displayed to the user after consulting the database for relevant contributing factors, with the most important listed first.

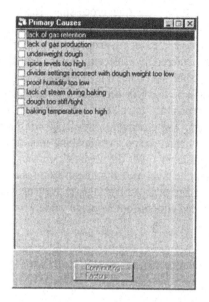

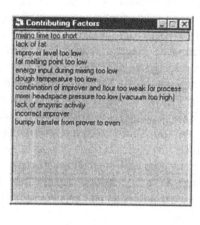

Figure 4 Primary Causes and Contributing Factors

The 'What-if?' module allows users to examine the likely effects of changing the processing details for a given breadmaking scenario. The application displays a list of generic queries which are categorised by processing step. The queries that are listed are dependent on the product and the processing method currently selected. When a user performs the query the application looks for the relevant generic message in the database and displays this to the user (Figure 5).

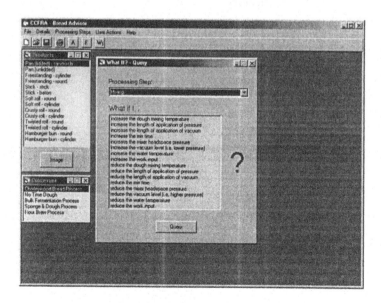

Figure 5 What-if? – Mixing

A more detailed 'What-if?' can be achieved by selecting processing details and entering values for the parameters displayed. This can also be used to check out a set of parameters for the step when it has been suggested as a potential fault in the fault diagnostic aspect. Processing details are entered by selecting the breadmaking processing step of interest. These steps, together with other relevant parameters (e.g. recipe) develop a 'Product profile' which will be used for subsequent consultations. The Product profile (Figure 6) acts as the repository for all the details that the user wishes to define, as a consultation is executed. The product profile can be considered as the 'DNA' of the product, containing the name, recipe, breadmaking method and processing steps. As users navigate between entry fields the application checks any input values against an allowable range from the database. If an input value is out of range an error message provides details of the acceptable range as well as likely effects manifested in the product and associated with the out-of-range value.

Product Profile

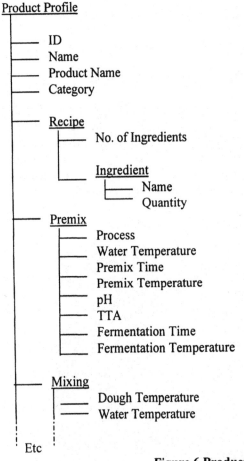

Figure 6 Product Profile

6.   Hardware and software

The hardware comprised a Windows NT server and 3 node PCs linked to form an intranet. These were required for the larger Intelligent Mediator project. Visual InterDev 6.0 was the development platform chosen as using it Visual Basic, XML and Database software etc could be used seamlessly. Dynamic HTML was used as for the user interface and data input aspects when the Bread Advisor was the back-end application used in the Intelligent Mediator scenario.

7.   Interface design

The interface designs for the same knowledge domain were different in display but the same in content. A web browser displaying dynamic HTML pages was used for access via the Intelligent Mediator (Figure 7). A more focussed windows design was used for the stand-alone version. In the latter case drop-down menus and icons were used to effect speedy use of the system. Care was taken in layout and screen colourings to enable the user to associate menus with actions. 'Help' is context sensitive and was also developed using HTML pages displayed on a browser.

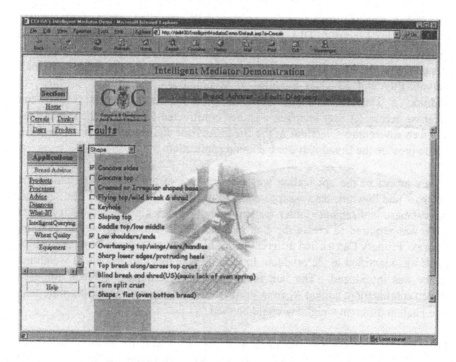

Figure 7 Fault Diagnosis uisng 'Intelligent Mediator'

8. Prototyping

The most difficult aspect of the design was to develop a mechanism whereby the knowledge and rules about breadmaking could be used in two different systems without need to provide two versions of code. Different techniques were suggested and small prototypes built to investigate the feasibility of approaches. The break through was the 'Product profile' whereby all the information and data needed during a consultation was carried and updated throughout a consultation. This enabled multi-enquiry by multi-user. It fulfilled the needs of both the Web-based Intelligent Mediator and the stand-alone versions.

9. Structure

With the constraint of this dual requirement in mind, it made sense to separate the Bread Advisor's functionality into it's own project file, with each of the stand-alone and web environment versions of the Bread Advisor having a different user interface. Having the program structured in this way meant that it was only necessary to write one version of the core Bread Advisor program.

The Bread Advisor functionality was essentially compiled into a single system Dynamic Link Library (a DLL file) and contained not only the structured Product Profile, but also the Bread Advisor program as a library of functions. Written in Visual Basic, the DLL file incorporated 7 class modules, for the Bread Advisor's functionality and 37 class modules to accommodate the product profile. In addition, a 'Data Environment Designer' provided all the necessary back-end database access. A user interface was then constructed for each of the stand-alone and web environment versions of the Bread Advisor and these referenced the DLL file to provide the Bread Advisor back-end application.

A key aspect of the application was the structure of the data in the underlying database and how this data was presented to the user as information. For instance, the database had separate tables for Faults and Primary Causes, although another table was required to create the link between Faults and their relevant Primary Causes. Primary Causes had different levels of importance, depending upon which Fault was identified in the product. In order to take this into account, a weighting factor was introduced. The link table provided this weighting factor for each linked combination, so that where a Primary Cause was associated with more than one Fault, a different weighting could be used.

For example, 'excess gas retention' is a primary cause for both of the faults 'creased or irregular shaped base' and 'keyhole'. However, the combination of 'excess gas retention' and 'creased or irregular shaped base' only has a weighting factor of 1, whereas the combination of 'excess gas retention' and 'keyhole' has a weighting factor of 3.

Updating the knowledge base is always a contentious issue. With this structure and with the type of knowledge we have in this domain it should be easier to add new knowledge as it comes on stream. However the interactions and rankings will still need to be validated.

10. Testing

The usual black and white box testing was undertaken. Particular testing was done to ensure that the diagnoses and rankings were sensible. The original rankings were modified to take into account the need to polarise and differentiate between the diagnoses, e.g. it was better to give causes of a fault over a wide number range so that when the list was displayed each item did not have the same score.

11. Commercialisation

Currently the final prototype version is out with our industry members for testing and feedback. The stand-alone Bread Advisor will be available on CD ROM from the Summer of 2001. It provides the baking industry with a much needed knowledge tool for novices, product developers and teachers. The number of images included has risen to about 100.

12. Approaches and Lessons

The way we tackle our knowledge systems has changed over the ten years. The cycle of developments in computing technology has been overlaid on our understanding and requirements for the knowledge domain itself. When the two come together then we have made greater leaps forward.

Our ability, as knowledge engineers/programmers, to elicit knowledge and work with experts and technologists has improved. In all of our successful systems, the computing staff and knowledge domain staff were integrated into the team. Where this was not the case we failed to achieve our goal.

If we had applied the traditional programming requirements of full specification before coding, we would not have been able to react to the rapidly changing computing environment and to the stimulation that prototyping generates in both the client (knowledge expert) and the design and programming team. Showing the client, albeit in simple screens, what the system can do and then involving them in the progress creates a feeling of 'ownership' throughout the projects. Listening to feedback in these situations can mean that a better system is produced in the end. The structuring of the knowledge and the design of the system in preparation for the coding is fundamental and an important part of a good system. The size of the domain should not be so ambitious as to be unachievable. Ambition with realism are good watch words. Linking smaller modules can be very successful and provides the whole team with the rungs to reach the top of the ladder (larger system). Linking the systems with conventional computing resources means we do not re-invent the wheel and at the same time provide a system with greater scope. We can use knowledge systems to link to process control in our industry. Intuitive modelling (e.g. directional changes) of knowledge is just as useful as mathematical modelling. No new technique should be overlooked before an assessment of its suitability in your own domain is made. The role that ease of use and user-friendliness play can never be underestimated. If the systems are easily navigated and the results are clear with access to additional help in the control of the user then successful systems and long life are more likely!

13. Benefits to the Baking Industry

The Bread Advisor PC tool has many benefits for the industry. These are both tangible and intangible and comprise:

1. More cost efficient processing leading to improved product quality for the consumer.
2. Reduced raw material wastage.
3. Greater product innovation leading to wider consumer choice.
4. Improvement to company and employee knowledge bases.
5. More rapid development of new products, e.g. to meet customer specifications.
6. Increased potential for exporting UK products and 'know how'.
7. On-the-job bread technology training tool for newcomers (Figure 8)

Figure 8 Bread Advisor in use for Training

14. Conclusion

In the Bread Advisor we have tackled the knowledge connected with breadmaking from both the manifestation of the finished product viewpoint and from the product/process development steps. The same representation of the knowledge is used for either case. The knowledge can be accessed via a CD ROM or from a more sophisticated system held on a server as was done with the Intelligent Mediator. Although the user interfaces look different the knowledge and rules behind the screens were the same.

The PC knowledge tool developed now enables product developers to enhance product quality when things go wrong and will tell them what will happen if some aspect or detail of processing or recipe is changed. This experimentation with feedback at the PC can enhance the users' own knowledge whether the user is an expert or a novice and can put back some of the knowledge that the industry has lost. The only thing it won't do – currently - is to provide an answer to the question 'How do I make a bread product that eats like....looks like....?' That is the next challenge!

15. Acknowledgements

This project was made possible through the financial support of MAFF and members of CCFRA. We thank the members of the Sponsoring Consortium and Industrial Steering Committee for their inputs to the technical detail and direction of the project. We thank the administrative and bakery staff for their assistance with the product imaging used.

References

[1] Young, L.S.(1998). Baking by Computer – Passing on the Knowledge, Proceedings of BCCCA 45th Technology Conference, London

[2]Young, L.S. and Cauvain, S.P. (1994). Advising the Baker, Proceedings of British Computer Society – Specialist Group on Expert Systems Annual Conference, Cambridge.

[3] Young, L.S., Petryszak, R. and Cauvain, S.P.(1995). Improving Cake Product Quality Proceedings of British Computer Society – Specialist Group on Expert Systems Annual Conference, Cambridge

[4] Young, L.S., Davies, P.R. and Cauvain, S.P. (1998) Cakes – Getting the Right Balance, Applications and Innovations in Expert Systems (Proceedings of British Computer Society Specialist Group on Expert Systems), Springer-Verlag, London

[5] Young, L.S. (2000) The Use of Interactive Computer Programs in the Baking Industry, Proceedings of 11th Cereals and Bread Congress, Australia

Generating Automotive Electrical System Models from Component Based Qualitative Simulation

Neal Snooke, Richard Shipman

Department of Computer Science, University of Wales

Aberystwyth, Ceredigion, SY23 3DB

email: nns@aber.ac.uk

Abstract

Model based reasoning applied to electrical systems has matured over recent years resulting in deployment of commercial design analysis tools in the automotive industry [1, 4]. These tools work at the component level on individual systems or subsystems. Analysis of multiple systems is becoming necessary because of the increase in system and subsystem interactions resulting from Electronic Control Unit based system architectures.

To address the resulting simulation complexity this paper considers the automated construction of black box system or subsystem models from envisionments produced by qualitative simulation. The models can then be used to improve efficiency of the repetitive simulation procedures required to perform automated Failure Mode Effects Analysis (FMEA).

The approach also has the potential to allow Sneak Circuit Analysis (SCA)[2, 3] to be extended to include systems with internal memory. It provides the basis of a useful visualization tool for complex system behaviour.

Keywords: Qualitative simulation; FMEA; State based model; System abstraction.

1 Introduction

FMEA is a repetitive design analysis task involving simulation for every component fault. The aim of this work is to allow the successfully deployed Autosteve FMEA tool [4] to work with larger groups of systems. The qualitative electrical representation used in the Autosteve tool allows analysis to be performed early in the design process for the majority of automotive systems and faults. Other work is currently in progress to provide targeted quantitative analysis when necessary and also late in the design process when numerical values are known. Systems that include communications bus protocols are also being considered in another current project [5].

Automotive industry practice generally requires only single fault scenarios to be considered. For FMEA this allows automatically abstracted system models to replace the component level simulation for systems that do not include the fault under consideration. This can provide big savings in simulation effort over an entire whole vehicle FMEA without losing the effects of a fault on other systems. The abstracted system models must adhere to the 'no function in structure' principle since faults in neighbouring systems could cause abnormal external environments to an unbroken system.

A simulation based envisionment provides a raw form of the system model, however the very large number of component based states produced by an envisionment is an inefficient representation due to the highly cohesive operation of system components. This paper describes an iterative approach, deriving a minimum number of *system level internal states* to produce a simpler, unambiguous system level model faithful to the original envisionment behaviour at the system boundary. The resulting model is far simpler than the envisionment because the envisionment includes the state of every component, and very few of these actually provide state significant at the level of system behaviour.

The method has several other potential benefits. Given a suitable interface it can provide an engineer with a much simpler model of the actual system behaviour. Anomalous behaviour is observed as unexpected system states or event transitions with unexpected conditions or dependencies. In the future the system level internal state information will be required to perform SCA, fault signature analysis [6], and automated scenario generation for FMEA. An important pragmatic consideration is that no additional model building effort is required from the engineer.

2 Simulation and Envisionment

The system models are comprised of a netlist generated from system schematics and a library of reusable component models. Each component model contains an electrical structure defined by network of qualitative resistances and optionally, a behaviour defined as a Finite State Machine (FSM) [7]. This work builds on our existing qualitative electrical simulation algorithm is known as the Qualitative Circuit Analysis Tool (QCAT) and is well documented in [8, 9, 10]. Simulation takes the form of a sequence of DC electrical analysis steps driven by external events and higher level component FSM behaviours. QCAT represents circuits as qualitative resistance networks with resistance values zero, load, and infinity, ensuring finite set of electrical states. Components and systems simulated using QCAT may have static or transient states typically attributable to the following sources in automotive systems:

Non electrical components An example is the toggle switch. The toggle button contacts change position for each complete press and release cycle.

Electronic Control Units ECU components are microprocessor based modules that may contain significant internal states. Software operation is modeled at a high level by FSM descriptions.

Feedback Emergent state can be produced by including feedback circuits even though the individual components have no internal state. An obvious example is a bistable constructed from 2 NAND gates.

Time based transitions Component models can include order of magnitude time constraints applied to events. This allows resolution of some of the potential qualitative ambiguity caused by multiple events. All events in each time period are run prior to those in the next longest time period regardless of how many there are. A typical automotive sequence of timeslots represents: instantaneous (electrical propagation); uS (ECU operations); mS (relay switching); S (user interaction); hour (battery discharge). These delays are equivalent to short term memory in the system.

The interactions with a system are provided by the set of variables that define its environment. This environment is a subset of the *components'* exogenous variables. It is a typical system characteristic to have relatively few inputs and outputs compared to the number of internal components thus ensuring that simplification/abstraction is possible.

2.1 Envisionment

The attainable envisionment is generated from an initial (usually powered down) default state corresponding to the default states of the components. It represents all states of the system reachable by exercising any sequence of normal inputs from the default state. Each of the possible input variable value changes (events) is provided to the system in turn and simulated. When the system changes state all the possible external events are again tried. Each of these system *envisionment states* is a composition of the state of all component states and variables. When the simulation encounters a state identical to one previously encountered it returns to another uncompleted behavioural branch, finishing when no uncompleted behavioural branches remain.

2.1.1 Component models and State matching

The QCAT component models comprise:

- An interface to the environment including electrical terminals and other enumerated variables.

- An optional electrical network represented by qualitative resistive loads (zero, load, infinite)

- An optional FSM representing behaviour

- A graphical symbol used on the system schematic

As an example the structure and behaviour is illustrated in figure 1 for the case of a typical automotive switch. The switch can be rotated through three twist positions by means of the **twist** input and also pressed using the button **position** input to toggle an electrical contact with each **pressed-released** cycle. The state diagram (left of figure) controls the behaviour by means of

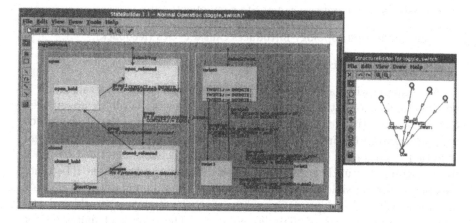

Figure 1: Toggle switch QCAT model

events that fire based on the condition of the inputs. The FSM expressions either refer to exogenous variables (ie. switch positions) of the component, or change elements of the underlying resistive model (right of figure). Notice that the twist behaviour only allows a few of the possible combinations of contact positions. Further details of the component modelling are presented in [8].

It is vital that the envisionment does not terminate a behavioural path until the system has returned to an *identical* state to ensure a complete and unambiguous exposition of the system behaviour. For our system envisionment state is a composition of:

- all component FSM model states;

- all resistive element values in the netlist;

- all input and output variables included in component models.

Redundancy between the parts of a component model will be removed by the system level simplification.

3   The System Perspective

By definition the components of a system will work together concurrently or in sequence to produce functions of the system that provide coherent effects in its environment [11]. This high degree of dependency in the operation of the individual components ensures that relatively few of the possible component state combinations will ever be realized during non-faulty operation of the system. The generated model must include only internal state significant at the *system level.* It is not generally possible to include this state directly from the components because:

- component behaviours are partially used within the system;

- system states comprise composite component state;

- the connection topology introduces causal cycles (feedback);

- the reflection of component internal states at the system interface.

An example will clarify the final point. Consider figure 2 (circuit A). It is possible to deduce that if the lamp is **off** and the switch becomes **closed** then after some time (**mS**) the lamp should change to the **on** state. If the switch becomes **open** in the intervening period the state does not change (**mS** event condition is no longer satisfied). The system is therefore described by the 2 state diagram. Circuit B is different. When the lamp is **off** and switch becomes **closed** it is not possible to determine when the lamp illuminates (immediately or after a **mS**). This depends upon how recently off state was achieved and hence the internal state of the relay contacts. The relay contributes no net internal state to the first system, but adds a transient state to the second.

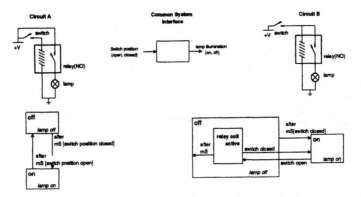

Figure 2: Reflecting component state at the system interface

The strategy used in this work is to produce an over simplified system model based on the system environment (black box) and then derive component based details (grey box) until the model no longer contains ambiguity. The major steps are depicted in figure 3 as follows:

Simplify Combine attainable envisionment states using system boundary.

Resolve Ambiguity The introduction of new state in this step may introduce new ambiguity resulting in an iterative algorithm.

Visualise Extract system level events between detected system states and orthogonalize the representation.

4 Example Circuits

To avoid unnecessary complexity we will use the two trivial circuits shown in figure 4 to illustrate the key points of the simplification process.

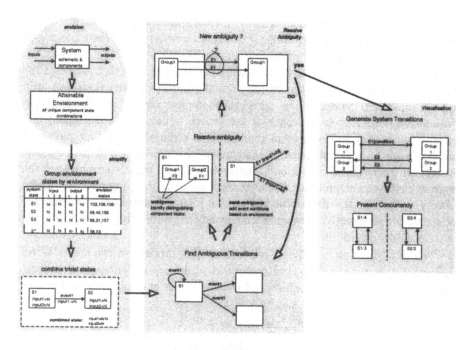

Figure 3: Simplification overview

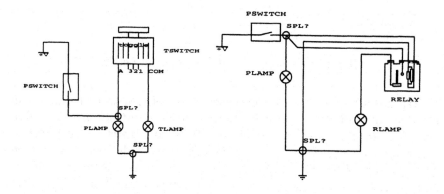

Figure 4: Toggle switch circuit (left) and relay circuit (right)

The 'toggle switch' circuit (figure 4) includes the compound multi contact toggle switch (figure 1) containing explicit internal state. When the toggle button is in the released position it is impossible to determine externally the position of the internal contacts. It is also interesting to note that although the twist position terminals of the switch are not connected, twist position is still a valid input and generates associated envisionment states. The simplification will discount this irrelevant part of the switch behaviour (twist input) and it will not appear in the system model. It is often the case that part of a module such as a switch pack or instrument cluster is relevant to a specific subsystem or mode of operation. The system model can determine that the system environment provided is too general allowing the pragmatically useful ability to 'generously' determine the system interface automatically from the schematic (unconnected component environment) and refine it based on the system model produced.

The second circuit includes a relay. The relay model has two states *active* and *inactive* to represent the switch contact positions. *activate* and *deactivate* events occur a qualitative 'millisecond timeslot' after current flows or ceases to flow through the coil.

5 Envisionment Simplification

The initial set of system states are obtained by grouping the envisionment states by the values at the system interface. The system interface for the example circuits is shown at the top left of figures 5 and 8. The envisionment details are in table 1.

Circuit	wires	non wire components	system variables	states	transitions
toggle circuit	7	7	20	24	96
relay circuit	8	7	14	8	12

Table 1: Example circuit envisionment details

Transitions between envisionment states are referred to as *envisionment transitions* and transitions between system states are *system transitions*. *System states* are sets of related envisionment states and therefore system transitions represent one or more envisionment transitions. A different system *event* represents each of the different changes that occur to the system environment during simulation. *Events* are common to both levels of transition and represent one or more changes to the system input variables.

5.1 Identification of Insignificant System States

Envisionment transitions leading to new states that represent only the environment change specified by the associated event are not interesting. Such states may be combined since the environment of the system can be used to distinguish multiple transitions of an event. Using a simple automotive example, it is clear that closing the ignition switch in the system 'off' state will cause a different transition dependent upon the existing position of the lighting switches. It is not desirable however for the system model to include these component states (switch contact resistances etc) when the ignition switch (and system) is off.

Table 2 shows how the states become grouped for the toggle switch circuit illustrating that the toggle switch button input can be in either position when both lamps are both on or both off. The twist switch is always uninteresting as expected since it is not used in the circuit.

System State	PLAMP .Light	PSWITCH .position	TLAMP .Light	TSWITCH .position	TSWITCH .twist
1-plus	TRUE	closed	TRUE	pressed released	off pos1 pos2
10-plus	FALSE	open	FALSE	pressed released	off pos1 pos2
3-plus	TRUE	closed	FALSE	released	off pos2 pos1

Table 2: System states for 'toggle circuit'

The lower section of figure 5 shows the 24 envisionment states as small filled boxes and initial system states as thick outlines. Each group represents the three positions of the twist switch. For diagrammatic clarity the twist positions are drawn as a single state to reduce the number of transitions drawn. The algorithm treats the envisionment as individual states and transitions.

5.2 Implicit Events

During the envisionment, transitions are not produced for external events that cause no state change. This provides a complete representation since all possible events are simulated from every state. An *implicit* transition loops back to its originating state for all unspecified events. Once envisionment states are combined, however, these implicit events must be considered since they lead to a source of ambiguity. Consider the **released** event in the state group marked **1-plus** in Figure 5. In the **closed-released** state the **released** event is implicit (shown dashed) however in the **open-held** states the same **released** event causes a system state change. These events need to be distinguished. For this reason all envisionment transitions that represent system state changes must be differentiated from all other envisionment states in the group by considering implicit events where necessary.

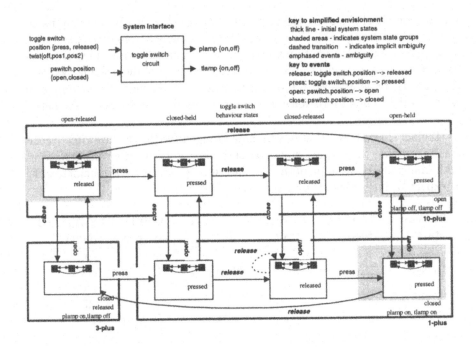

Figure 5: Toggle circuit simplification example

5.3 Transition Ambiguity

Ambiguous transitions are those that cause alternative behaviours in the model. The ambiguous transitions are divided into two categories; ambiguous, and semi-ambiguous. Ambiguous transition pairs represent the same event from the same source leading to different destinations. Semi-ambiguous transitions can be distinguished by a difference in the system environment. They occur primarily due to system states that represent the multiple valued environment variables (section 5.1). Ambiguous transitions occur because of missing internal system state and will be considered in section 5.5.

It has been assumed that different system events cannot be ambiguous. This assumption is true if system events represent single (unique) input changes. Where multiple simultaneous changes are used an event (E1) may represent a subset of the changes associated with another event (E2). E1 is therefore ambiguous with E2. The uniqueness properties of events used in an envisionment are determined at the outset of simplification and are taken into account when subsequent transition ambiguity is checked.

5.4 Semi-ambiguous events

Appropriate environment condition(s) can be added to remove semi-ambiguous transitions. These additional conditions do not represent any additional changes to the device (input) environment, they are merely checks to determine behaviour based on the existing environment. Environment conditions are shown in square brackets after events in the final model. The sole distinguishing environment value can be the one that is responsible for the event and therefore the extra conditions refer to the system environment before the event occurred. Environment conditions are determined as follows:

1. One or more external factors that can distinguish each ambiguous pair of transitions are found.

2. Any factors common to all the ambiguous pairs associated with each *system transition* are determined. Transitions internal to a system state are not of interest since they cannot affect system level behaviour.

3. If stage 2 fails to find common factor(s) for all pairs an exhaustive search of the factor combinations found in stage 1 is performed.

4. The most compact set of factors is then chosen.

The process of removing remaining ambiguity (section 5.5) will introduce additional state into the system model. The identification of semi-ambiguous transitions is therefore likely to be pessimistic and to avoid unnecessary environment conditions their selection is delayed until any internal states have been generated.

5.5   Internal State and Memory

System memory will lead to ambiguous events in the model. There is guaranteed to be at least one distinguishing feature between any two ambiguous events in a deterministic system since no two envisionment states can be identical, and any given event applied to an envisionment state must always cause the same effect. If no distinguishing factors are found for an ambiguous event there must be state 'hidden' in the component models or random elements in the system.

The system state may represent a single feature or combination of features (variable value or state) belonging to the component models, and is represented using sub groups of envisionment states within each system state. We have used the term *state group* to reflect this relationship with the environment based states. The state groups are however independent additional states of the system and do not provide an additional event hierarchy. For example in figure 7 the transition **PSWITCH.position closed** from state **1-plus** to **3** does not represent an event from the state group **1-plus:RELAY.active**.

The aim is to keep the model as compact as possible while allowing unambiguous behaviour predictions.

5.5.1   Ambiguous transitions

Ambiguous transitions are resolved using a similar procedure to the semi-ambiguous ones in section 5.4 except that:

- Transition pairs that have previously been identified as semi ambiguous are not considered.

- Distinguishing factors are drawn from the component model variables (described in section 2.1).

- The aim is to group the envisionment states in each system state (rather than add conditions to events). Therefore a set of *component factors* (rather than environment factors) that can distinguish all pairs in the state is required.

- Where a number of choices of internal factors are available the same set of group names are chosen for each of the system states.

- Many factors are associated with the same behaviour and therefore have a system wide direct mapping of values for the envisionment states of interest. These are treated as composite factors to assist in the final search for the best factors.

The minimum number of factors on a system wide basis are chosen, new system states are generated, and the ambiguous states are allocated to the new state groups. Notice that envisionment states are allocated to groups only to resolve ambiguity, and not because they contain the factor values associated with the group. This ensures that groups represent 'actual system memory *use*' rather than 'component memory *capability*' i.e. the memory must be significant to the future system behaviour.

When no system wide common group factor emerges the selection is currently done by exhaustive search of the (combinations of) differentiating factors associated with all ambiguous pairs. Typically there are not too many factors to search because the same few factors are usually responsible for all ambiguity. This is unsurprising because the ambiguity is caused by system memory and in the systems we are considering this is memory is limited to special ECU or mechanical states. When several minimum sized sets are found the one with the most abstract (highest level in the component hierarchy) factors are chosen.

5.5.2 Expanding the model

The introduction of state subgroups might lead to additional ambiguities. Consider the toggle switch example in figure 5. During the first resolution of state groups the **release** events in state **10-plus** are all internal and hence not ambiguous. The state groups (grey boxes) are introduced to resolve the **close** ambiguity. Now the **release** event from the **open-held** state is potentially ambiguous with the implicit **release** event from the **open-released** state. Since their destinations are the same state group the ambiguity is avoided, however. The ambiguity resolution process is carried out repeatedly, progressively selecting ambiguous transitions and reselecting new sets of distinguishing states until only semi-ambiguous events remain. These are then resolved as in section 5.4 to provide the finished model.

6 Generating the System Events

System transitions are those connecting system states or substates. The system transitions are generated from envisionment transitions by:

- Removing those internal to a system state group.

- Removing duplicate transitions.

- Combining multiple transitions for the same event between the same system states.

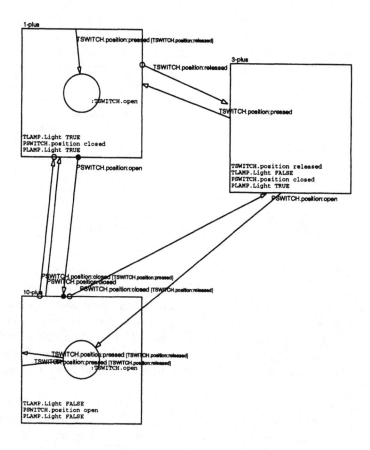

Figure 6: Generated states for toggle switch circuit

The final (automatically produced) system state charts for the examples are shown in figures 6 and 7. The squares represent the external environment based states(only single valued variables shown). The circles represent state groups. The circles at transition ends indicate multiple transitions (of benefit when several state groups exist). The event lines with empty circles indicate that transitions for this event exist that originate/terminate at matching state

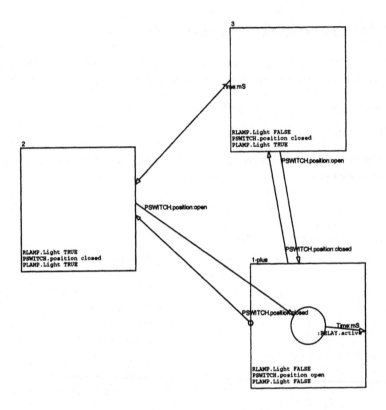

Figure 7: Generated states for relay circuit

groups inside the state. The filled circle is similar but includes the topmost system state transition as well as the state groups. An event from a system state with no circle applies only to the top system state and does not apply if the system is in one of the group states. The system can only be in either the state *or* one state group at any one time. The notation simply indicates inheritance by the groups of the system state external properties. (Perhaps an additional state group and junction connectors [7] should have been included to avoid this).

We can observe several interesting aspects to the behaviours. The toggle switch circuit has three main states both lamps on, both off and a state where only the power indicator is on. The on and off states require a system state to represent the toggle position since the switch when released can remain on or go off. When only the power indicator lamp is on (**3-plus**), the switch can only be released and as soon as it is pressed the other lamp is activated (switch toggle operation is not symmetric, see figure 1). Extra conditions are required on the **pressed** events in state **10-plus** to ensure the switch is released prior to the next press event occurring. The **PSWITCH.position.open** event when both lamps are on causes both lamps to go off but the switch maintains its internal state of TSWITCH.open. Note that TSWITCH.open is not a bottom level state in the toggle switch behaviour FSM.

7 Discussion

The system state chart produced so far is essentially a 'flat' set of states and the system can be in only one of them at a given time. Therefore for complex systems it is likely there will be a state explosion.

Many systems have several almost independent behaviours or sub behaviours and this orthogonality can be used to simplify the description using a concurrency notation. This is currently an area of development, however the result of this process for the relay circuit is shown in figure 8.

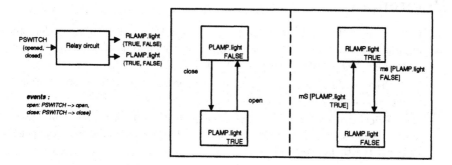

Figure 8: Relay circuit concurrent states

The algorithm described in this paper has been implemented (in Java) and several automotive system circuits have been successfully analysed. We expect to be able to utilize these models in a more efficient version of the AutoSteve FMEA tool aimed at whole vehicle FMEA. This ability is significant because

- Groups of interacting systems are becoming prevelent in modern vehicles.

- Many of the most dangerous faults are caused by unexpected and subtle interactions between systems designed by different engineering teams.

- The qualitative nature of the simulation allows the above design flaws to be detected early.

The results of this work will be applied to tasks such as SCA and fault signature analysis that require the internal system states to be known. The current graphical presentation has scalability issues but we expect that with further development the descriptions should provide a valuable additional abstraction facility to virtual yellow boarding and design verification tools [12, 13]. The ability to interactively view specific events, conditions or states could be provided with such a tool to help an engineer gain an overview of a system or investigate specific behavioural issues.

The only part of the algorithm that has scalability issues worse than the envisionment generation (a prerequisite), is the selection of best factors. The complete search of a large set of possible factors becomes prohibitive very rapidly. There are a number of enhancements possible such as ordering the search by minimum number of factors first, providing heuristics to prioritise factor combinations by occurence in the transition pairs, or subdividing the systems.

Acknowledgements

This work has been supported by the UK Engineering and Physical Sciences Research Council (GR/N06052 - Whole Vehicle Whole Life-cycle Electrical Design Analysis), Ford Motor Company, and First Earth Ltd.

References

[1] C. J. Price, D. R. Pugh, N. A. Snooke, J. E. Hunt, and M. S. Wilson. Combining functional and structural reasoning for safety analysis of electrical designs. *Knowledge Engineering Review*, 12(3):271–287, 1997.

[2] C. J. Price, N. Snooke, and J. Landry. Automated sneak identification. *Engineering Applications of Artificial Intelligence*, 9(4):423–427, 1996.

[3] C. J. Price and N. A. Snooke. Identifying design glitches through automated design analysis. In *Annual Reliability and Maintainability Symposium*, pages 277–282. IEEE, January 1999.

[4] FirstEarth Limited, http://www.firstearth.co.uk/. *AutoSteve*.

[5] N. A. Snooke and C. J. Price. Softfmea - automated safety analysis of automated embedded systems. EPSRC grant GR/R2388.

[6] C. S. Spangler. Equivalence relations within the failure mode and effects analysis. In *RAMS 99*. IEEE, IEEE Press, January 1999.

[7] D. Harel and M. Politi. *Modelling Reactive Systems with Statecharts*. McGraw-Hill, first edition, 1998.

[8] N. A. Snooke. Simulating electrical devices with complex behaviour. *AI Communications special issue on model based reasoning*, 12(1-2):44–59, 1999.

[9] C. J. Price, N. Snooke, D. R. Pugh, and J. E. Hunt and. S. Wilson. Combining functional and structural reasoning for safety analysis of electrical designs. *Knowledge Engineering Review*, 12(3):271–287, 1997.

[10] M. Lee and A. Ormsby. Qualitative modelling of the effects of electrical circuit faults. *Artificial Intelligence in Engineering*, 8:293–300, 1993.

[11] B. Chandrasekaran and R. Josephson. Representing function as effect: assigning functions to objects in context and out. In *AAAI Workshop on modelling and reasoning*, 1996.

[12] C. J. Price, N. A. Snooke, and D. J. Ellis. Identifying design glitches through automated design analysis. In *Invited paper in Innovative CAE track, Procs 44th Annual Reliability and Maintainability Symposium*. RAMS, January 1999.

[13] A. G. McManus, C. J. Price, N. Snooke, and R. Joseph. Design verification of automotive electrical circuits. In *13th International Workshop on Qualitative Reasoning*. Lock Awe, 1999.

Automated Control of an Actively Compensated Langmuir Probe System Using Simulated Annealing

L. Nolle[1] A. Goodyear[1] A. A. Hopgood[2] P. D. Picton[3] N. St.J. Braithwaite[1]

[1]Oxford Research Unit, The Open University
Berkley Road, Oxford, OX1 5HR, UK

[2]Department of Computing, The Nottingham Trent University
Burton Street, Nottingham, NG1 4BU, UK

[3]School of Technology and Design, University College Northampton
Northampton, NN2 6JD, UK

Abstract

A simulated annealing (SA) method has been developed to deduce fourteen Fourier terms in a radio-frequency (RF) waveform. Langmuir probes are important electrostatic diagnostics for RF-driven gas discharge plasmas. These RF plasmas are inherently non-linear, and many harmonics of the fundamental are generated in the plasma. RF components across the probe sheath distort the measurements made by the probes. To improve the accuracy of the measurements, these RF components must be removed. This has been achieved in this application by active compensation, i.e. by applying an RF signal to the probe tip. Not only do amplitude and phase of the applied signal have to match that of the exciting RF, but also its waveform has to match that of the harmonics generated in the plasma. The active compensation system uses seven harmonics to generate the required waveform. Therefore, fourteen heavily interacting parameters (seven amplitudes and seven phases) need to be tuned before measurements can be taken. Because of the magnitude of the resulting search space, it is virtually impossible to test all possible solutions within an acceptable time. An automated control system employing simulated annealing has been developed for online tuning of the waveform. This control system has been shown to find better solutions in less time than skilled human operators. The results are also more reproducible and hence more reliable.

1 Problem Description

This article concerns the use of simulated annealing (SA) to control a diagnostic measurement system for a range of important industrial processes based on plasma technology. The plasmas in question are produced by the passage of electricity through a gas at low pressure, resulting in a partially ionised medium comprising electrons, ions, radicals and neutrals, according to which gases are involved.

The semiconductor industry has been a major exploiter of plasma technology. It uses plasma processes to etch and deposit the different thin layers of semiconductor, insulator and metal that make up integrated circuits. The demand for the ability to maintain uniformity and yield while scaling up for larger-area processing has promoted a considerable research effort in real-time assessments and control of the uniformity of technological plasmas.

Under the prevailing conditions, the plasmas used in materials processing are not in thermal equilibrium so considerable energy (typically equivalent to tens of thousands of Kelvin in temperature) resides in the electrons. Through interactions with these electrons, material can be broken into its constituent atoms. Thus gases and solids can be 'activated' electrically by means of a plasma. The heavier particles in plasmas tend to remain relatively cool so that the plasma medium facilitates the treatment of thermally sensitive surfaces and bulk materials. For a number of operational reasons, considerable use is made of radio frequency (RF) power supplies in the generation of technological plasmas. Basic electrical measurements on the distribution of charged particles in a plasma is a fundamental requirement for process developers and has potential as a routine control parameter in future.

The problem that is tackled in this article concerns the adaptation of a basic electrical measurement of uniformity that is much used in plasmas generated by direct current. When radio-frequency power is used to create the plasma, the electrical environment requires special attention. It transpires that one of the approaches, the one adopted here, though simple in principle, calls for a level of optimisation and control for which some kind of AI is essential.

1.1 Radio-Frequency Driven Discharge Plasmas

Under normal conditions, gases do not conduct electrically. Almost all electrons are bound to an atom or molecule. However, if electrons are introduced and given enough energy by an external energy source, like electro-magnetic fields, light, heat, etc., then they have the potential on collision with gas atoms or surfaces to release more electrons, which themselves may release other electrons. This resulting electrical breakdown is known as an avalanche effect. The so-formed ionised gas or plasma is now conducting.

In industrial radio-frequency powered plasmas, an RF generator is used as an external power-source, usually operating at 13.56 MHz. The use of RF rather than DC has developed for a number of reasons including efficiency and compatibility with systems in which direct electrical contact with the plasma is not feasible. The frequency of 13.56 MHz is assigned for industrial, non-telecommunications, use. The RF is inductively or capacitively coupled into a constant gas flow through a vacuum vessel using electrodes (Figure 1).

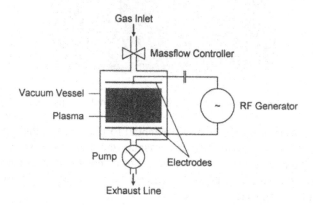

Figure 1 – Capacitively coupled RF-powered plasma.

The electrons have only a fraction of the mass of the atoms, hence the can follow the electric field, while the ions respond only to slower variations in electrical structure. Electrons near the electrodes can escape. This results in electric fields, pointing from the plasma to the electrodes. These fields generate a flux of energetic ions, which can be applied continuously to a large area of workpiece, e.g. for etching or deposition.

1.2 Langmuir Probes

Electrostatic or Langmuir probes were developed by Langmuir in 1924 and are one of the oldest diagnostic tools used to obtain information about properties of low pressure plasmas [1]. Such a probe consists of a small metallic electrode that is inserted into the plasma (Figure 2).

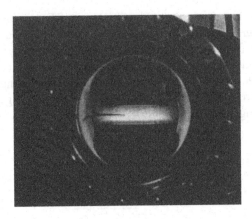

Figure 2 – Langmuir probe inserted into an Argon plasma.

By applying a positive or negative DC potential to the probe, either an ion or an electron current can be drawn from the plasma, returning via a large conducting surface such as the walls of the vacuum vessel or an electrode. This current can be used to analyse the plasma, e.g. for the determination of the energy of electrons, electron particle density, etc.

The region of space-charge (or sheath) that forms around a probe immersed in a plasma has a highly non-linear electrical characteristic. As a result, harmonic components of potential across this layer give rise to serious distortion of the probe's signal. In RF-generated plasmas this is a major issue as the excitation process necessarily leads to the space potential in the plasma having RF components.

1.3 Active Compensation in RF-driven Plasmas

In order to compensate for the time variation of RF potential difference between probe and plasma, the probe potential has to follow that of the exciting RF signal [2]. This can be achieved by superimposing a synchronous signal of appropriate amplitude and phase onto the probe tip. Plasmas are inherently non-linear and therefore they generate many harmonics of the exciting fundamental. As a consequence of that, the RF signal necessary for satisfactory compensation has not only to match in amplitude and in phase that of the exciting RF, it also has to match the waveform of the harmonics generated in the plasma.

Conveniently, the electrostatic probe and the plasma spontaneously generate a useful control signal. In the presence of a plasma, an isolated electrostatic probe adopts a 'floating potential', at which it draws zero current. The effect of inadequate compensation on a probe in an RF plasma is to drive the DC potential of the probe less positive (or less negative). Thus, optimal tuning is identical with the probe adopting the most positive (or least negative) potential. The 'floating potential' is also referred to here as a DC bias.

2 Automated Control System

Previous work reported by Dyson et. al. [3] involved the use of three harmonics for waveform synthesis. In this application, an additive synthesiser (harmonic box) with seven harmonics has been used to generate the appropriate waveform for a Langmuir probe system attached to a *Gaseous Electronics Conference* (GEC) reference reactor [4]. Figure 3 shows the schematics of the control system for waveform tuning. The fourteen input parameters (seven amplitudes and seven phases) are heavily interacting due to the technical realisation of the synthesiser.

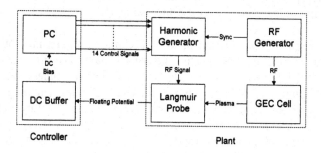

Figure 3 – Closed control loop for waveform tuning.

For example, the slightest departure from an ideal sinusoidal shape in one of the channels introduces harmonics itself. In practice, even after careful electronic design, it is found that there is a weak but significant coupling between the control of amplitude and phase. As a consequence of this, the number of points in the discrete search space has to be calculated as follows:

$$n = (2^b)^p \qquad (1)$$

Where:

n	number of points in search space
b	resolution per channel in bits
p	number of parameters to be optimised

The D/A and A/D converters used in this project had a resolution of 12 bits and the dimensionality of the search space was 14. Hence, the search space consisted of $n \approx 3.7 \times 10^{50}$ search points. In this case, mapping out the entire search space would take approximately 10^{41} years. This was clearly not an option!

In order to tune the Langmuir system within an acceptable timescale, a suitable search algorithm had to be found. In selecting an appropriate algorithm, two requirements emerged. Firstly, the algorithm had to be capable of dealing with a high degree of epistatis (the degree of parameter interaction). Secondly, because of the absence of auxiliary information about the plasma, like its transfer function etc., the prospective algorithm had to be a black box search algorithm.

Previous research has shown that both requirements are met by simulated annealing [5]. Therefore, this algorithm was selected.

2.1 Simulated Annealing

This general optimisation method was first introduced by Kirkpatrick et. al. [6], based on the work of Metropolis et. al. [7]. It simulates the softening process ('annealing') of metal. The metal is heated-up to a temperature near its melting point and then slowly cooled-down. This allows the particles to move towards an optimum energy state, with a more uniform crystalline structure. The process therefore permits some control over the microstructure.

Simulated annealing is a variation of the hill-climbing algorithm. Both start off from a randomly selected point within the search space. The difference between them is that if the fitness of a trial solution is less than the fitness of the current one, the trial solution is not automatically rejected, as in hill climbing. Instead it becomes the current solution with a certain transition probability $p(T)$, which depends on the difference in fitness and on the temperature T. Here, 'temperature' is an abstract control parameter for the algorithm rather than a real physical measure. In this research, the transition probability $p(T)$ for a given temperature and a given difference in fitness ΔF is determined as follows:

$$p(T) = \frac{1}{1 + e^{\frac{\Delta F}{T}}} \tag{2}$$

Where:

T temperature: control parameter for cooling schedule
$p(T)$ probability of transition for temperature T
ΔF difference in fitness between current candidate solution and trial solution

The algorithm starts with a high temperature, which then has to be reduced subsequently in steps.

$$T_{n+1} = \alpha T_n \tag{3}$$

Where:
T_n temperature at step n
α cooling coefficient

On each step, the temperature must be held constant for an appropriate period of time (i.e. number of iterations) in order to allow the algorithm to settle in a 'thermal equilibrium', i.e. in a balanced state. If this time is too short, the algorithm is likely to converge against a local minimum. The combination of temperature steps and cooling times is known as the 'annealing schedule', which is usually selected empirically. Figure 4 shows the flowchart of the basic simulated annealing algorithm.

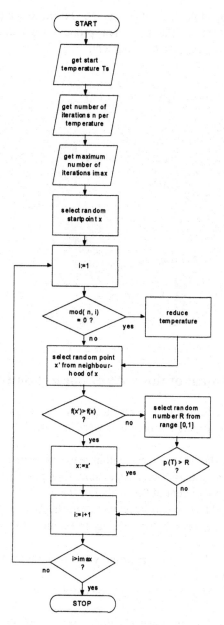

Figure 4 – Flow-chart of the basic SA algorithm.

3 The Implementation of the Control System

The system was set up at the laboratories at the Oxford Research Unit of the Open University. Figure 5 shows the Langmuir probe system attached to the GEC reference reactor used during the development.

Figure 5 – Experiment set-up.

3.1 The Development of the XWOS Control Software

Before the XWOS (X Windows Waveform Optimisation System) control software was developed, the following requirements were identified:

- the optimisation should take place within reasonable time,
- the search results (fitness) over time should be plotted on-line on screen in order to allow a judgement of the quality of the result,
- the operator should be able to select values for the SA parameters,
- the operator should have the opportunity to set any of the fourteen parameters manually,
- the operator should have the opportunity to fine-tune the settings found by the automated system,
- the DC bias (fitness parameter) had to be monitored.

The control software (Figure 6) was developed in C++ on a 500 MHz Pentium III PC running the Linux 2.2 operating system. The graphical user interface was coded using X-Windows and OSF/Motif.

XWOS allows the operator to start a search from the main window. During the search, the fitness over time (i.e. iterations) is plotted in real-time. After the algorithm has been stopped (either by reaching the maximum number of iterations or by the operator), the inputs for the waveform synthesiser, as well as the corresponding sliders on the main screen, are set to the best solution found during the search. The DC bias gained is displayed numerically and on an 'analogue' meter. The operator may then change the settings determined by the algorithm by hand, while observing the DC bias on the meter.

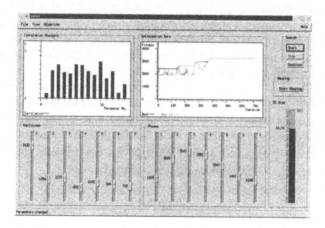

Figure 6 – XWOS main window.

After a search, the history data of the run is used to perform a correlation analysis between the input parameters and the fitness function. The correlation coefficients are graphically displayed in a separate window and may be used as an indicator of the sensitivity of each channel for the given plasma parameters.

The search parameters can be manipulated by the operator using the search parameter dialog box (Figure 7). Here, the operator can also adapt the software to the plasma equipment by selecting an appropriate time constant for the plasma system.

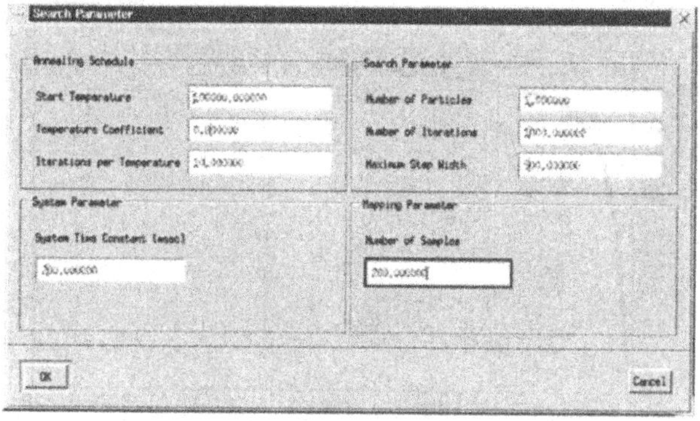

Figure 7 – Search parameter dialog box.

XWOS also provides the facility for random mapping of the search space for a more meaningful correlation analysis.

3.2 Choosing SA parameters

A sigmoid probability function (equation 2) has been used in conjunction with the standard cooling function (equation 3). The cooling coefficient α has been chosen to be 0.8. The maximum number of iterations was 1000, while the number of iterations per temperature was 20. The maximum step width, i.e. the maximum difference between the current solution and a new trial solution, has been set to 500. The selection of a suitable value for the start temperature T_S is most important for the success of SA. If it is not sufficiently large, the system starts in an already 'frozen' state. Hence, it is more likely to get stuck in a local optimum. If it is too large, the algorithm performs a random walk rather than a random guided search. Previous research has shown that a value of 0.5 for the initial transition probability $p(T_s)$ is a good compromise for a small ΔF, decaying towards zero for larger values of ΔF [8]. Therefore, T_S has been calculated as follows:

$$p(T_s) \approx 0.5$$

Using equation 2

$$\frac{1}{1+e^{\frac{\Delta F}{T_s}}} = 0.49$$

Results in

$$T_s \approx 25\Delta F \qquad (4)$$

Figure 8 shows the graphical representation of the normalised probability function for $\Delta F = 1$ together with $p(T_s) = 49\%$.

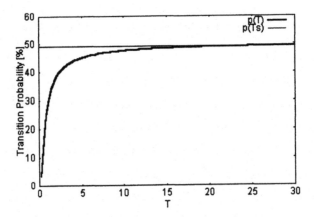

Figure 8 – Transition probability versus temperature.

It can be seen that equation 4 can always be used to estimate the required start temperature T_S for expected values of ΔF if Equation 2 is chosen to be the probability function.

4 System Performance

Argon gas is used at a pressure of 100 mTorr. The plasma is usually produced using a power output from the RF generator of 50 W.

Figure 9 shows a typical run of the algorithm. The dotted line represents the best solution found so far, the thick line represents the fitness on each iteration.

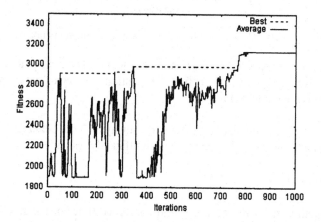

Figure 9 – Typical run of the SA algorithm.

It can be observed that the algorithm initially explores the search space, while later on (after approximately 400 iterations) it exploits the most promising region. Hence, the behaviour of the algorithm at the beginning of the search is similar to random walk, while towards the end it performs like ordinary hill climbing.

The results gained during test trials by SA are compared with the results gained by different human operators in Figure 10.

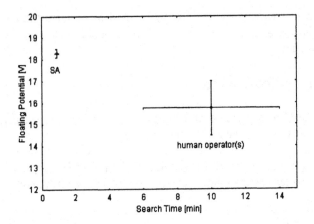

Figure 10 – Comparison between XWOS and human operators.

The data points represent the average achieved DC bias (floating potential) plotted against the average time it took to find the solution. The error bars represent the deviations of these parameters.

It can be seen that simulated annealing has always found better solutions than human operators, but has achieved these in significantly less time.

4.1   Discussion

While the quality (achieved fitness within consumed time) of the solutions found by SA shows only minor variations, the variation in quality for solutions found by human operators is quite dramatic. This is due to human aspects, like the operator's mood or experience. Hence, SA is more reliable in finding the global optimum and its solutions are more reliable. However, the existence of variations in fitness for SA indicate that the algorithm did not always find the global solution, even if it always came quite close to it.

It has been observed during the experiments that the selection of an appropriate step width is crucial to the performance of the simulated annealing algorithm. If the step width is too small, the algorithm has insufficient time to explore the whole search space, and is therefore likely to get stuck in a local optimum. If the step width is too large, the algorithm settles in the region of the global optimum, but if it is already near to the peak, new trial solutions are likely to 'fall off' the peak and hence miss the top of it.

Further work should include an examination of whether the step width can be adapted to the search space during the optimisation process and what effects this adaptation would have on the results achieved.

4.2 Conclusions

In this paper, a novel system for active compensation of a Langmuir probe system in an RF plasma has been presented. Seven harmonics have been used to synthesise the waveform of the potential as it appears in the plasma. Tuning of the fourteen parameters (seven amplitudes and seven phases of the harmonics) by hand is not a straightforward task. The quality of the results depends on a number of human factors, like the operator's mood or experience. A software package has been developed to automate the tuning by simulated annealing. This type of optimisation algorithm was chosen because it offers two desired properties: it can cope with epistatis and noisy inputs and it is a black box optimisation method, i.e. it does not rely on auxiliary information about the system to be optimised.

The software has been used successfully for the tuning, and the results were compared with the results gained by human operators. SA clearly outperformed the human operators in both the fitness of the results and the time needed for the optimisation.

4.3 Further Work

The next stage of this project will be the implementation of step-width adaptation. The effectiveness of such an adaptive system will be compared with the current system.

5 Acknowledgements

This work was funded by the Engineering and Physical Sciences Research Council (EPSRC) under grant reference GR/M71039/01. The authors wish to express their thanks to Fraser G Robertson, Faculty of Technology, the Open University, for assistance with the RF equipment,, and to Pierre Barroy, Oxford Research Unit, the Open University, for his assistance in setting-up the experiment.

References

1. Swift J D S, Schwar M J R: Electrical Probes for Plasma Diagnostics, Ilitte, London, 1970
2. Benjamin N M P, Braithwaite N St J, Allen J E: Self bias of an r.f. driven probe in an r.f. plasma, Mat. Res. Soc. Symp. Proc. 117, 1988, pp 275-280
3. Dyson A, Bryant P, Allen J E: Multiple harmonic compensation of Langmuir probes in rf discharges, Meas. Sci. Technol. 11(2000), pp 554-559
4. Sobolewski M A: Electrical Characterization of Radio Frequency Discharges in the Gaseous Electronics Conference Reference Cell, Journal of Vacuum Science & Technology A – Vacuum Surfaces and Films, 10: (6) 3550-3562 Nov-Dec 1992

5. Nolle L, Walters M, Armstrong D A, Ware J A: Optimum Finisher Mill Set-up in the Hot Rolling of Wide Steel Strip Using Simulated Annealing, Proceedings. of the 5th International Mendel Conference, Brno, 1999, pp 100-105

6. Kirkpatrick S, Gelatt Jr C D, Vecchi M P: Optimization by Simulated Annealing, Science, 13 May 1983, Vol. 220, No. 4598, pp 671-680

7. Metropolis A, Rosenbluth W, Rosenbluth M N, Teller H, Teller E: Equation of State Calculations by Fast Computing Machines, The Journal of Chemical Physics, Vol. 21, No. 6, June 1953, pp 1087-1092

8. Nolle L, Armstrong D A, Hopgood A A, Ware J A: Optimum Work Roll Profile Selection in the Hot Rolling of Wide Steel Strip Using Computational Intelligence, Lecture Notes in Computer Science, Vol. 1625, Springer, 1999, pp 435-452

Rhythm Pattern Accuracy Diagnosis System Using Cluster Analysis and Music Experts' Knowledge Base

Takahiro YONEKAWA

Graduate School of Decision Science and Technology,
Tokyo Institute of Technology

2-12-1, O-okayama, Meguro-ku, Tokyo, 152-8552 Japan

Atsuhiro NISHIKATA

Center for Research and Development of Educational Technology (CRADLE),
Tokyo Institute of Technology

2-12-1, O-okayama, Meguro-ku, Tokyo, 152-8552 Japan

Abstract

This paper investigates the objective appraisal and feedback method for human music rhythm ability. Twelve adult subjects performed eight rhythm patterns in four-four time, by tapping an electric drum pad. The deviation of note length for each note in a bar was obtained which is the evaluation for the rhythm accuracy. To process the measured data which involve human errors or fluctuations, the rhythm pattern matching algorithm using cluster analysis was developed. As a result of analyses, the deviations of note lengths could be statistically analyzed in detail, depending on the rhythm patterns, tempos, as well as the subjects. The rhythm pattern accuracy diagnosis system was developed by utilizing SVM technique. It uses music experts' knowledge base concerning rhythm evaluation, and generates comments and advice for each subject's performances as well as quantitative diagnosis. The feedback by the system during musical rhythm training was shown to be effective.

1   Introduction

Computer-Aided Instruction (CAI) provides useful environment in various coursework and lifelong learning. It seems to be effective also in learning musical skill. Usually, in music classes, musical abilities of students are evaluated based on the experiences of music teachers. For some instructional items, however, the objective evaluation may be possible. Especially in musical basic ability, some features in musical performance may be suitable for objective evaluation.

The aim of this research is to establish the objective appraisal method of music ability in a realizable way. It is important to evaluate one's musical skill (Colwell 1970). But there are few educational materials or tools to evaluate easily and to get intelligent instruction on students' musical performances. This paper focuses on the evaluation of rhythm ability; which is especially important among musical abilities.

The actual musical piece is constituted by a stable tempo and various rhythm patterns. The authors have reported the appraisal method of tempo stability (Yonekawa *et al.* 2000) (Yonekawa *et al.* 2001). In this paper, the evaluation and feedback methods for the accuracy of beated rhythm patterns are investigated. In the feedback method, the knowledge-based engine is used, which is incorporated music experts' knowledge concerning rhythm pattern accuracy evaluation.

2 Pattern recognition of beated rhythms

2.1 Measurements of performance data

2.1.1 Apparatus for measurement

Each subject is seated in front of a rubber pad of electric drum set. The subjects were twelve persons who were mainly faculty and graduate students. Seven persons were good at playing the piano, drums, clarinet, guitar and so on. Two of them had experience in using this kind of drums. When he or she strikes the pad using a drum stick with his or her own right hand, a MIDI drum controller sends MIDI messages to PC-UNIX via a MIDI synthesizer (Figure 1). A simple MIDI recording program (written in C language) on PC-UNIX receives messages, and writes down the time data to a file; data consist of a time train describing when the subject struck the pad. Time data that the computer receives have a resolution of 0.2 ms.

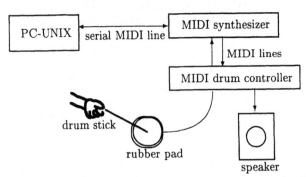

Figure 1: Apparatus for experiment

2.1.2 Rhythm patterns

Eight rhythm patterns in four-four time were composed by using restricted set of notes listed in Table 1. They are shown in Table 2. Criteria of selection are simplicity of pattern and frequent appearance in general musical compositions.

2.1.3 Procedure

The procedure of the experiment is as follows:

1. A subject strikes an assigned rhythm pattern (Table 2), with hearing the metronome sound. Prior to this, they are allowed to refer to tick sound of desirable rhythm pattern any number of times. Tempo and the rhythm pattern are to be memorized at this time.

Table 1: Used notes and their relative lengths

name of note	musical notation	length
dotted half note	𝅗𝅥.	3.0
half note	𝅗𝅥	2.0
dotted quarter note	♩.	1.5
quarter note	♩	1.0
eighth note	♪	0.5

Table 2: Patterns of rhythms in four-four time

(a)	$\mid^4_4$ 𝅗𝅥. ♩ $\mid$	(b)	$\mid^4_4$ 𝅗𝅥. ♪♪ $\mid$
(c)	$\mid^4_4$ 𝅗𝅥 ♩. ♪ $\mid$	(d)	$\mid^4_4$ 𝅗𝅥 ♩ ♩ $\mid$
(e)	$\mid^4_4$ 𝅗𝅥 ♩ ♪♪ $\mid$	(f)	$\mid^4_4$ 𝅗𝅥 ♪♪♩ $\mid$
(g)	$\mid^4_4$ 𝅗𝅥 ♪♩ ♪ $\mid$	(h)	$\mid^4_4$ 𝅗𝅥 ♪♪♪♪ $\mid$

2. The subject is then asked to repeatedly strike the rhythm pattern at the stable tempo for 120 seconds as accurate as possible.

1. and 2. are performed for every rhythm pattern. Tempo is 90 BPM at first half, and 120 BPM afterward.

2.2 Rhythm pattern recognition algorithm

2.2.1 Time train in data file

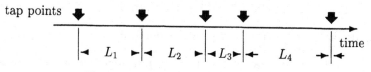

Figure 2: Time train $\{L_i\}$ in data file

The time train $\{L_i\}, i = 1, 2, \cdots$ which is stored in a data file represents the intervals between successive two taps (Figure 2). Tap point is defined as the time when a drum stick just touches a drum pad. Therefore, each interval is equivalent to the note length. Each element of $\{L_i\}$ may correspond to one of the notes in a bar. The measured data $\{L_i\}$ involve human errors or fluctuations — subjects might strike a wrong tap occasionally or recover from missing taps. To determine the correspondence between L_i and notes, pattern recognition algorithm is needed.

2.2.2 Pattern recognition algorithm

The algorithm to recognize a one-bar rhythm pattern were shown in Figure 3. A time train $\{L_i\}$ was given at the beginning. Then, its normalized partial time train vector $\{M_i\}$ is prepared. The number of elements in each M_i is equal to n, where n is the number of notes in a bar. The 1-norm of each M_i is normalized to 1 (See Figure 3).

Next, $\{M_i\}$ are divided into groups by cluster analysis under the following conditions: the number of cluster is n, and the distances between clusters are calculated using centroid method. On the other hand, the reference vectors $P_j, j = 1, 2, \cdots, n$ are defined which represent correct note-length sequences.

Given:

- a time train $\{L_i\}, i = 1, 2, \cdots, N$, where N is the number of received time interval data

- number of notes in a bar: n

- note identifier: A, B, C, $\cdots$

- reference vectors: $\{P_j\}, j = 1, 2, \cdots, n$ (See Figure 4)

Algorithm:

1. Define normalized partial time train $\{M_i\}$:

$$M_i = (\tilde{L}_i, \tilde{L}_{i+1}, \cdots, \tilde{L}_{i+n-1}),$$
$$\text{where } \tilde{L}_k = \alpha L_k, \quad \sum_{k=i}^{i+n-1} \tilde{L}_k = 1, \ \alpha : constant$$

2. Do cluster analysis on $\{M_i\}$ under the conditions as follows:

   - number of cluster: n

   - clustering method: centroid method (no square)

3. Choose a cluster nearest to P_1 , and name it as C_1.

4. Now, each M_i in that cluster ($i \in C_1$) is identified to be a one-bar sequence.

5. Do correction of the note lengths for each one-bar sequence M_i in cluster C_1 by multiplying a correction coefficient η, so that $\displaystyle\sum_{i \in C_1} \sum_{j=1}^{n} |\log \frac{\eta M_{ij}}{P_{1j}}|$ is minimized with respect to η.

Figure 3: Rhythm pattern recognition algorithm

Thus, the vectors $\{M_i\}$ which are derived from input data and the reference vectors $\{P_j\}$ are mapped on the same n-dimensional space (See Figure 4, bottom). Next, the one-to-one correspondence between clusters and reference vectors are determined based on their distances. Then the cluster C_1 corresponding to the reference vector P_1 contains one-bar sequences starting from the first note in a bar. Experimental result showed that 96.8 % of notes performed by twelve subjects were successfully identified.

Due to the normalization constraint, $\tilde{L}_i$ may be biased owing to extreme deviations of certain elements. To reduce the bias, $\tilde{L}_i$ are corrected as described in the step 5 of Figure 3.

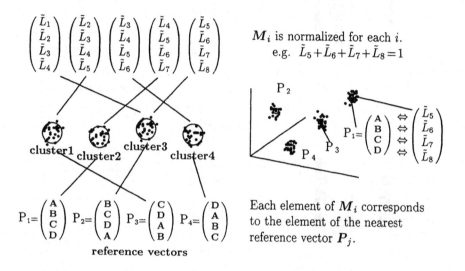

M_i is normalized for each i.

e.g. $\tilde{L}_5 + \tilde{L}_6 + \tilde{L}_7 + \tilde{L}_8 = 1$

Each element of M_i corresponds to the element of the nearest reference vector P_j.

Figure 4: Diagram of the pattern recognition algorithm using cluster analysis

3 Analyses of performance data

3.1 Deviation and instability of note lengths

Typical two subjects' scatter charts of M_i are shown in Figure 5 (left). Stability of note length of subject YT (upper left) was higher than that of subject KM (lower left); when the clusters have smaller diameters and are closer to each reference vector, the note lengths are more stable and more accurate.

The distributions of all the notes in bars are shown in Figure 5 (right). Accuracy of each note length in each bar that a subject performed is evaluated by the deviation of note length from its ideal length (the ideal length equals to the ideal partition of the actual length of the bar in question) as:

deviation of note length $\tilde{L}_j^*$ [%]

$$= \frac{\text{subject's note length } \tilde{L}_j - \text{ideal length } \tilde{T}_j}{\text{ideal length } \tilde{T}_j} \times 100 \quad , j = 1, 2, \cdots, n$$

$\tilde{L}_j^*$ vanishes when the subject's note length equals to the ideal one. When the subject's are longer than the ideal one, it takes positive value.

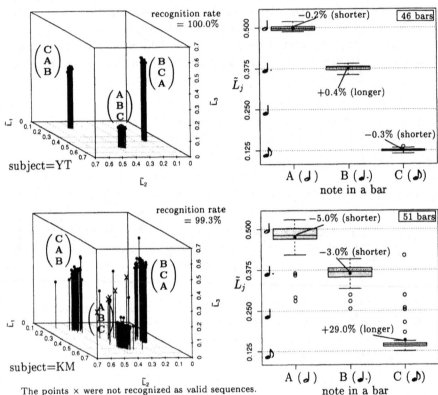

The points × were not recognized as valid sequences.

Figure 5: Results of the cluster analysis (left) and performance accuracy (right)

3.2 Relationship between deviation and instability

There are two aspects of evaluation in the note length distribution. One is the note length deviation in average, which shows the accuracy of note length as a whole. The other is the note lengths' standard deviation which corresponds to the stability of note length. In Figure 6, each piece of performance is expressed by a dot on a surface whose horizontal and vertical axes corresponds to the note length deviation and note length instability, respectively. As it is expected, there is a medium positive correlation ($r = 0.43$) between the deviation and instability. Still, however, the exceptional case "the more accurate, the more stable" exists such as the case "accurate but instable" or "stable but inaccurate".

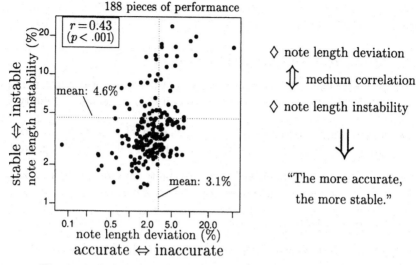

Figure 6: Relationship between deviation and instability

3.3 Tendency of inaccuracy

The tendency of inaccuracy was shown in Table 3, which classifies twelve subjects into four categories depending on their bias features. Seven persons performed accurately, and the other were not. The note "B" were played shorter by four persons, and note "C" were played longer by two of them.

These features were found also in other patterns and tempos. It was found that the evaluation output by this algorithm was similar to one evaluated by musical experts.

Table 3: Tendency of incuracy: pattern (f) , 120 BPM

Description \ Note	A ♩	B ♪	C ♪	D ♩	person(s) 12 subjects
Accurate	○	○	○	○	7 (58 %)
B was inaccurate.	○	short	○	○	2 (17 %)
B and C were inaccurate.	○	short	long	○	2 (17 %)
All were inaccurate.	short	long	long	long	1 (8 %)

Less than 4% of inaccuracy is marked by ○.

4 Feedback method using musical experts' knowledge base

It is important to consider the feedback method of the evaluation in rhythm accuracy. It is easy for leaners to understand the meaning of feedback if it is made as music experts do. In this section, the method to generate "the evaluation as well as experts' advice" from leaners' performance profiles is described.

4.1 Quantitative evaluation indices

Learners' performance data are summarized in three types of evaluation indices, "note length deviation", "note length instability" and "tempo instability":

- **"note length deviation"** $\tilde{L}_j^*$: deviation of each note in a rhythm pattern, $j = 1, 2, \cdots, N$, N: the number of valid note length data.

- **"note length instability"** S_k : instability of note length in a pattern, $k = 1, 2, \cdots, n$, n: the number of notes in a bar.

- **"tempo instability"** K_1, K_2 : two kinds of tempo instability.

The note length instability S_k is calculated by the following equation:

$$S_k = \frac{1}{m} \sum_{l \in C_1} |M_{lk} - \frac{1}{m} \sum_{i \in C_1} M_{ik}| \ ,$$

m : the number of vectors M_i beginning with first note length in a bar

The S_k means the distribution size of leaner's feature vectors M_j around the center of gravity of the vectors $\frac{1}{m} \Sigma_{i=1}^m M_i$. If a leaner's performance is instable throughout the measurement time, the distribution size is large.

K_1 and K_2 are the indices concerning tempo stability and are calculated as:

$$K_1 \, [\%/\text{min.}] = \frac{T(t_m) - T(t_1)}{T(t_1)} \times \frac{1}{t_m - t_1} \times 100 \ ,$$

$$K_2 \, [\%] = \text{S.D.}[T(t_b) - \{T(t_1) + K_1(t_b - t_1)\}, \ \forall_{t_b}]$$

where t_b : start time at b-th bar, T_{t_b} : tempo at the time t_b ,

S.D.: standard deviation

If the final tempo is faster than the initial tempo, K_1 is positive value.

These quantities as objective evaluation values are useful themselves. The music experts' knowledge base (described afterward), in addition to these indices, provide more understandable and effective advice for learners.

4.2 Musical Experts' Rhythm Pattern Diagnosis Model (MERPDM)

4.2.1 Performance feature vector

One's performance feature of the specific rhythm pattern and tempo is represented by the $2n + 2$ dimensional (n is the number of notes in a bar) vector $F_{p,t}$:

$$\boldsymbol{F}_{p,t} = \begin{pmatrix} \frac{1}{m}\Sigma_{i\in C_1} \tilde{L}_i^* \\ \frac{1}{m}\Sigma_{i\in C_1} \tilde{L}_{i+1}^* \\ \vdots \\ \frac{1}{m}\Sigma_{i\in C_1} \tilde{L}_{i+n-1}^* \\ S_1 \\ S_2 \\ \vdots \\ S_n \\ K_1 \\ K_2 \end{pmatrix}$$, p: rhythm pattern identifier, t: tempo identifier

$\boldsymbol{F}_{p,t}$ are represented by points in $2n+2$ dimensional space. Similar performance feature vectors are, therefore, placed close to each other in the space.

4.2.2 Machine learning process with performance feature vectors and experts' evaluation

For each performance, an expert evaluates it from several points of view. The expert labels commentaries, which are prepared in advance, as "true" or "false". As a result, pairs of binary values and performance feature vectors $(\boldsymbol{F}_{p,t})$ are collected. These pairs are training data for the learning program of SVM. If they are learnt completely, either of "true" or "false" for the commentary will be predicted for an unknown performance. In this way, all the corresponding commentaries will be classified and answered.

5 Rhythm pattern accuracy diagnosis system

When a learner practices rhythm patterns using the evaluation system to get better with his or her play, appropriate diagnoses will help him or her a great deal. In this section, the feature of the rhythm pattern accuracy diagnosis system with knowledge-based engine using SVM technique is described. This system will generate appropriate suggestion or advice for learners' rhythm performance as a feedback.

5.1 Flow of the system

The main program (diagnosis.pl) opens a GUI window (Figure 7). It runs as the flow chart shown in Figure 8. At first, a learner is instructed about the functions of the system with voice. After that, the rhythm pattern and tempo are selected by a learner. Before the measurement of his or her performance, the learner can perform with hearing the metronome sound as preparation. The measurement is done for sixty seconds without metronome sound. When the performance is finished, the system generates the evaluation as a performance profile for feedback. They are presented by voice, graphics, and text form.

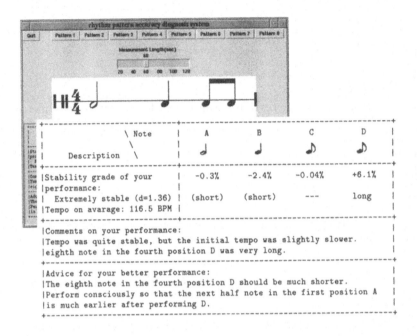

Figure 7: A GUI window of the rhythm pattern accuracy diagnosis system

In this process, a knowledge-based analysis is used for generating the evaluations. The system has the Music Experts' Rhythm Pattern Diagnosis Model (MERPDM) as knowledge base.

5.2 System configuration

- OS: FreeBSD 4.0
- Applications required:
  - splay 0.8.2 (for playing voice files)
  - perl 5.005
  - p5-Tk-800.008 (Tk library for perl5)
  - SVM^{light} Version: 3.02
- MIDI Synthesizer: YAMAHA DTXPRESS

This diagnosis system consists of four programs. The main program is a perl script diagnosis.pl using Tk module; Tk library provides GUI functions to perl in X-Window environment. The other three programs (diagnosis.sh, cluster.c and merpdm.c) run as module for the main program. The C program cluster.c is mainly for cluster analysis concerning this diagnosis system. The merpdm.c is the inference engine to operate the music experts' rhythm diagnosis model. SVM commands (svm_learn and svm_classify) are called from merpdm.c.

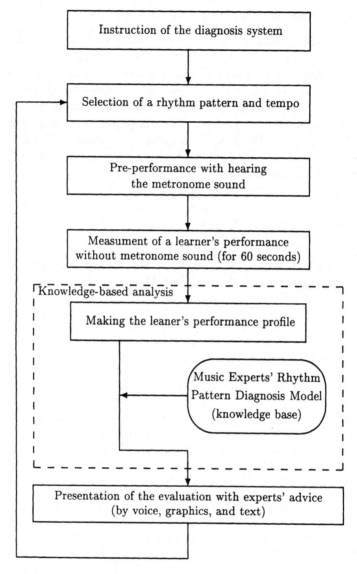

Figure 8: System flow of the rhythm pattern accuracy diagnosis system

5.3   An evaluation sample generated by the system

The evaluation sample generated by the system is shown in Figure 7. Quantitative indices are presented at first. The stability of note length is indicated in grade.

Comments and Advice for learner's performance are shown below. They are generated using the MERPDM.

5.4 Training effects using the system

Training effects using the system was experimented for twelve subjects. In this experiment, the section "Advice for your performance" in Figure 7 was not used for a feedback to a learner. They are devided into two groups, feedback group (six persons) and non-feedback group (six persons). No significant difference of deviations of note lengths were found between the groups before the training.

One-minute rhythm performance of the pattern(c) were measured in 90BPM for eight times. Only for feedback group, evaluation of their performance was presented by voice after each one-minute performance. Each performer's effectiveness E is defined as:

$$E = \max(-\ln(D_k/D_1)) \quad , k=2, \cdots, 8 ,$$

$$\text{where} \quad D_k = \sum_j |\tilde{L}_j^*| \quad , k=1, 2, \cdots, 8$$

As a result (See Figure 9), accuracy appeared greater in the feedback group than that of non-feedback group ($p < .1$).

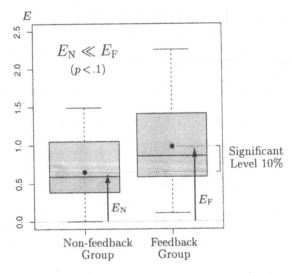

Figure 9: Training effect between feedback group and non-feedback group

6 Conclusion

This paper proposed an objective evaluation method on human musical basic ability and its method of feedback. Through the experiment using twelve subjects, it was shown that the proposed method could successfully extract the statistical features of each subject's accuracy of the rhythm performance. The feedback was generated which shows quantitative diagnosis for each performance.

The future subject is to reinforce the Musical Experts' Rhythm Pattern Diagnosis Model (MERPDM) as a knowledge base. It is also to be discussed on the method to interpret the quantitative statistics into more understandable diagnosis or advices for the learners.

References

[1] Bentley, A. (1966), *Measures of Musical Ability*, October House, New York

[2] Malcolm Tait & Paul Haack (1984), *Principles and Processes of Music Education*, Teachers College Press, Columbia University

[3] Moore, B.C.J. (1989), *An Introduction to the Psychology of Hearing (Third Ed.)*, Academic Press, London

[4] Rita Aiello (1994), *Musical Perceptions*, Oxford University Press

[5] Seashore, C.E., Lewis, D.L. and Saetveit, J.G. (1960), *Seashore Measure of Musical Talents (revised)*, The Psychological Corporation, New York

[6] Colwell, R. (1970), *The Evaluation of Music Teaching and Learning*, Prentice-Hall, Inc., Englewood Cliffs, New Jersey

[7] Nello Cristianini & John Shawe-Taylor (2000), *An Introduction to Support Vector Machines and other kernel-based learning methods*, Cambridge University Press, Cambridge

[8] Thorsten Joachims (1999), *Making large-Scale SVM Learning Practical. Advances in Kernel Methods – Support Vector Learning*, B. Schölkopf and C. Burges and A. Smola (ed.), http://www-ai.cs.uni-dortmund.de/DOKUMENTE/joachims_99a.pdf, MIT-Press, Cambridge

[9] T. Yonekawa, A. Nishikata, M. Nakayama, Y. Shimizu (2000), *An Evaluation of Basic Rhythm Aptitude Based on Tempo Fluctuation*, Japan Journal of Educational Technology, Vol.24, No.3, pp.173-181

[10] T. Yonekawa, A. Nishikata, M. Nakayama, Y. Shimizu (2001), *An Accuracy Evaluation of Beated Rhythm Patterns*, IEICE General Conference, D-15-3, p.203

SESSION 4:

KNOWLEDGE AND INFORMATION MANAGEMENT

An Expert System for Evaluating the 'Knowledge Potential' of Databases

Stephen Potter and Stuart Aitken,
AIAI, University of Edinburgh, Edinburgh, United Kingdom
stephenp@aiai.ed.ac.uk
http://www.aiai.ed.ac.uk/

Abstract

Data Mining techniques can, under favourable conditions, extract valuable knowledge from an organisation's databases. However, the precise nature of these favourable conditions is poorly articulated, and as a result organisations run the risk of instigating costly and time-consuming data mining episodes upon inappropriate or irrelevant data. In response to this problem, the authors have applied expert systems technologies to the task of predicting the extent to which a given database contains knowledge that is both valuable and susceptible to mining. It is intended that this system will form a component of a 'knowledge auditing' method for appraising an organisation's (existing and potential) knowledge resources. This paper describes this application, along with some of the particular issues surrounding its implementation, testing and delivery to prospective users.

1. Introduction

Alongside the increasing capacities and decreasing prices of data storage media there has been a commensurate growth in the number and size of databases that are generated and maintained within organisations. Whilst these undoubtedly provide a useful historical record of the organisation's transactions and entities, there has been a growing recognition that, when considered as a whole, these records can implicitly constitute more general knowledge of the relationships that hold amongst these transactions and entities. This knowledge is potentially of immense value to the organisation, enabling it to better understand and reason about its processes and customers, and then act so as to maximise its profits. Accordingly, the question then becomes one of how this implicit knowledge might be made explicit.

There are several techniques by which information of the sort found in databases might be 'converted' into actionable knowledge. The work described in this paper concerns the application of Data Mining (DM) techniques to databases for the purposes of acquiring knowledge. These techniques exploit algorithms developed through AI research into machine learning and more traditional statistical data analysis algorithms in order to generate useful knowledge inductively, that is, to extract general relationships from a given set of examples of these relationships (provided by the records in the database).

Hence, when successful, a DM episode can convert an organisation's existing database resources into useful knowledge. However, there are many reasons why an application of DM to a particular database might not produce the desired results: the algorithms might be applied inappropriately; the data may be too noisy; or the database records may contain irrelevant or incidental information. Moreover, even if knowledge is extracted, unless it is of practical use to the organisation then the episode cannot be considered a success. Since DM is frequently performed by experts from outside the organisation, and the process of understanding and then applying algorithms to the database can be time-consuming, any failure - regardless of the reason for it - can prove costly.

This factor provided one of the motivations for the work reported here. It was realised that the ability to evaluate a particular database with respect to its 'knowledge potential' (that is, the potential that it has to provide useful knowledge if DM is applied appropriately to it *but without actually applying DM to it*) would be of great value to organisations that possess databases and lack the resources or the inclination to pay to be told that their data are of little worth. Furthermore, if this ability were embodied within an expert system, it would enable it to be effectively transmitted to remote locations where and when it is required. This paper describes such a system, along with issues raised by the use and delivery of its knowledge. It is envisaged that this expert system would form an element in a wider 'knowledge auditing' methodology; since this would be a factor which influenced a number of the choices made in the system, this idea will now be discussed briefly.

1.1 The Knowledge Audit

Since nowadays it is widely accepted that knowledge is a valuable (and in many cases the most valuable) organisational resource, its audit, in order to form a picture of the nature and extent of this resource, would seem as worthwhile to an organisation as would be the audit of any more tangible resource. However, therein lies the difficulty: knowledge is rarely explicit in the manner of these more tangible resources, and is often evinced, if at all, through the processes of the organisation.

Although a browse of the internet reveals a number of knowledge management organisations offering 'knowledge auditing' services, the precise nature of these services is rarely clear (often as an understandable result of their commercial sensitivity), and it was felt to be a worthwhile endeavour, under the umbrella of the *Advanced Knowledge Technologies* initiative[1], drawing on the project members' wide-ranging knowledge research experience, to try to establish a coherent and sound methodology, along with the necessary tools, for performing an audit.

---

[1] The Advanced Knowledge Technologies (AKT) project is a long-term interdisciplinary collaboration between research groups at 5 UK universities which aims to tackle fundamental problems associated with knowledge management.

Databases, when viewed as repositories of (potential) knowledge, constitute resources that fall within the remit of the audit and which should be included within the overall assessment of the organisation's knowledge. Although the wider knowledge auditing research is still very much in its infancy, it was felt that an auditing tool for assessing databases could be constructed in a relatively short period of time and would provide a useful experimental test bed for exploring the various technologies that might play a role in performing the knowledge audit. As such, two principle factors have been influential in its construction:

- First, there is a desire to exploit the information- and knowledge-sharing facilities afforded by the World-Wide Web: the ability to perform a knowledge audit over the internet would, it is hoped, lead to a more efficient (and less costly to implement) procedure.
- Secondly, since commerce is being conducted at increasing rates, and organisations are becoming increasingly dynamic in terms of information (and hence knowledge) flow, it is clear that there is a real need for any auditing process to be quick and efficient to be of any use to these organisations.

Hence, this database auditing tool would be available to the organisation via the medium of the internet, and it should be able to judge a database's worth rapidly, especially when one considers that the organisation might have many databases that it wished to audit. (Although conceived as a component of a knowledge audit methodology, it was also thought desirable that, if possible, the tool should be able to function as a 'stand-alone' application, able to offer useful advice regardless of whether or not it was being used as part of an audit of the organisation in question.)

1.2   Structure of this Paper

In the following section, the Data Mining task, and the processes involved, will be described in some detail. The third section describes the sort of information and knowledge required for an expert system to audit a database. Subsequent sections describe the implementation of this system and some of the particular issues that are raised by the implementation and the testing of this and similar knowledge-based applications. Finally, some conclusions are drawn about the work.

2.   Data Mining

According to Berry and Linoff [1] Data Mining can be defined as:
"...the process of exploration and analysis, by automatic or semi-automatic means, of large quantities of data in order to discover meaningful patterns and rules."

They go on to remark that some people have been misled into thinking that DM is "a product that can be bought rather than a discipline that must be mastered." This comment highlights the fact that DM relies as much on the expertise and experience of its practitioners as it does on the availability of particular algorithms – and, consequently, why expert systems might have a role to play in this process. This section is devoted to describing the DM task in greater detail, so providing the background necessary for understanding both the motivation for an expert system and the system itself. To begin with, however, it will be advantageous to discuss briefly databases, and the accompanying terminology used throughout this paper.

2.1 Databases

To simplify matters, a database is considered here to be a collection of one or more *records*. Each record describes some event or entity, in terms of the values that it possesses for each of a number of pre-defined attributes or *fields*, which are common to all records. There are a number of characteristics of databases that can cause particular problems for DM or else influence the decisions that are made. These include the extent to which values are missing in the data, the amount of noise in the values, and the number of records contained in the database and the degree to which these records form a representative sample of the whole. Inasmuch as they have a bearing on the work presented here, these characteristics will be discussed in greater detail in a later section.

2.2 The Data Mining Process

The Data Mining task is one of extracting useful knowledge from a (usually large, but not necessarily so) database. This is an *inductive* process: each record in the data represents some event, and the DM task is to produce some generalised description of these events that is in some way useful to the organisation that owns the database. There is a range of tools for performing this induction; these include algorithms originating from the AI discipline of machine learning (typically, these algorithms will represent attempts to mimic some aspect of human learning capabilities) and from statistical analysis. Limitations of space preclude a detailed discussion of the various algorithms here.

At the highest level, this process is represented by Berry and Linoff's 'virtuous circle' of DM (Figure 1). Here DM is viewed as a continuous cycle, with earlier results being used to modify the business processes, generating more (and perhaps different types) of data, which, in their turn, can then be mined. The work presented here is concerned with the very earliest stages of DM, before such a cycle has been initiated, at the time when the organisation's existing database resources are to be assessed so as to decide whether they contain data that might be transformed into knowledge that is both actionable and useful.

2.2.1 Step 1: Identify Business Problems – and DM Solutions

This initial step involves establishing the goals or the purpose of a DM exercise. This is a poorly defined task, which usually takes as its starting point some particular database, and which involves devising some hypothesis about what might be usefully learned from the database. This notion of 'useful' knowledge is obviously not a uniform one; it depends as much upon the organisation's wider goals and resources, upon the ML algorithms that are available, and upon the DM practitioner's experience and creativity, as it does upon the nature and content of the database itself. Hence, the task at this stage is more one of communication and understanding than one of data analysis: the DM practitioner must gain an understanding of the meaning of the data and its place within the context of the organisation. Only then can notions emerge of what might represent useful knowledge for the organisation.

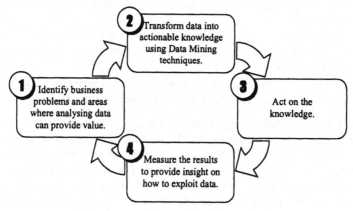

Figure 1. The 'virtuous circle' of Data Mining (after Berry and Linoff [1]).

If these (potentially conflicting) factors can be reconciled, the outcome of this stage will be one or more models or descriptions of the knowledge that might be learned from the data: the in the next stage the DM task becomes one of learning these models. The quality of the analysis and choices made during this step will have a major bearing on the efficiency and success of the endeavour.

2.2.2 Step 2: Transform Data into Actionable Knowledge

This step involves a number of sub-tasks, applied for each knowledge model in turn. First, a particular DM algorithm is selected as being suitable for learning the knowledge (in practice this will have had a bearing on the previous step, influencing the construction of the knowledge descriptions, and the choice may well have been (implicitly) made already). With the algorithm selected, the next sub-task is to construct the appropriate datasets from the database. Depending on the algorithm chosen, three datasets may be needed:

- The *training set* –contains the data to be used to try to learn the knowledge.
- The *validation set* – this has the same form as the training set, but consists of distinct sets of values. It is used when applying certain algorithms to set parameters or guide the acquisition process (not all algorithms require this set).
- The *test set* – a third disjoint set drawn from the database that shares the form of the previous two. This set is used to assess the quality of the learned knowledge once training has concluded.

Together these sets may include all the records in the relevant subset of the database, or else some sample of them: a representative smaller sample may provide the desired knowledge more efficiently. Ensuring that each sample/subset is representative of the whole is extremely difficult, if not impossible. (It is sometimes appropriate to manipulate the datasets so that they are no longer representative, so as to emphasise certain rare – but crucial – events in the data.)

Before these datasets can be constructed, however, it will usually be necessary to preprocess the data. This preprocessing can be a difficult task, and requires a certain amount of expertise to do well – as it must be done if the DM exercise is to succeed. Han and Kamber [2] identify four different forms of data preprocessing:

- *Data cleaning* – remove (or reduce) noise and correct inconsistencies and incompleteness.
- *Data integration* – merge data from a number of sources.
- *Data transformation* – manipulate data into forms more suited to the DM algorithm in question.
- *Data reduction* – reduce numbers of data to more manageable levels, and in such a way as to preserve as far as possible its potential for DM purposes.

The next step is to apply the algorithm to the suitably processed datasets. In order to do this, values must be chosen for the particular learning parameters of the algorithm. Generally, there is little assistance available for selecting these values, and DM practitioners must rely on their experience or intuition; nevertheless, there will usually be some degree of trial-and-error and 'tweaking' of values involved, until either apposite settings are found and the knowledge is successfully learned, or else the attempt is abandoned in the wake of repeated failure. During the actual learning process little human interaction will, in general, be needed. If learning terminates successfully, and evaluation using the test data suggests that the resulting knowledge conforms to the description of the desired knowledge, then the task may be considered to have concluded satisfactorily - the knowledge has been 'mined' successfully from the database. If not, then an alternative choice must be made at one of the previous stages in the DM process, and the task repeated accordingly. Once the knowledge has been validated, it will be necessary to analyse it as a precursor to acting upon the knowledge. In order to facilitate this, it may be necessary to 'visualise' the knowledge, that is, to make it more immediately comprehensible through the use of graphical representations, etc.

2.2.3 Step 3: Act upon the Mined Knowledge

Armed with this new knowledge, the organisation must put it into practice. How this is done obviously depends on both the organisation and the nature and content of the knowledge. The knowledge may merely serve to confirm that the organisation's existing beliefs and operations are well-founded and so increase the confidence with which they are applied, or it may lead to the modification of existing operations so as to move into more profitable regions, or even to the introduction of entirely new operations to exploit hitherto unrecognised areas into which the organisation can expand.

2.2.4 Step 4: Measure Results

If the value of the knowledge – and of DM, in general – to the organisation is to be ascertained, the results of its use must be monitored. Analysis of these results may provide interesting insights, and if the organisation is convinced of the worth of DM and committed to its application, they may suggest additional areas in which data may be mined, and, indeed, the sort of data that should be collected to optimise the returns from future DM episodes.

3. Data Mining and the Knowledge Audit

Under the right circumstances and with the right resources available, then, the discipline of Data Mining can transform data into knowledge that can improve the operations and activities of an organisation. For this reason, it was thought that as yet unmined databases should be included within the remit of a knowledge audit of an organisation, with some measure of their potential value as repositories of knowledge being incorporated into this assessment. However, a DM episode on a single database might be a lengthy process, requiring DM expertise and resources - and even then, a failure to extract useful knowledge might not necessary mean that the database is worthless as a store of knowledge: poor decisions may have undermined the attempt where better ones would have resulted in success. When, in addition, one considers that an organisation might have a great number of databases, it is clear that this audit must be done, if it is to be done at all, without recourse to actually performing DM on the database.

The authors, drawing on their practical experience of DM applications, feel that it is possible to perform an appraisal of a database in this manner, and, moreover, that the knowledge for performing this audit might usefully be embodied within an expert system, providing a means by which the audit might be automated - hence the work reported in this paper. This section gives an overview of the knowledge used to build this system; the sources of this knowledge were the authors themselves, DM textbooks (chiefly [1] and [2]) and Microsoft's Object Linking and Embedding (OLE) description of DM [3].

The assumption was made that the user of the system would be an employee of the organisation that is undergoing the knowledge audit, and that the system will be executed once for each database that is included within the scope of the audit. This user is expected to be familiar with the database and its contents, and with its place in the wider context of the organisation, and able to answer questions about these: the system would ask a sequence of relevant questions, and make an evaluation of the database on the basis of the answers supplied by the user. Since the system would be part of a general-purpose auditing methodology, the questions would necessarily refer to organisations and databases in the abstract, since it would be infeasible to incorporate specific knowledge of each organisation and its databases.

Furthermore, since this system will be operating as a component in a wider knowledge audit of the organisation, and there may be a number of databases that require auditing, there exists an added practical consideration: the system should be able to make its evaluation without the need for drawn out, time-consuming interaction with the user. In other words, there is a need to find some compromise between, on the one hand, gathering enough information to make an accurate assessment of the database and, on the other, asking as few questions as is possible.

Finally, although this expert system would form but a component in a knowledge auditing methodology, it would, presumably, be of great practical advantage if the system were able to draw conclusions and make recommendations that in some way 'stand alone'; that is, if the system were able to offer general advice on the suitability of databases for DM. With these considerations and assumptions in mind, and taking into consideration the foregoing discussion of the DM process, the relevant information required from the user can be thought of as falling into three general categories:

- The relationship that exists between the database, knowledge and the organisation;
- The availability and nature of background knowledge of the domain that may assist DM, and;
- The nature and content of the database itself.

Each of these will now be considered in turn.

3.1 The Relationship between Database, Knowledge and Organisation

Assuming that the user has some database, from a DM perspective the knowledge audit task is to try to answer the following question: *to what extent do the data in this database contain knowledge that: (a) might be data-mined, and (b) would (potentially) be of value to the organisation?* To answer this question, it is necessary to first consider – at a generic level - about what sorts of knowledge can be acquired through DM. The literature contains several classifications of the types of knowledge that can be mined; there is some degree of consensus to suggest that, at the highest level, this knowledge falls into two categories, which may be termed (following Han and Kamber [2]) *predictive* and *descriptive* knowledge:

- *Predictive knowledge* – this sort of knowledge allows some value to be suggested for one or more attributes (each attribute will correspond directly to a field in the database or else will be derived from some combination of fields by some known operation) of a particular record, based on the values of the other fields of the record. So, this form of knowledge might be used to make predictions about the behaviour of certain attributes, or to otherwise supply values where they are missing for whatever reason.
- *Descriptive knowledge* – this knowledge is in the form of some useful general description or representation of the database or some subset of the data contained therein. This description will make evident general patterns and relationships that occur in the data that were either previously unknown, or else were suspected and are now confirmed.

Any given database might contain both predictive and descriptive knowledge. The first question of the expert system, then, would simply ask the user whether or not, on the basis of the sort of information recorded in the database fields, he/she believes that one or both of these types of knowledge may be present in the database under consideration, and if so, whether this knowledge would be of use to the organisation if it were to be made explicit. Since a negative answer to either the first or second part of this question would indicate that DM could extract nothing of use from the database, the database is adjudged worthless and the session ceases.

Following a positive response to both parts, the interrogation of the user proceeds to the next question, which also concerns the nature of knowledge learnt through DM. Since DM algorithms operate inductively and, accordingly, any knowledge they acquire remains susceptible to invalidation by the occurrence of a single counter-example, this knowledge cannot be guaranteed to be wholly and completely accurate; rather, confidence in its correctness grows with the number of examples – with no counter-examples – seen. Hence, at this stage user should be asked if all the (prescriptive and descriptive) knowledge gained from the database would only be of use if it were wholly correct – if so, the database has no value from a DM perspective, and questioning ceases.

Since, for the purposes of the audit, it is necessary to quantify the potential value of the knowledge in the database, it is necessary to gain some idea of the possible extent of knowledge in the database. Therefore, the next question asks how many 'scraps' (that is, distinct elements) of knowledge of both types are thought potentially to exist in the database, and how many record fields are 'involved' in each scrap of knowledge, on average. This latter question is an attempt to gain some sort of idea of the complexity of the knowledge (and so, the number of data necessary to acquire it) – as a rule of thumb, it is assumed that complexity is proportional to the number of involved fields, though this is not necessarily so.

Now that the some idea has been gained of the 'amount' of knowledge that the database may contain, attention can turn to the question of its worth - any DM exercise can be considered a success only if the knowledge it derives from the data is of value to the organisation. Failure to consider the resources and goals of the organisation can lead to situations in which, for example, valid, seemingly 'good' knowledge is mined, but since it is already well-known within the organisation the DM effort confers no additional value. Hence, the value of the potential knowledge can only be assessed by some agent (in this case, the system user) familiar with the objectives and operations of the organisation. The user is asked to judge the relative worth of the knowledge scraps, if they were made available as a whole, on a scale of 1 ("knowledge of minor usefulness, perhaps confirming existing knowledge and validating current procedures") to 5 ("knowledge of the utmost importance to the future of the organisation"). Once a clearer picture has been gained in this way of the relationship between organisation, database and potential knowledge, attention can turn to the next area of questioning.

3.2 Background Knowledge of the Domain

The existence and availability of additional background domain knowledge can also have a bearing on the data mining exercise. This might be quite generic in nature, or else be specific to the organisation and to the data stored in the database. The next phase in the questioning involves asking about background knowledge. During DM background knowledge may be used for two general purposes:

- When preprocessing of the data, background knowledge can be used to 'clean' or to better represent the data for the chosen algorithm (its most common use).
- During the operation of the algorithm, to guide and suggest possible generalisations that might hold across the data.

The existence of this background knowledge is *not* a necessary condition for successful data mining – useful knowledge can be mined in its absence. However, in a typical DM application, its presence will facilitate the exploitation of the database, will make the process more efficient (and thereby reduce costs) by reducing the amount of analysis of the data necessary to preprocess it, and may increase the quality and value of the acquired knowledge by expressing it in more readily comprehensible terms, suited to both the domain and the organisation.

Hence, the availability of background knowledge will, in general, serve to enhance the potential of the database for DM, and so increase the value of the database from the perspective of a knowledge audit. Accordingly, the system should ask its user about the availability of background knowledge. In order to do this, thought needs to be given the to nature of this knowledge. It is considered that background knowledge in DM applications can be classified as one of the following:

- Knowledge of useful or appropriate categories or ranges into which (particularly numerical) values fall.
- Knowledge of potentially useful attributes that can be derived from the fields of the database, and of how such attributes are derived.
- The definitions of any potentially useful (taxonomic, hierarchical, etc) relationships describing the fields of the data.

For the purposes of the system, the user is not required to supply any of this knowledge, but merely to be able to indicate its availability or otherwise.

3.3 The Database and its Contents

Now the focus can turn to the database itself. Obviously, the nature and the content of the database will be a major factor governing the success of the DM enterprise – if the knowledge is simply not present in the data, then no amount of effort can acquire it. The system user has already expressed a belief that the fields of the database are such that useful relationships amongst them potentially exist; here, then, the task is to try to gather more information about the database and the values it contains so as to evaluate the suitability of the database for acquiring this knowledge. To this end, the user is asked for the following information:

- The number of records in the database - knowledge needs to be well-exemplified if it is to be learned, and, in general, the more complex the knowledge, the greater the number of examples that are needed to learn it.
- The number, if any, of 'missing' fields – attributes that the user thinks of as possible factors in the potential knowledge but which – for whatever reason – have not been recorded.
- An indication of the extent to which values are missing from relevant fields – for a number of reasons, values are often go unrecorded; this can serve to limit the usefulness of a record, in the worst case rendering it entirely useless.
- The accuracy of the recorded values – inaccurate values can result in the learning of inaccurate knowledge. Unfortunately, inaccuracy is not apparent from the database itself – rather, some external knowledge of the methods of gathering and recording values is needed. Accuracy can be considered to manifest itself in two related forms, called here *precision* (the degree by which numerical values differ from the corresponding 'actual' values) and *correctness* (the degree to which non-numerical values are 'right').
- The content of the relevant fields – on the whole, current DM algorithms operate on symbols and numbers; any other forms of data – for example,

images, or complete English sentences, either need to be preprocessed extensively using background knowledge or else disregarded for the purposes of DM. The user is asked to indicate whether the fields contain information beyond simple symbolic and numerical values.

Once these questions have been asked the consultation of the user is completed. Many more questions could be asked and more information gathered, but the need for a quick assessment process should once again be emphasised – the authors consider the above questions sufficient to form an evaluation of the database.

3.4 Evaluating the Database

The answers supplied are used to generate an overall score for the database. 'Positive' characteristics of the database and its context increase its score, while 'negative' characteristics diminish it. Once everything has been considered, the database will have been awarded a score for its 'knowledge potential' on a scale of 0 ("The nature and content of the database render it of little or no use to your organisation for DM purposes") to 5 ("Your answers suggest that the database represents an extremely valuable source of organisational knowledge, and one that would amply repay the costs incurred as a result of a DM episode"). At a later stage, it will almost certainly be necessary to 'normalise' this score to bring it into line with the wider knowledge auditing evaluation (perhaps expressing it in more concrete financial terms). This will not be a trivial task, and will require detailed analysis of the return generated by knowledge and the costs of implementing new knowledge within organisations, as well as of the costs of DM itself.

4. Implementation

The knowledge described above can most naturally be described in terms of forward-chaining rules. This, coupled with the desire to investigate the possibility of performing the audit remotely using the internet led the authors to the use of the Jess shell [4] for the implementation of the system. Jess is a rule engine and scripting environment written in Sun System's Java language. Originally inspired by the CLIPS shell, it provides an inference engine based (like CLIPS) on the Rete algorithm. Being written in Java, it offers programmers the opportunity to embed the shell within an applet, and so, to make their expert systems available across the WWW using standard web browsers. GUI facilities permit remote users to interact with the system, providing it with the requested information, and, later, to be presented with the results of the system's reasoning.

The relatively small number of rules permitted the rapid implementation of a prototype expect system; it was felt desirable that the system should be developed in this manner so as to provide a useful experimental platform for exploring the potential and testing the viability of 'delivering' knowledge via the internet – one of the key concepts underlying the notion of the knowledge audit as a whole. The system was developed along fairly typical lines, incorporating rules to ask the various questions outlined above and then to evaluate these answers. Routines for displaying additional information and advice to users was incorporated into the latter rules, explaining, for instance, that the proportion of missing values in the database hamper its worth or that the evaluation of the database as a whole suggests that a limited preliminary DM study might be worthwhile before embarking on a full-blown exercise. In doing this, the intention is to increase the usefulness of the system as a 'stand-alone' system, independent of the goals of the knowledge audit.

This system was constructed into an applet complete with user interface, offering drop-down menus and the like to simplify communication with the user. This was incorporated within a web-page (Figure 2), which also included links to further information and to provide feedback via email, along with a glossary of the technical terms used within the expert system, implemented in such a way (using frames) as to allow a user to look-up a definition in the course of using the system.

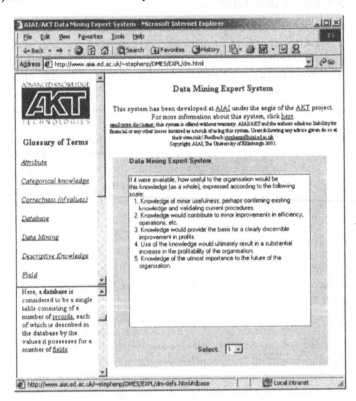

Figure 2. The expert system applet in a browser (in this case Microsoft's Internet Explorer).

5. Testing the Application

The implementation and intended use of this system – in particular, the use of the internet – throw up challenges (and opportunities) for testing beyond those normally encountered in the course of expert system development. Testing of a more conventional expert system can be thought of as a process of confirming that the system can be used as intended to solve real problems. Beyond the detection of bugs in the operation of the various components of the system and interface, this involves, on one hand, validating as far as possible that the knowledge embodied in the system is correct and complete, and is that required to solve the problem in question, and, on the other hand, testing that the system can be (and will be) used effectively by its intended users. Although comprehensive testing of the system described in this paper is still very much in its early stages, each of these testing objectives has interesting implications for applications of this sort.

5.1 Testing the Knowledge

Typical conventional approaches to validating the knowledge in an expert system include comparing the performance of the system on a set of test cases with the expected performance, and asking experts to criticise the knowledge base. The former approach is problematic in this case, since this audit task is, in some respects, a new one – no cases exist of the 'correct' appraisal of databases in the fashion proposed here. Furthermore, it would not be adequate merely to seek out examples of applications (both successful and otherwise) of DM, since, for example, the failure of a particular application does not necessarily mean that the database contains no knowledge that might be mined.

Consequently, the authors' attention has turned to the second form of testing, the employment of experts to criticise the knowledge. One of the chief problems encountered during this form of testing is the difficulty of gaining access to experts; with the various demands placed upon their expertise, finding the time necessary to perform this evaluation can be difficult. Here, however, the use of the internet suggests an alternative approach. The system can easily be made available to a greater number of experts, at geographically remote sites, than is usually available for appraisals, and, furthermore, since the system would be constantly on-line, the appraisal can be performed when at any time of the expert's choosing.

For such an approach to succeed it will probably be necessary, at the very least, to implement an alternative version of the expert system in which the knowledge is made much more explicit, or even to dispense with the system entirely, and simply 'publish' the knowledge in some sort of on-line discussion forum, opening the possibility of experts critiquing the knowledge collaboratively. Such an approach raises interesting practical and theoretical issues – about, for example, how experts might be encouraged to interact in this fashion, and where ownership of collectively developed knowledge would rest – but the authors think that this approach to the knowledge assessment has great potential, and intend to pursue it in the near future.

5.2 Testing the System

An important task during the early stages of conventional expert system development is to obtain a clear idea of the prospective users of the system, in terms of their capabilities, resources and context. This should influence the implementation and, in particular, the interface, of the resulting system. However, in this case this is difficult, since the system is intended for use by a variety of people in a variety of organisational contexts, and, as such, the idea of the user is at most, a vague, generic one. Once again, this makes testing the system problematic. Questions raised range from the technical to the sociological; they include:

- Can the system be accessed (in an acceptable amount of time) and run on a range of different platforms using different browsers? Does the appearance of the interface remain as uniform as possible? Do users understand the interface concepts (links, menus, buttons, etc) with which they are presented?
- Can the system be used by the full range of prospective users, whose context, abilities and knowledge might vary substantially?
- Assuming that the system can be used, is the knowledge it contains delivered in the right form? Can users answer the questions and then act upon the advice they are given? Do users trust knowledge delivered in this manner?

While there has been some work in remote evaluation of software systems (e.g. see [5]), there has, so far, been little reported by way of methodologies for testing the delivery of knowledge-based systems over the internet in this manner. The authors believe that as the internet continues to grow and its exploitation becomes more sophisticated, 'knowledge publishing' ventures, such as the one reported here, will gain in prominence, and, as a consequence, techniques for their evaluation will come to be of great importance. As with the testing of the knowledge, in the near future the authors intend to try to develop methodologies to assist in this task.

6. Conclusions

This paper describes an expert system application for evaluating the extent to which a database contains knowledge that Data Mining algorithms might be used to acquire. While the implementation of this system is quite straightforward and conventional, the desire to use internet technologies and the notion of the system as being a single component in a wider knowledge auditing methodology have imposed certain constraints on this system, influencing many of the decisions made, and have interesting implications for the application and testing of the system.

Acknowledgements

This work is supported under the Advanced Knowledge Technologies (AKT) Interdisciplinary Research Collaboration (IRC), which is sponsored by the UK Engineering and Physical Sciences Research Council under grant number GR/N15764/01. The AKT IRC comprises the Universities of Aberdeen, Edinburgh, Sheffield, Southampton and the Open University. Java, Jess, CLIPS and Microsoft Explorer are registered trademarks.

References

1. Berry, M. J. A. & Linoff, G. Mastering data-mining: the art and science of customer relationship management, Wiley, New York, 2000.
2. Han, J. & Kamber, M. Data mining: concepts and techniques, Morgan Kaufmann, San Francisco, CA, 2001
3. Microsoft, Inc. OLE DB for data mining specification, 2000. Available online at: http://www.microsoft.com/data/oledb/dm.htm.
4. Jess, the Java Expert System Shell, v.5.2, http://herzberg.ca.sandia.gov/jess/. (Jess is available free of charge for academic research purposes.)
5. Hartson, H.R., Castillo, J.C., Kelso, J., Kamler, J., & Neale, W.C. Remote Evaluation: The Network as an Extension of the Usability Laboratory. Procs. CHI'96 Human Factors in Computing Systems, 1996, pp. 228-235.

ESTHER – expert system for the diagnostics of acute drug poisonings

Oleg Larichev[1], Artyom Asanov[1], Yevgeny Naryzhny[1]
Sergey Strahov[2]

[1] Institute for Systems Analysis, Russian Academy of Sciences, 9, pr. 60 let Octjabrja, 117312, Moscow, Russia
{oil, art, nev}@isa.ru

[2] Filatov Children's Hospital, Moscow, Russia

Abstract

In recent years, there were a lot of cases of acute drug intoxications in Russia, and there exists a lack of qualified specialists capable of correct intoxication diagnosing. That is why this research was aimed at developing an expert system for diagnostics of poisonings caused by overdose or misuse of widespread medicines. Such medicines are available in every family and it is very easy to exceed the critical dosage that may lead to a fatal issue. According to some estimates nearly a half of all poisonings are provoked by improper use of medicines.

This paper presents main concepts of an Expert System for Toxicological Help (ESTHER). The most widespread medicines were combined into 25 groups according to the similarity in poisonings diagnostics and treatment. More than 60 clinical signs used by an expert in diagnostics of intoxications were included. The system was deliberately designed to use only clinical signs of poisonings with the view of using it in ambulance cars and hospitals of small towns where accurate laboratory analyses are not available.

The system imitates reasoning of a physician – an expert in toxicology. The ideas of method for knowledge base construction are presented. The architecture of the expert system is discussed in detail as well.

1. Introduction

Recent years in Russia revealed a trend toward fast increasing of a number of poisoning cases for adults as well as for children. This situation makes more urgent and important the problem of poisonings diagnostics and treatment. A considerable change in acute poisonings pattern has occurred in the last decade. Pharmaceuticals (particularly psychotic drugs), alcohol and surrogates replaced as the main poisonings causes acetic acid and other corrosives, organophosphorous pesticides and other household agents. Approximately one half of all poisoning cases are connected with drug poisoning.

This situation with a large number of intoxications could be significantly softened by availability of good expertise in hospitals and in ambulance cars. But unfortunately the majority of physicians working in the ambulance service and in hospitals don't know enough about the reasons of intoxications, their diagnostics and treatment.

Therefore, the important aim of the research is development of an expert system based on the knowledge of experienced physician. Such system could be applied as a useful source of advices for young physicians and physicians of different specialisations.

This paper presents main ideas of ESTHER (Expert System for Toxicological Help). Now the system is being in the process of testing at the Toxicological Centre of Russian Health Ministry.

2. Particular features of diagnostics for acute drug poisonings problem

Specific features of diagnostics for drug poisonings problem are as follows:

1. There are a lot of different medicines. They could be allocated into approx. 25 groups on the basis of their influence on human organism. Usually a typical representative for each group can be defined.

2. A set of 5-12 diagnostic signs can be used for the diagnostics of poisonings caused by medicines belonging to one group. The total number of the diagnostic signs is more than 60. They can be divided into several groups: medical examination, patient's complaints, anamnesis, state of central nervous system, cardiovascular system, respiratory system, urinary system, gastrointestinal tract. Each diagnostic sign has a scale of possible values. For example, pulse rate can be described as: tachycardia, normal pulse or bradycardia.

3. In the process of diagnostics a physician creates a holistic image of patient's state on the basis of description in terms of diagnostic signs' values. Generally knowledge about some subset of values is not sufficient for the diagnostics.

4. There are certain groups of drug poisonings described by similar diagnostic signs. For the differentiation among them it is necessary to solve a series of differential diagnostics problems.

5. There are several courses of patient's treatment depending on a type of a drug, severity of patient's state, and a degree of affection on certain systems of human organism.

3. Difficulties in the development of an expert system for the diagnostics of acute medicinal poisoning

From the formal point of view, the diagnostics problem may be presented in the following way. There is a multi-dimensional space of combinations of diagnostic signs' values. With 63 diagnostic signs having in average 3 values on each scale, the total number of such combinations is equal to 3^{63}. It is necessary to allocate these combinations (clinical situations – CS) into different classes of poisonings. Let us note that such classes may intersect. Moreover, it is necessary to distinguish among the degrees of intoxication for each class: mild poisoning or severe poisoning, because this is needed when selecting a treatment course.

Main difficulties in the application of Artificial Intelligence approach for a solution of this problem are:

1. In order to be useful an expert system should closely imitate expert reasoning in the process of diagnostics for all clinical situations. However, direct presentation of all CSs to an expert is impossible due to the large dimension of the problem.

2. One cannot expect receiving expert rules used in diagnosing in the explicit form. It is well known that expert's knowledge is predominantly unconscious.

3. A decision for each CS depends on a combination of diagnostic signs values (holistic image of a possible patient) and cannot be obtained by asking an expert to nominate some coefficients of importance for each diagnostic sign value.

4. At any stage of the expert knowledge elicitation process an expert can make different kinds of errors. It is very desirable to have means that allow discovering errors and eliminating them.

These specific features don't allow using one of the well-known approaches (i.e. [1, 2, 3]) that have many successful applications in other areas. A new approach was to be developed.

4. Methodological approach to the construction of expert knowledge base

Main features of our approach to the construction of expert knowledge base for the drug poisonings diagnostics problem are as follows:

1. 25 knowledge bases imitating expert diagnostics skills are constructed successively for each class of poisonings.

2. For each class of poisonings an expert defines a subset of diagnostic signs and their values needed for the diagnostics. All combinations of the diagnostic signs values define the space of possible patient states.

3. An expert collates values of diagnostic signs by typicality with respect to each class of intoxication.

4. An expert's knowledge is elicited by presenting on a computer screen a description of different CSs in terms of diagnostic signs values. An expert has to

assign each CS into one of three classes: strong intoxication with a drug of a corresponding class, mild intoxication, no intoxication by a drug of a corresponding class (different cause of intoxication).

5. In order to save valuable expert efforts, binary relation of domination by typicality is used. If an expert assigns one CS to certain class of intoxication, some other CSs with diagnostic signs values (from the subset used) that are not less typical for this class, can also be allocated into the same class. Use of this binary relation allows classifying several CSs on the basis of one expert decision. In other words a cone of dominance by typicality is constructed in the space of CSs.

6. Fortunately such cones are intersecting ones. This creates a possibility to check expert's decisions for the absence of contradictions and to find special cases of diagnostic signs interdependence. For each contradictory case the corresponding information is presented to an expert on a computer screen for the detailed analysis.

7. A special algorithm is used when choosing the next CS to be presented to an expert for the classification. The algorithm aims at minimising a number of questions needed for classification of all CSs.

8. For the classes of poisonings that are described with similar sets of diagnostics signs special knowledge bases for differential diagnostics are constructed.

The new approach to the problems of expert knowledge elicitation has been tested previously on different practical tasks [4, 5]. A group of methods based on this approach was developed [5, 6]. The most advanced of them allow obtaining (directly and indirectly) expert classification of 700-800 CSs per hour [6].

After construction the knowledge bases were tested by presenting a number of difficult cases to computer and to an expert. The results demonstrated close imitation of expert reasoning.

5. Formal statement of the problem

Given:
$K = 1, 2, ..., N$ – the set of diagnostic signs; n_q – the number of values on the scale of the q-th diagnostic sign ($q \in K$).

L_1, L_2, L_3 – ordered decision classes. L_1 – severe intoxication with some medicine X; L_2 – mild intoxication with medicine X; L_3 – no intoxication with X.

S_q – the set of values on the scale of the q-th diagnostic sign; values on each scale are ordered by typicality for each decision class; the ordering by typicality on the scale of one diagnostic sign does not depend on the values of the other signs.

Cartesian product of the diagnostic signs' scales: $Y = S_1 \otimes S_2 \otimes ... \otimes S_N$ creates the set of clinical situations (CS). One CS may be represented as $y^i = (y_1^i, y_2^i, ..., y_N^i)$ and $y_q^i \in S_q$.

Needed:

On the basis of information obtained from an expert it is needed to construct the complete (all CSs are classified) and noncontradictory classification.

Let us explain the notion of noncontradictory classification. Having ordered diagnostic signs' scales, it is possible to define anti-reflexive and transitive binary relation P of domination by typicality (for one decision class):

$$P = \{(y^i, y^j) \mid \forall s \in K \ y_s^i \geq y_s^j, \exists s' \ y_{s'}^i > y_{s'}^j\},$$

where $\geq$, $>$ – weak and strong relations of domination by typicality between values on the diagnostic signs' scales.

If $(y^i, y^j) \in P$, then y^i cannot belong to lower class (in the order) than y^j does, and vice versa: y^j cannot belong to higher class than y^i. If this condition is true for any pair $(y^i, y^j) \in P$, then the classification is noncontradictory.

6. Structure of the knowledge base

Knowledge base of ESTHER system consists of 25 knowledge bases for the decision classes (different classes of poisonings) and 40 knowledge bases for differential diagnostics. After expert knowledge has been stored in the knowledge base of the system, it becomes possible for arbitrary CS with any combination of diagnostic signs' values to find out a decision class (or several ones) and severity degree of intoxication.

After the construction of complete and noncontradictory knowledge base, methods of questionnaire theory [7] have been used to produce an optimal decision tree for each class of medicines. Criterion of optimality here is a minimum average number of questions needed to arrive to a conclusion about the existence and severity of poisoning by the drug of this class [8]. Decision tree presents a strategy of putting questions about values of clinical signs with the goal to ascertain the fact of intoxication and state of a patient. Each node of the tree is a question about a value of a diagnostic sign. Depending on the answer the following node is chosen. One of the decision trees embedded into the ESTHER knowledge base is presented on Fig 1.

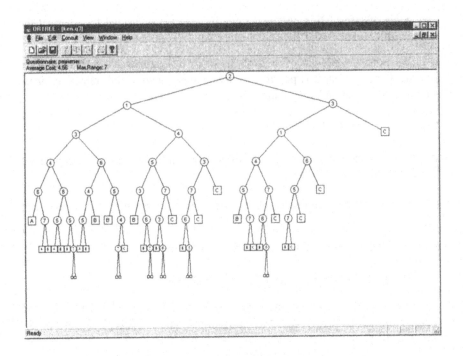

Fig. 1. The constructed optimal decision tree for diagnosing of poisoning by one of the medicines.

In the process of the knowledge base construction, the expert gave information about the most typical values of diagnostic signs for each decision class as well as impossible signs' values. Tables of prohibited values for pairs: "diagnostic sign – decision class" are the important constituent part of the knowledge base. Such tables allow speeding up the diagnostics process.

For the decision classes with similar sets of diagnostic signs the additional knowledge bases have been constructed. The corresponding optimal decision trees allow one to make decision in complex situations when intoxications by several drugs are possible. For such cases ESTHER gives the conclusions like "intoxication by drug A is more probable than one by drug B", "intoxication by drugs A and B is possible". An expert who tested the system noted that these answers increase the quality of system's answers in difficult cases of poisonings.

7. System architecture

Principal modules of ESTHER system and their interactions are represented at the diagram (see Fig. 2).

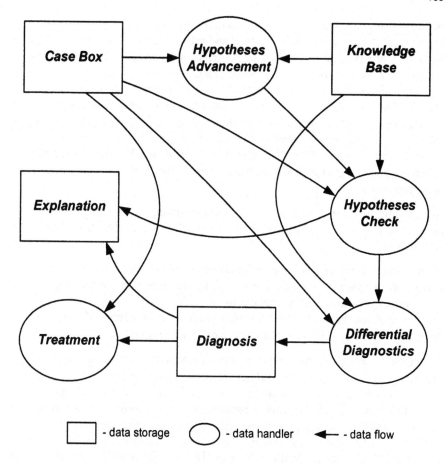

Fig 2. ESTHER principal modules and their interactions

There are two basic modes of a user's work with ESTHER system – data input mode and consultation mode. In the data input mode a user sees a list of clinical signs grouped under the titles: "External examination data", "Anamnesis", "Cardiovascular system", etc. All information about a patient including his/her state, illness history, complaints and so on is stored in the "**Case Box**" module. A user, for example an ambulance physician, successively enters values of clinical signs that are relevant to a particular case. "**Hypotheses Advancement**" module monitors this information and makes suppositions about a possible poisoning cause. If such a supposition arises, it notifies a user and suggests switching to consultation mode for hypotheses checking.

Hypotheses advancement module examines a patient's case with the purpose of discovering typical signs of poisoning by one or another drug. If there are several concurrent hypotheses it selects the one that is supported by the largest number of typical signs' values. When a hypothesis for checking is formed, the hypotheses advancement module either notifies a user about its readiness to switch to consultation mode when system is in the data input mode or transfers the arisen hypothesis to the "**Hypotheses Checking**" module when system is in the consultation mode.

In the consultation mode the system successively checks and puts forward new hypotheses. It takes initiative upon itself and asks the user about values of clinical signs that are needed to confirm or to reject a hypothesis. While checking a hypothesis about a poisoning by some drug, the system uses the constructed optimal decision trees. A pass through the tree is accomplished and at the nodes, where values of clinical signs are still unknown, a user is questioned about values of appropriate signs to reach a conclusion. As a result of this pass one of the following conclusions is drawn: "Serious poisoning by medicine X", "Mild poisoning by medicine X" or "No poisoning by medicine X". The last means that either the poisoning was caused by the medicine other than X or there is no drug poisoning at all.

At any time user can break the mode of consultation, switch back to data input mode, add and/or change values of any clinical signs and after that resume the consultation.

While advancing and checking hypotheses the so-called exclusions are used intensively. Exclusion is a rule formulated by the expert in the following form: "Poisoning by the medicine X cannot cause the clinical signs' values a, b, c..." Our practice revealed that such rules decrease significantly the number of hypotheses to be checked as well as the time necessary to reach a diagnosis.

In general case it may happen as a result of hypotheses checking that several hypotheses about poisonings by different medicines are confirmed. This may be the case if patient actually has taken several medicines as well as when different medicines result in similar clinical pattern. In order to refine the diagnosis the "**Differential Diagnostics**" module is applied. There are special expert rules stored in the knowledge base of the system. They allow distinguishing among medicines similar in clinical patterns in difficult cases. These rules are also stored as optimal decision trees. An oriented graph is constructed in the "**Differential Diagnosis**" module. Nodes of the graph correspond to confirmed hypotheses and arcs correspond to the relations of poisonings' probabilities between different medicines. For example, if differential diagnostics rules state that poisoning by medicine X_1 is more probable than poisoning by medicine X_2, then nodes X_1 and X_2 in the graph are connected by the arc that originates at node X_1 and enters node X_2. After that, the graph is condensed, that is a kernel of undominated nodes is extracted. For each node X belonging to the kernel the string "Poisoning by medicine X is most probable" is written to the final diagnosis (module "**Diagnosis**"). For the other nodes X' the string "Poisoning by medicine X' is not excluded" is written to the diagnosis. Our discussion with expert revealed that these two wordings are sufficient for practical purposes and there is no need in more precise distinguishing among poisonings' probabilities.

The ESTHER system allows explaining the diagnosis. While passing through a decision tree in the "**Hypotheses Check**" module information about passed tree nodes is stored. That is information about values of clinical signs that were used in diagnosing is recorded. The "**Explanation**" module stores arguments "pro" for each confirmed or rejected hypothesis as well as arguments "contra". The system provides explanations in the following form: "*There is poisoning with medicine X* *with degree of gravity D **because** sign S_1 has value s_{11}, sign S_2 has value s_{21} ... **in spite of** the fact that sign S_3 has value s_{32} etc.".* This allows explaining in a natural way from the user's viewpoint both confirmed and rejected hypotheses. It is important to remark, that physicians use this explanation style as well when explaining their own decisions – usually they enumerate symptoms of poisoning and then say that these symptoms are sufficient for diagnosing.

There is also the module of recommendations on treatment as a constituent part of the ESTHER system (**"Treatment"** on the diagram). It can be used as a reference manual for getting acquainted with basic methods of treatment of poisonings by one or another medicine. Another, more important feature is its ability to give recommendations on the particular given case of poisoning. Using a diagnosis made by other modules of the system and extracting clinical pattern of poisoning from the **"Case Box"** module it is able to recommend treatment with regard to the gravity of poisoning, degree of damage to the systems of human organism. It can also prescribe a symptomatic therapy. Moreover, when prescribing treatment methods and dosage of antidote medicines it is possible to take into account age, weight and illness history of the patient.

Openness of ESTHER system's architecture was an important objective of its designing. Openness principle was followed when designing the knowledge base of the system, inference, explanation and treatment subsystems. Therefore, for example, it is rather simple now to include new groups of medicines that could cause poisonings. This feature is of great importance, because new medicines are emerging continuously.

The system's design provides for separation and encapsulation of a user interface environment shell and the system's knowledge base that was implemented in a specialised high-level scripting language. This guarantees high reusability of the knowledge base handling components and allows easy modification of rules and algorithms included in the system.

8. Conclusion

From our point of view the ability of expert system to behave like a human is the critical factor for its successful application. The developed ESTHER system includes large knowledge base that closely imitates expert knowledge and reasoning in the problem of drug poisonings diagnostics.

The system gives to a user a possibility to use active and passive ways of interaction. When ESTHER takes initiative upon itself and starts questioning a user he or she has a good chance of self-education. A user can compare his/her preliminary conclusion with one of the expert – the author of the knowledge base.

It is important to note that the open architecture of ESTHER provides a possibility to add new decision classes (causes of intoxications) and new diagnostic signs for such classes. A revision of individual knowledge bases is also possible for any decision class using knowledge of more experienced (for this class of poisonings) physician.

The expert system for the diagnostics of acute drug poisonings is the example of "knowledge distribution" for large groups of specialists. We believe that appearances of new diseases and new drugs make the problem of "knowledge distribution" for large areas more important.

References

1. Pople, H.E. The Formation of Composite Hypotheses in Diagnostic Problem Solving: An Exercise in Synthetic Reasoning, The Fifth International Joint Conference on Artificial Intelligence, Boston, MIT, 1977.

2. Shortliffe, E.H. Computer-based Medical Consultations: MYCIN, New York, American Elsevier, 1976.

3. Schreiber, A.Th., Wielinga, B.J., Akkermans, J.M., Van de Velde, W. CommonKads: A comprehensive methodology for KBS development. IEEE Expert, 9, 1994.

4. Larichev, O.I., Mechitov, A.I., Moshkovich, H.M., Furems E.M. The Elicitation of Expert Knowledge, Nauka, Moscow, 1989 (in Russian).

5. Larichev, O.I., Moshkovich, H.M., Furems, E.M., Mechitov, A.I., Morgoev, V.K.: Knowledge Acquisition for the Construction of the Full and Contradictions Free Knowledge Bases, IEC ProGAMMA, Groningen, The Netherlands, 1991.

6. Larichev, O.I., Bolotov, A.A. The DIFKLASS System: Construction of Complete and Noncontradictory Expert Knowledge Bases in Problems of Differential Classification, Automatic Documentation and Mathematical Linguistics, Vol. 30, N. 5, Allerton Press, New York, 1996.

7. Parhomenko, P.P. The Questionnaires Theory: Review, Automatics and Telemechanics, N. 4, Moscow, 1970.(in Russian)

8. Naryzhnyi, E.V. Construction of the Optimum Questioning Strategy for a Complete Expert Data Base, Automatic Documentation and Mathematical Linguistics, Vol. 30, N. 5, Allerton Press, New York, 1996.

Interpreting Aerial Images: A Knowledge-Level Analysis

A. Darwish, T. Pridmore, and D. Elliman
School of Computer Science & Information Technology,
Jubilee Campus, Wollaton Road, University of Nottingham,
axd@cs.nott.ac.uk
Nottingham, UK, NG8 1BB

Abstract

Many image understanding systems rely heavily on a priori knowledge of their domain of application, drawing parallels with and exploiting techniques developed in the wider field of knowledge-based systems (KBSs). Attempts, typified by the KADS/CommonKADS projects, have recently been made to develop a structured, knowledge engineering approach to KBS development. Those working in image understanding, however, continue to employ 1st generation KBS methods. The current paper presents an analysis of existing image understanding systems; specifically those concerned with aerial image interpretation, from a knowledge engineering perspective. Attention is focused on the relationship between the structure of the systems considered and the existing KADS/CommonKADS models of expertise, sometimes called "generic task models". Mappings are identified between each system and an appropriate task model, identifying common inference structures and use of knowledge.

1   Introduction

Early knowledge-based, sometimes called "expert", systems typically comprised large, unstructured collections of simple, supposedly independent, rules. These were generally applied to input data by a monolithic inference engine. It was often argued that this design allowed such systems to make flexible use of their knowledge, be developed incrementally and/or provide explanations of their reasoning. In practice the unstructured nature of 1st generation expert systems made them extremely difficult to develop, maintain and understand.

In recent years significant attempts have been made to replace the ad hoc tools and techniques underlying classic, 1st generation expert systems with a more structured knowledge engineering approach. A number of knowledge engineering methodologies have appeared, though KADS/CommonKADS [7, 9, 10, 13] is arguably the best developed.

Key to the KADS/CommonKADS methodology is the notion of the generic task model, or model of expertise, which describes the knowledge, inference and control structures which may be used to perform instances of particular classes (design, diagnosis, etc.) of task. An early step in the development of a new system using KADS/CommonKADS is the identification of which library of task models is most applicable to the problem at hand. Subsequent design decisions are then made with reference to this template, which may be modified if the task at hand does not fit an existing model with sufficient accuracy.

Knowledge engineering in general and KADS/CommonKADS in particular have had a significant impact on the development and subsequent uptake of knowledge-based systems. Knowledge-based image understanding systems, however, continue to rely upon 1st generation techniques and design methodologies; unstructured rule bases remain the norm (see, for example [3]).

The longer term aims of the research reported here are 1) to examine the possibility of applying knowledge engineering methodologies to the development of image understanding systems and 2) to produce an aerial image understanding system based on sound design principles.

The current paper presents an analysis of existing image understanding systems, specifically those concerned with aerial image interpretation, from a knowledge engineering perspective. Attention is focused on the relationship between the structure of the systems considered and the existing KADS/CommonKADS models of expertise. A mapping is sought between each system and an appropriate task model, the intention being to identify common inference structures and use of knowledge. In this we follow Clancey's [1] early work on medical diagnosis systems. Section 2 introduces three generic task models - simple classification, heuristic classification, and systematic refinement. Section 3 presents an overview and analysis, in terms of these models, of six aerial image-understanding systems. Results are then discussed in section 4 before conclusions are drawn in section 5.

2. Models Of Classification Expertise

2.1. Heuristic Classification

The present KADS/CommonKADS methodology grew out of a series of European research projects active throughout the 1980s and 90s. Over this period a number of different notations and formalisms were developed and used to describe models of expertise [7, 9]. Although it is not the most recent, in what follows we adopt the notation employed by Tansley and Hayball [10] for its simplicity and clarity. In this form, a generic task model comprises an *inference structure, task structure* and *strategies*. The inference structure takes the form of a diagram in which rectangular boxes represent domain roles - the knowledge and data available to and manipulated by the system - and ovals denote inferences made over those roles. Arrows linking these components highlight possible, though not compulsory, chains of inference.

Inference structure diagrams are supplemented by short descriptions of each of the domain roles and inference types. In heuristic classification (Figure 1), for example, the domain role *observables* contain "any observable phenomenon" while *variables* represent "the value placed on the observed data, from the system's perspective". *Solution abstractions* are "an abstract classification of a problem (or other concept)" and *solutions* are "a specific, identified solution".

Each inference type description contains a brief textual description of the inference performed, its inputs, outputs, knowledge used/required and possible implementation methods. During *abstract*, for example "observable data are abstracted into variables". This requires definitional knowledge and may be achieved via definitional abstraction, based on essential and necessary features of a concept, qualitative abstraction, a form of definition involving quantitative data, or generalization in a subtype hierarchy [1].

Similarly, *match* matches abstracted data "heuristically by non-hierarchical association with a concept in another classification hierarchy". This exploits heuristic knowledge and may be achieved using heuristic rules. Finally, specialize refines abstract solutions into more specific ones, again exploiting heuristic knowledge, possibly to traverse a classification hierarchy [10].

The *task structure* component of a generic task model describes ways in which the inference structure might be traversed. For heuristic classification two possibilities are identified; forward reasoning, following the abstract, match, specialize route just described, or backward reasoning. Backward reasoning selects possible solutions and works backwards through specialize, match and abstract to determine whether or not the patient's observable condition supports the hypothesis made. These two routes represent extremes in the space of possible task structures, one can imagine many ways of integrating forward and backward reasoning to achieve (heuristic) classification.

Few KADS/CommonKADS task models include a detailed strategy layer; mainly because strategy level knowledge, though intended to be higher level, is often also strongly domain dependent. The strategy level of the heuristic classification model, merely suggests that level of refinement required varies significantly with application, affecting the specialize inference, and that the cost of obtaining data is the most important factor to consider when choosing a task structure.

Heuristic classification was first described by Clancey [1], who found that it adequately described the majority of medical diagnosis expert systems considered in his review of that area. Models have been proposed for design, monitoring, diagnosis, prediction, repair, configuration, planning and many other task types. In what follows, however, we shall be concerned only with the various models of classification.

2.2. Simple Classification

Simple classification (Figure 2) is the most basic classification task model, comprising only a single inference type: *classify*. This aims to transform observables into variables that are recognised by the system. Simple classification selects one of a flat set of pre-enumerated solutions, it is essentially a pattern matching operation but may involve abstraction, aggregation, etc depending upon the relationship between the observables and variables. Though its inference structure is trivial, simple classification may also be run in data- or goal-driven fashion.

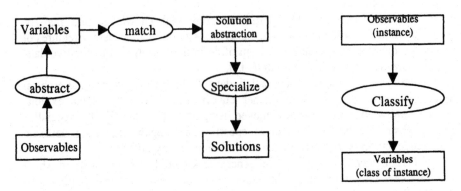

Fig. 1. Heuristic Classification

Fig. 2. Simple Classification

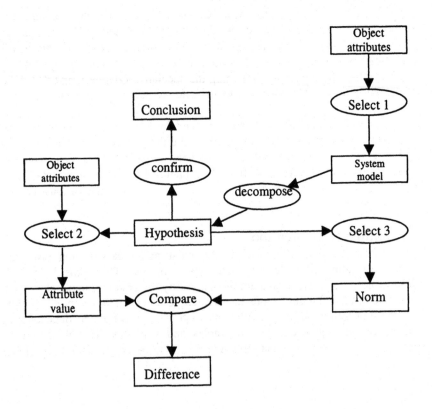

Fig. 3. Systematic Refinement

2.3. Systematic Refinement

The inference structure of systematic refinement (Figure 3) is noticeably more complex. This is due in part to this model's ability to employ different is-a hierarchies to describe different input data, and partly to its systematic nature: operations that are (implicitly) subsumed within the match inference of heuristic classification are explicitly represented in systematic refinement. Processing begins with a statement about some entity that requires more detailed description. A *select* inference then chooses an appropriate hierarchy (system model) which is *decomposed* to generate a hypothesis, a possible description of the input data. If the bottom of the hierarchy has been reached the hypothesis is *confirmed*. If not, the hypothesis is used to control the *selection* of attributes from both the input object description and the norm, the a priori expectation of the appearance of objects of a particular class. Finally, these attributes are *compared*, producing a description of the fit of the current hypothesis to the input data. The traditional task structure of systematic refinement is iterative, repeatedly decomposing the system model until a confirmed hypothesis arises. Its ability to employ multiple classification hierarchies means that systematic refinement is particularly appropriate when the problem at hand cannot be adequately managed using a single model.

3. Task Models For Aerial Image Interpretation

In the present study, six aerial image interpretation systems have been examined. These were randomly selected from a larger review of the literature in this area and are believed to be typical of that literature.

3.1 A Spectral-Knowledge-Based Approach For Urban Land-Cover Discrimination (SKU) [12]

The prototype SKU knowledge based system was developed in the early 1980s in the Earth Resources branch of NASA. Its main objective was to test the feasibility of using spectral knowledge to classify remotely sensed data. The system comprises two phases. The first calibrates the data to ground reflectance using linear regression within each band, then it spatially averages the calibrated data to produce a mean pyramid whose bottom level is the full resolution image.

The second phase attempts to classify each pixel individually using a spectral knowledge base consisting of rules characterising spectral relationships within and between categories and local frequency distributions of the spectral properties of classified pixels. The process is iterative. The rules, which are conditional on local frequency distributions, are applied to produce an evidence array that is used to classify the mean pyramid data. The local frequency distributions are then updated to reflect the newly classified pixels and the rules are applied again. The process continues until less than 5% of pixels change classification between iterations (see Figure 4).

This is clearly a classification system; its function is to assign a label to (i.e. classify) each image pixel. The initial calibration phase does not map directly onto any CommonKADS classification model, but can be incorporated as an additional *Transform* inference [10]. The pyramid formation step, however, is a form of the *Abstract* inference found in heuristic classification.

The second phase of SKB is effectively an iterative *match* operation. Heuristic rules are applied to match pixel descriptions to abstract types such as uniform, noise and outlier. There is no explicit specialisation phase in this system, the iterative process seeks to make the correct classifications but does not systematically search for more specific labels. Specialisation may occur, but this is achieved by repeated application of match. The task structure employed is simple forward classification; although the system is iterative the iteration is contained within the match inference.

3.2 IRS: A Hierarchical Knowledge Based System for Aerial Image Interpretation [2]

IRS is based on a multiresolution perceptual clustering methodology. Interpretation proceeds both bottom-up and top-down: initial features generated using kernel and primary perceptual grouping operations provide input to model-driven analysis. The system (Figure 5) can be divided into four main processes. In the first a 2 x 2 non-overlapping, averaging mask is used to create a multiresolution image pyramid.

The second process is primary feature generation. Here, linear features are extracted, independently, from each pyramid level. This is achieved via edge detection and contour tracking, which produces linked lists of data points marking the boundaries of significant image structures. Finally, linear interpolation is used to generate a memory efficient description (length, orientation and end point location) of any straight lines in the image.

The third process is perceptual clustering, this aims to reduce the complexity of the interpretation problem by identifying clusters of adjacent lines. Measures of proximity, collinearity and parallelism between these lines are then calculated. Knowledge-based analysis is the final step. This begins by forming more complex structures by clustering the previously created perceptual groupings. Making use of ancillary knowledge of the resolution of the original image, the system determines scale dependent parameter ranges, which are then rescaled for each resolution level. Finally, object recognition is performed.

IRS may also be considered a heuristic classification KBS. The data abstraction process is multi-stage that begins (like SKB) with the creation of an image pyramid and ends with the production of a database of straight line descriptions. Two system components, image representation and primary feature generation, are responsible for this task.

A transitional process, *sort*, [10] is needed to reorganize the collection of objects in order to reduce the computation time. Finally, the knowledge-based analysis process may be considered to perform a *match* inference and is used to perform contextual reasoning. Again, there is no explicit specialisation step in IRS, and the process is driven forwards.

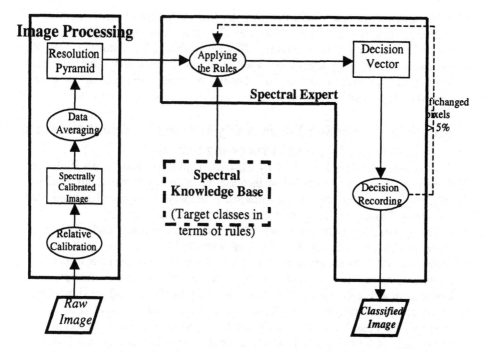

Fig. 4. A Spectral Knowledge-Based Approach
for Urban Land-Cover Discrimination

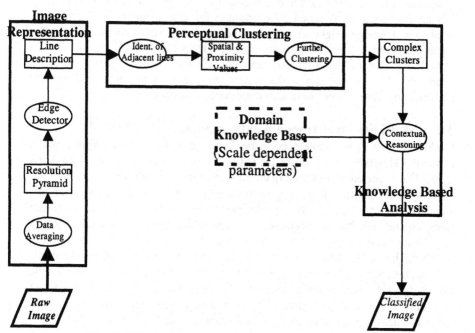

Fig. 5. IRS: A Hierarchical Knowledge-Based System
for Aerial Image Interpretation

An alternative view would consider the knowledge-based analysis phase an implementation of the *classify* inference. The abstraction process then becomes pre-processing for a simple classifier. Strictly speaking, the distinction between the two interpretations hinges on whether or not there exists some (implicit) hierarchical structure in the set of classes considered. For present purposes, however, either view is acceptable.

3.3 Remote Sensing Image Analysis Using A Neural Network & Knowledge-Based Processing (NNK) [8]

This system, developed in 1994 by Shikoku University and Osaka Prefecture University, Japan, was intended to increase the accuracy of extracting land use information from remotely sensed images. It employs both neural network and knowledge-based processing and was tested on a Landsat-5 image.

The system (Figure 6) is composed of three major components and a foundation phase in which three bands, 3, 4 and 5, are extracted from the raw, multi-spectral image. The other bands are omitted either because they are considered too noisy, redundant, or unable to differentiate between the desired classes. Interpretation begins with a 'Preprocessing Phase', in which a primary training set is generated by roughly clustering the input image using the K-means method. The second 'Recognition Phase' aims to classify pixel data, using a neural network, into 10 categories. Back-propagation is used to train the network. It is expected, however, that atmospheric and other 3D effects such as cloud shadows will, along with low image resolution, introduce misclassifications. The third 'Error Correcting Phase' aims to reduce misclassification. It is sub-divided into two steps. In the first, likely misclassifications are detected by examining the classifications assigned to the local (3 x 3)-image neighborhood surrounding each pixel. . The second process attempts to correct misclassifications using IF THEN rules.

At the centre of the inference structure of NNK is the *classify* inference, implemented by the neural net. The system may therefore be considered a simple classification system with some additional post-processing.

3.4 Multi Spectral Image Analysis System (MSAIS) [4]

MSAIS (Figure 7) was developed to facilitate the process of classifying surface materials using rules that describe the expected appearance of materials in relative terms. The expected classes are organised hierarchically in a decision tree.

The system comprises three major components. The first is the 'image analyser', which examines image histograms and spectral signatures to gather new decision rules. The second, the 'tree organiser', is responsible for building the classification tree. Using the tree organizer the user can add, delete or modify either a node or a rule in the hierarchical decision tree. The third component is the 'image classifier'. It compares each pixel in the image to the first level of decision rules stored in the knowledge base and classifies them to the three major surface classes, water, vegetation and soil-like materials. The second step is to attempt to classify those classes to sub-classes and so on until the system reaches the end of the tree.

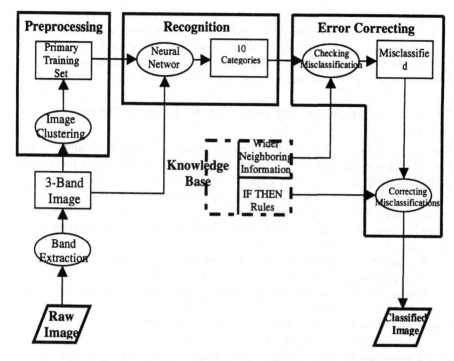

Fig.6. Remote Sensing Image Analysis Using A Neural Network
& Knowledge-Based processing

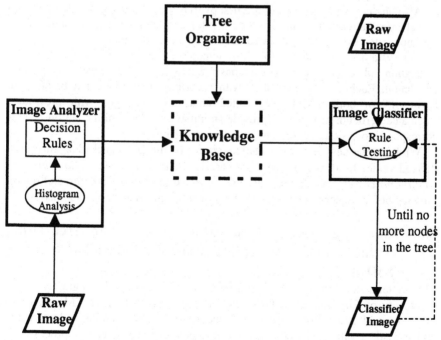

Fig.7. Multi Spectral Image Analysis System

Leaving the early knowledge acquisition stages to one side, it might be argued that it this system performs simple classification - it comprises a single inference that directly assigns each pixel a certain label. The set of target classes are, however, not flatly but hierarchically organised. The system is therefore better described as a very basic implementation of systematic refinement.

3.5 Knowledge-Based Segmentation of Landsat Images (KBL) [11]

This system is the result of work funded by National Science Foundation of the United States in the late 1980s. Its objective is to combine image-processing techniques with semantic knowledge of the image to successfully classify a township-sized portion (256 x 256 pixels) of a Landsat image.

The system (Figure 8) is divided into two parts: category oriented segmentation, where spectral and spatial knowledge is integrated with image segmentation techniques to extract targeted classes, and image oriented segmentation, during which a hierarchical segmentation is integrated with the previously identified regions to further specialise the classification of the vegetation areas.

The system starts by dividing the input image into vegetation and non-vegetation regions. Kernel information is extracted to provide an initial interpretation of the image and the two types of region are then dealt with separately.

Previously extracted vegetation areas are first overlaid with the generated kernel information before using spatial clustering, seed detection and region growing techniques to obtain consistent regions. Finally, spectral rules from the knowledge base are used to classify these regions to a pre-defined set of sub-vegetation classes.

Also, the non-vegetation areas are first overlayed with the previously generated kernel information before using spectral rules and contextual information, from the knowledge base to separate urban areas from bare land areas.

This system maps neatly onto the systematic refinement task model. Initially, vegetation indices are used to select a basic system model, e.g. vegetation, or non-vegetation. Each area is then dealt with according to the model it belongs to. However, for both models, segmented areas are overlayed with previously calculated kernel information to provide an initial hypothesis of the land-use. This corresponds to systematic refinement's *decompose* inference.

While properties of non-vegetation areas are directly checked against pre-defined values to identify urban from bare land (*select 2, select 3, compare and confirm processes*), vegetation areas are subjected to spatial clustering and region growing before undergoing the same test to identify the vegetation sub-classes.

3.6 Knowledge-Based Classification of an Urban Area Using Texture and Context Information in Landsat-TM Imagery (KBUA) [6]

This system, developed in the late 1980s by the Institute of Geography at the University of Copenhagen in Denmark, aims to classify Landsat-TM images of urban areas of Third World countries. It incorporates both quantitative knowledge and heuristic assumptions and aims to reflect the human interpretation process.

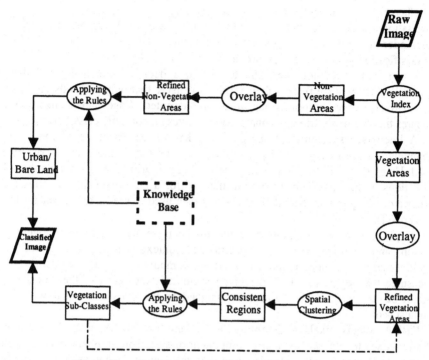

Fig.8. Knowledge-Based Segmentation of Landsat Images

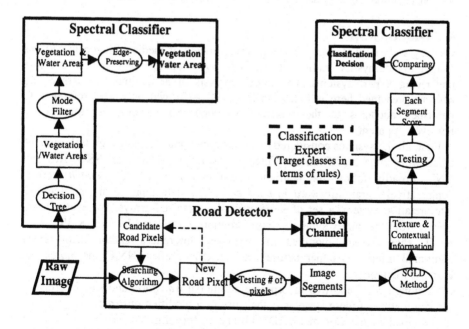

Fig.9. Knowledge-Based Classification of an Urban Area
Using Texture and Context Information in Landsat-TM Imagery

Classification proceeds in four phases (Figure 9). First, areas of water and vegetation are extracted. In the second and third phases roads are detected and the remainder of the image segmented into homogenous regions respectively. Finally, a classification system labels the previously generated segments.

Water and vegetation are extracted using a decision tree and pre-defined spectral rules. A mode filter is then applied to ensure that only pixels that are part of relatively large, homogeneous areas are accepted. Edge enhancement then ensures that the mode filter (permanently) removes no correctly classified pixels.

A line-based segmentation approach is taken to the extraction of roads and channels. The process begins by identifying a pixel that is likely to be part of a road. Using this as a starting point, a line tracking algorithm searches a number of directions within a certain maximum distance for a new pixel that satisfies the criteria of being part of a road. This pixel is then used to seed a search for further road pixels.

In phase three the remainder of the image is segmented into homogenous regions and measures of texture, spectral and contextual features calculated for each. Finally, a simple numerical score is computed for each segment. This measures the degree to which the given region matches each of the labels that might be assigned. Each segment is assigned to the class associated with the highest score.

KBUA selects pixels representing major land-use classes, then decomposes those classes to sub-classes; a key component of systematic refinement. It should be noted, however, that in classic systematic refinement decomposition is simply the traversal of an is-a hierarchy. KBUA uses several methods, e.g. decision tree and linear search algorithms, to achieve the corresponding result.

4. Discussion

Clancey's [1] now classic knowledge-level review of medical diagnosis systems sought to "demystify traditional practice" by revealing the common structure underlying expert systems. The initial analysis of aerial image understanding systems presented here is much smaller, and performed only with reference to published accounts of the systems examined. Some common structure is, however, apparent.

First, all the systems considered can be mapped onto classification task models, albeit with some modifications. Three of the reviewed systems, SKU, IRS and NNK, broadly follow the heuristic classification model. The *match* step is comparatively straightforward in each case. The data input to an aerial image interpretation system, a set of large spatially-organised arrays, however, differs greatly from the purely symbolic representations considered by most KBSs. As a result, each system modifies the expected inferences and/or incorporates additional inferences either before (SKU, IRS) or after (NNK) the *match* (or *classify)* inference.

Although SKU and IRS incorporate additional *transform* and *sort* inferences, the key feature of these systems is their use of a modified *abstract* step. Abstract is described in the CommonKADS library as forming "an instance of a more general class", a definition clearly tuned to the symbolic (rather than spatial) data commonly dealt with by KBSs. Note, however, that replacing a pixel value with its local average does constitute (spatial) abstraction. The new value describes a larger subset of the input data just as a concept higher up a classification tree describes a larger set of concepts.

It should be noted that CommonKADS also recognises the *aggregate* inference. This combines a collection of objects to produce a structured arrangement of objects. A pixel grouping operation that produced region descriptions that were subsequently used instead of individual pixels would be performing aggregation. Pyramid formation, however, constitutes abstraction because it represents each pixel at multiple (spatial) resolutions.

One of the key challenges of image interpretation is how best to obtain and exploit the contextual information implicit in the spatial organisation of the image. The analysis performed to date suggests that systems based around heuristic or simple classification can incorporate spatial context, but do not appear to couple this tightly or in any systematic fashion to the core classification inference. These systems can be described reasonably well using existing generic task models, though it might be beneficial to introduce spatial forms of some of the basic inference types to make description and comparison more transparent. NNK, for example, initially considers each pixel independently, only examining the surrounding context after a classification has been made, to recover from errors. This inference step could be considered a particular (spatial) form of the *change_value* inference [10].

While heuristic and simple classification approaches can usefully be adopted, analysis suggests that systematic refinement might offer more opportunities for cleanly incorporating contextual information. Within the land-use classification problem, which is hierarchical in nature, each sub-category has separate and distinct spectral, textural and spatial characteristics. Urban sub categories for example, bear little relation to vegetation sub categories. Within these categories, however, close similarities can arise – it can be very hard, for instance, to distinguish forestry and fields. It is therefore unlikely that any single system model will be able to adequately describe all the different land-use sub categories. The core step of dynamically selecting a system model, along with the subsequent stepwise model decomposition and comparison phases, make systematic refinement particularly well suited to this class of problem.

KBL is perhaps the closest match to systematic refinement as described by Tansley and Hayball [10]. Moreover the system neatly incorporates spatial context by overlaying kernel measures on a (spatially) segmented image. The structure of KBUA also corresponds reasonably well to the systematic refinement model, though different processes are employed to achieve model selection. This is not expected to occur in more traditional KBSs. Together, KBL and KBUA illustrate a variety of ways in which spatial information may be incorporated into an aerial image understanding system based upon systematic refinement. Future research in this area will be directed towards mapping out the space of such possibilities and seeking an optimal arrangement.

5. Conclusion

Image interpretation systems exploit domain knowledge to such an extent that they can be considered KBSs. Most, however, continue to rely on 1st generation expert system technologies and methodologies. We have presented analyses of a small number of aerial image interpretation systems from a KADS/CommonKADS perspective. These systems can be described using existing generic task models, and those descriptions used to compare systems at the knowledge level, though the process might be eased by the introduction of spatial forms of some of the basic inference types. Our initial analysis suggests that systems based upon heuristic or simple classification struggle to couple spatial context to the core classification inference, but that systematic refinement offers significant opportunities in this area.

REFERENCES

1. W.J. Clancey, *"Heuristic Classification,"* Artificial Intelligence, vol. 27, pp. 215-251, 1985

2. S. J. Cosby and R. Thomas, *"IRS: A Hierarchical Knowledge Based System for aerial Image Interpretation,"* 3rd International Conference on Industrial Engineering Applications of Artificial Intelligence and Expert Systems, Charleston, SC, USA, July 16-19, 1990

3. D. Crevier, and R. Lepage, "Knowledge-Based Image Understanding Systems: A Survey," Computer Vision & Image Understanding, vol. 67, no. 2, pp. 161-185, Aug. 1997

4. R. D. Ferrante et. al., *"Multi-Spectral Image Analysis System,"* 1st Conference on Artificial Intelligence, Denver, Co, USA, 1984

5. T. Matsuyama and V. S. Hwang, *SIGMA: A Knowledge-Based Aerial Image Understanding System.* New York, Plenum Press, 1990

6. L. Moller-Jensen, *"Knowledge-Based Classification of an Urban Area Using Texture and Context Information in Landsat-TM Imagery,"* Photogrammetric Engineering & Remote Sensing, vol. 56, no. 6, June 1990, pp. 889-904

7. G. Schreiber, et. al., *Knowledge Engineering and Management: The CommonKADS Methodology.* Cambridge, Mass.: MIT Press, 1999

8. H. Murai and S. Omatu, *"Remote Sensing Image Analysis Using a Neural network & Knowledge-Based Processing,"* International Journal of Remote Sensing, vol. 18, no. 4, May 1997, pp. 811-828

9. G. Schreiber, B. Wielinga and J. Breuker, (ed.), *KADS: A Principled Approach to Knowledge-Based System Development.* London: Academic Press Ltd., 1993

10. D. S. W. Tansley and C. C. Hayball, *Knowledge-Based Systems Analysis & Design: A KADS Developer's Handbook.* Hertfordshire, Hemel Hempstead: Prentice Hall International (UK) Ltd., 1993

11. J. Ton et. al.: "Knowledge-Based Segmentation of Landsat Images", IEEE Transactions on Geoscience & Remote Sensing, vol. 29, no. 2, March 1991

12. S. W. Wharton, *"A Spectral-Knowledge-Based Approach for Urban Land-Cover Discrimination,"* IEEE Transactions on Geoscience & Remote Sensing, vol. 25, no. 3, May 1987, pp. 273-282

13. B. Wielinga, A. Th. Schreiber and J. A. Breuker, "KADS: A Modeling Approach to Knowledge Engineering," Knowledge Acquisition, vol. 5, pp. 5-53, 1992

Modelling the Task of Summarising Time Series Data Using KA Techniques

Somayajulu G. Sripada, Ehud Reiter,
Jim Hunter, and Jin Yu
Dept of Computing Science
University of Aberdeen, Aberdeen, UK
{ssripada,ereiter,jhunter,jyu}@csd.abdn.ac.uk

Ian P. Davy
WNI Oceanroutes
Oceanroutes (U.K.) Ltd.
Aberdeen, UK
iand@abd.wni.com

Abstract

The SUMTIME project aims to develop better techniques for producing natural language summaries of time-series data. The initial phase of the project has focused on understanding how human experts perform this task, via knowledge acquisition and corpus analysis exercises. This has led to a number of observations, of which the most important is that producing human like summaries involves as much processing of domain knowledge as that of communicative and linguistic knowledge. Summarisation is not simply a verbalisation of how a set of numbers changes over time. Instead it is the process in which the author adds value to the raw data using his expertise and presents exactly the information that is relevant to the end-user.

1. Introduction

Time-series data (TSD) is ubiquitous in the modern world. Currently, such data is usually presented to humans either graphically or as tables of raw numbers. In the SUMTIME project at Aberdeen University (www.csd.abdn.ac.uk/research/sumtime/), we are attempting to develop better models and techniques for generating textual summaries of time-series data, using a combination of natural-language generation (NLG) and automatic time-series analysis techniques in the light of knowledge derived from observing humans summarising TSD. In this paper we discuss some of the observations we have made during our study of how humans produce textual summaries of time-series data (which has been our main activity to date), including the impact of domain and user knowledge on the summarisation task.

2. Background

2.1 Time-Series Data

A time-series data set is a collection of values of a set of parameters over time. For example, regular measurements of the temperature and blood pressure of a hospital patient would constitute a time series data set. Time-series data sets can range in size from 5-10 measurements on one parameter (for example, enrolment over the past ten years in CS1001) to millions of measurements on tens of thousands of parameters (for example, sensor data from a space shuttle mission).

Human beings frequently need to examine and make inferences from a time-series data set. For example, a hospital doctor will look at time-series patient data when trying to diagnose and treat a patient, and a university administrator will look at time-series data about course enrolment when estimating how much lab resources a particular course is likely to require. Currently, human examination of time-series data is generally done either by direct inspection of the data (for small data sets), by graphical visualisation, or by statistical analyses.

2.2 Textual Summaries of Time-Series Data

Sometimes people want textual summaries of time-series data as well as graphical summaries or statistical analyses. For example, newspapers publish textual summaries of weather predictions, the results of polls and surveys, and stock market activity, instead of just showing numbers and graphs. This may be because graphical depictions of time-series data require time and skill to interpret, which is not always available. For example, a doctor rushing to the side of a patient who is suffering from a heart attack may not have time to examine a set of graphs, and a newspaper reader may not have the statistical knowledge necessary to interpret raw poll results. Also, some data sets (such as the space shuttle one mentioned above) are simply too large to present graphically as a whole in any meaningful fashion.

Currently textual descriptions of time-series data must be produced manually, which makes them expensive and also means they can not be produced instantly. Graphical depictions of data, in contrast, can be produced quickly and cheaply using off-the-shelf computer software; this may be one reason why they are so popular. If textual summaries of time-series data could be automatically produced by software as cheaply and as quickly as graphical depictions, then they might be more widely used.

Summarising time-series data is also interesting from the perspective of natural-language generation because the input data is truly non-linguistic. Many NLG systems are components of text-to-text systems (such as machine translation and text summarisation), which means that the conceptual structure of their inputs is already linguistic; this is also often the case for NLG systems which use AI knowledge bases as their inputs. Such systems may, for example, need to decide whether the concept INCREASING should be expressed lexically as *increasing*, *rising*, or *going up*, but they do not need to determine whether the concept INCREASING is an appropriate description of a data set. A time-series summarisation system, in contrast, must make such decisions, which means that it must represent and reason about the meaning of 'close-to-linguistic' concepts such as INCREASING[1].

2.3 SUMTIME

SUMTIME is a new project at the University of Aberdeen, whose goal is to develop better models and techniques for generating textual summaries of time-series data, in part by trying to integrate leading edge techniques for natural language generation and time-series analysis. We are initially working in two domains:

- **Meteorology**: Producing weather forecasts from numerical weather simulations, in collaboration with WNI Oceanroutes, a private-sector meteorological services organisation.

- **Gas Turbines**: Summarising sensor readings from a gas turbine, in collaboration with Intelligent Applications, a leading developer of monitoring software for gas turbines.

We will start working on a third domain in the second half of the project. This is likely to be in the medical area, perhaps summarising clinical patient data from babies in neo-natal units, although this is not definite.

The meteorological and gas turbine domains differ in the amount of data that needs to be summarised. Generally a weather forecast is based on a time series data set which contains tens of parameters (the exact number depends on the type of forecast). The numerical simulation generally gives parameter values at hourly or 3-hourly intervals, so a 7-day weather forecast would be based on tens of values for each of these tens of parameters, or on the order of magnitude of a thousand numbers in all. The gas-turbine domain, in contrast, involves much more data. Again detailed numbers depend on the particular turbine being monitored, but as an order or magnitude we get hundreds of parameters measured at one second intervals over a period of a day or so, which means on the order of ten million numbers in all.

The first year of SUMTIME has primarily been devoted to trying to understand how human experts summarise time-series data, via a combination of knowledge acquisition techniques and corpus analysis. This is discussed below.

2.4 Previous Work

There have been a number of previous systems, which summarised time-series data, of which perhaps the best known is FOG [2]. FOG also produced weather forecasts from numerical weather simulations, and is in operational use in Environment Canada. At least as described in the published papers, FOG's research emphasis

---

[1] Note that we cannot simply say that a time-series is increasing if the last value is higher than the first value. The time series -1, 1, -1, 1, -1, 1, -1, 1, -1, 1, for example, satisfies this criteria but would not normally be described as *increasing*.

was on multi-lingual microplanning and realisation (using the terminology of Reiter and Dale [9]) using Meaning-Text Theory [8] models. The research emphasis in SumTime, in contrast, is on content determination and document planning. In other words, our research will focus on determining the conceptual content of a forecast, and we plan to use existing techniques where possible to decide how to express this content linguistically. FOG, in contrast, focused from a research perspective on the issue of how a conceptual representation of a forecast could be expressed in both English and French.

Closer in spirit to SumTime is TREND [1], which produced text summaries of historical weather data (for example, the weather over the past month). TREND, like SumTime, focused on content determination and conceptual issues, and it also, like SumTime, used sophisticated time-series analysis techniques (wavelets). Perhaps the main difference between TREND and SumTime is that TREND described the visual appearance of a graph without reference to a domain or user model, or an underlying task. That is, TREND's goal was to describe what a time-series graph 'looked like' to a human viewer, and it was partially based on models of how people visually perceived graphs. SumTime, in contrast, has the goal of producing a text summary that is useful to a human user, which means that the system, like a human meteorologist (see Section 4 below), will need to take into account knowledge about the domain and the user.

Systems, which summarise time-series data, have also been built in other domains, such as stock market reports [6] and statistical summaries [4]. Again to the best of our knowledge, these systems used relatively simple techniques for concept formation, although many of them used sophisticated techniques for microplanning and realisation.

There has also been a considerable amount of research on sophisticated techniques for analysing and abstracting time-series data, such as Shahar [13]. However, these systems have not been connected to text generators, instead their output has generally been displayed graphically [12] or as raw abstractions.

The goal of SumTime is in part to bridge the gap between these two strands of research, NLG and time-series analysis, and do this in a way which to some degree replicates the manner in which a human expert would summarise time-series data.

3.   Knowledge Acquisition

The first year of SumTime has focused, after an initial literature review, on trying to understand how human experts summarise time-series data. The main objectives of the Knowledge Acquisition (KA) activities have been [3, 11]:

1.   To determine the task model of summarisation

2.   To determine the types of knowledge required for the task model.

3.   To acquire all the required types of knowledge in detail.

The KA activities in the two domains (meteorology & gas turbine) have been different because the two domains differ in the following aspects:

1. Gas-turbine engineers do not currently write textual summaries of sensor readings, which makes corpus acquisition and expert observation difficult. On the other hand, in the domain of meteorology we have access to a large corpus of human-written forecasts.

2. The large amount of data in the gas-turbine domain meant that we had to spend a considerable amount of time developing tools for displaying data to experts in KA sessions. In the domain of meteorology the data sets are much smaller.

In SUMTIME, we have carried out the following KA activities tailored to the needs of the individual domains:

- Discussions with experts.

- Think-aloud sessions, in which experts were asked to 'think-aloud' as they examined and summarised a data set.

- Observation of experts as they wrote summaries in their workplace environment.

- Corpus analysis of a collection of time-series data sets and corresponding manual written summaries.

- Collaborative prototype development, in which we essentially built an initial system to an expert's specification, and then compared its output to manually written summaries of same data sets.

day	hour	wind dir	wind speed
2-3-01	6	W	10
2-3-01	9	W	11
2-3-01	12	W	13
2-3-01	15	WNW	14
2-3-01	18	WNW	15
2-3-01	21	WNW	11
3-3-01	0	NW	9
3-3-01	3	NW	8
3-3-01	6	WSW	9
3-3-01	9	SSW	11
3-3-01	12	SSW	21
3-3-01	15	SSW	22
3-3-01	18	SSW	24
3-3-01	21	SW	26
4-3-01	0	SW	27
4-3-01	3	SW	24
4-3-01	6	WSW	22
4-3-01	9	W	21
4-3-01	12	W	21
4-3-01	15	W	16
4-3-01	18	WSW	10
4-3-01	21	SSW	14
5-3-01	0	S	22

Table 1. Wind predictions from TAB model on 2-3-01

```
06-24 GMT, 02-Mar 2001:
WSW 10-14 RISING 14-18 AND VEERING WNW THIS
AFTERNOON, VEERING NW 8-12 THIS EVENING

00-24 GMT, 03-Mar 2001:
NW 8-12 BACKING SSW 18-22 IN THE MORNING THEN RISING 26-30 IN
THE EVENING

00-24 GMT, 04-Mar 2001:
SSW 26-30 VEERING W 18-22 IN THE MORNING, BACKING WSW
10-14 BY EVENING THEN BACKING S 22-26 LATE EVENING

5-Mar 2001 and 6-Mar 2001:
SSW 22-26 RISING 35-40 ON MONDAY, VEERING WSW 28-32
TUESDAY MORNING THEN BACKING SW 20-24 LATER

7-Mar 2001 and 8-Mar 2001:
SW 20-24 BACKING SE 32-38 WEDNESDAY AFTERNOON,
VEERING S-SW 20-24 EARLY ON THURSDAY
```

Figure 1. Wind texts from human-written forecast for 2-3-01

4.   Observations Made

A more complete description of the results of our knowledge acquisition activities is given in [14].   Here we just summarise some of the more important and interesting observations. We first describe the domain independent observations followed by domain dependent observations. Data sets in the Gas turbine domain are very large (nearly two hundred parameters sampled every second) and therefore for simplicity's sake we describe the domain independent observations with the help of example data set from the weather domain. We will focus on the particular task of producing textual summaries of wind speed and direction, in weather forecasts intended for offshore oilrigs.

Table 1 shows wind speed and wind direction predictions extracted from the 'TAB' model file produced by the numerical simulation on 2 March 2001,[2] and Figure 1 shows the text summaries produced by a human forecaster on 2 March 2001. This forecast is broken up into 5 forecast periods. The forecasts for the first three forecast periods (up to the end of 4 Mar) are based on the TAB model data shown in Table 1. The forecasts for the last two forecast periods (5 March to 8 March) are based on the less accurate MMO model, which we have not shown in this paper. Note that a complete forecast for an offshore oil rig would describe many other meteorological parameters, including wind at 50M altitude, visibility, waves, temperature, cloud cover, and precipitation.

---

[2] In fact the TAB file was extracted from a model built by a human forecaster from a numerical simulation; the forecaster used a graphical editor, which allowed him to interpolate and adjust the numbers produced by the numerical simulation.

4.1   Domain Independent Observations

4.1.1 Qualitative Overview

One of the most interesting observations in our KA sessions was that experts usually formed a qualitative overview of the underlying system as a whole before writing summaries. This overview is used to decide what to do about boundary cases or unusual situations. For example, if a forecaster sees an outlier in a data set, such as a N wind becoming NE for one time period and then reverting to N, he or she will use the qualitative overview to decide whether this is realistic and should be reported, or whether it is an artefact of the numerical simulation and should be ignored.

When asked about the role of an overview in writing the summaries the expert has replied that it's main role is to facilitate reasoning with the input data. This ability to reason with input data helps to draw inferences about the state of the underlying system. When included in the summaries, these inferences would be more useful to the end user than just the raw data. Details about our observations on qualitative overviews, and a 'two-stage' model for content determination based on these observations, are given in [15].

While inferring the overview, during a KA session, the expert focused entirely on domain reasoning as if he were solving a meteorological problem. He has ignored the communicative issues indicating that the creation of the overview is more like a problem solving activity than like a communicating one. The objective of this problem solving activity seems to be the determination of the overall state of the underlying system (gas turbine or atmosphere).

The above observation suggests that the task of overview creation is a knowledge-based activity, which can be studied in its own right as a task of building an expert system. In SUMTIME, we intend to scale down the problem and make it a component in a system SUMTIME-MOUSAM that we are currently building. SUMTIME-MOUSAM would act as a test bed for carrying out experiments with summarising weather data (initially) and gas turbine data (later). This is explained further in the Section 5.1.3 below.

We have observed overview formation by human experts in other domains as well, including the SUMTIME gas turbine domain and a previous project on generating personalised smoking-cessation letters [10].

4.1.2 Impact of User

Another fact that emerged from our knowledge acquisition efforts was that forecasters sometimes consider how users (rig staff) will use the forecast when deciding on its content (same with the gas turbine domain as well, where the personnel in charge of the particular turbine need to act based on the summaries and the summaries need to take this into consideration). Of course, anyone who has looked at weather forecasts, realises that the kind of information present in a forecast depends on the user; for example, oil rig forecasts include information about wind at 50m altitude which is not present in newspaper forecasts, because it is not of interest to the general public. However, forecasters may also adjust the detailed content of forecasts depending on user and task models.

For example, during one of our think-aloud sessions, where experts spoke their thoughts aloud while writing a forecast, the forecaster decided to use the phrase *19-24* to describe wind speed when the TAB file predicted a wind speed of 19kt. This is because the forecaster knew that even if the average wind speed in the period was 19kt, the actual speed was going to vary minute by minute and often be above 20kt, and he also knew that rig staff used different operational procedures (for example for docking supply boats) when the wind exceeded 20kt. Hence he decided to emphasise that the wind was likely at times to exceed 20kt by using a wind speed range of "19-24", instead of a range centred around 19kt, such as "17-21".

It is possible that the fact that the forecast in Figure 1 starts with WSW instead of W (which is what the input data in Table 1 suggests) is due to user factors. In particular, if the forecaster is unsure whether the wind will be coming from W or WSW, it probably makes sense for him to state the broadest variety of wind directions in the phrase (that is *WSW ..... veering WNW* instead of *W ..... veering WNW*), in order to warn rig staff that the wind might be WSW and they shouldn't count on it being W or WNW.

User needs also influence the level of detail of forecasts. For example, if the wind is less than 10kt, then the exact wind speed and direction usually have no impact on rig operations (with some exceptions, such as when a rig is flaring gas); this is one reason why many forecasters use generic phrases such as *less than 10* for light winds (Sect 4.2.1).

4.1.3 Data Reliability

One of the first observations we made is that forecasters do not treat the numbers in the TAB and MMO files as gospel. For example they may adjust the numbers based on their knowledge of local geographical effects which are not considered in the numerical simulation, such as the effect of peninsulas on wind speed at nearby off-shore sites. Forecasters may also adjust numbers based on their own experience; for example, the specification given to us by one of the forecasters for wind text production adjusted the wind speed in the TAB file using another parameter, lapse rate (a measure of the stability of the atmosphere), because the forecaster felt that this adjustment improved the accuracy of the prediction.

Perhaps more subtly, forecasters also made judgements about the reliability of the numbers, especially temporally. For example, it might be clear that a storm is going to move through an area, thus increasing wind speeds, and a forecaster might agree with the model's prediction of how high wind speeds will rise but feel less confident about the model's prediction of when this will happen, that is when the storm will actually reach the oil rig. Thus forecasts usually use relatively precise (given the 3-hour granularity of the TAB file) temporal terms such as *early afternoon*, but sometimes use less precise terms such as *later* or *for a time*. This can again be observed in Figure 1 where the forecast for 5 and 6 March uses vague terms such as *on Monday* and *later*.

In the gas turbine domain, the issue of data reliability may be either due to noise in data transmission or due to sensor failure.

4.2 Domain Dependent Observations

4.2.1 Forecaster Variations

One surprise to us was the degree of variation between individual forecasters. This included

- lexical variations: For example, some forecasters describe an increase in wind speed as *increasing*, whereas others use the term *rising*. Another example is that some forecasters always use a four knot range for wind speed, such as *12-16*, while others vary the size of the range depending on the circumstances. The forecaster who wrote the text in figure 1 for example, generally used four knot ranges but used some larger ranges (*35-40, 32-38*) in later forecast periods.

- content variations: For example, some forecasters use phrases such as *less than 10* for low wind speeds, without going into details, whereas others give detailed descriptions such as *2-6*. Another example is that when the wind is varying a lot, some forecasters report every change explicitly, while others use general terms such as *occasionally* or *mainly*.

Variations among individual forecasters are, in fact, one of the reasons why forecasting organisations are interested in computer text generation. For example forecaster variations means that an offshore oil rig could one day get a forecast predicting a wind speed of *less than 10* and the next day get a forecast predicting a wind speed of *2-6*, when the wind in fact is identical on both days. This could perhaps confuse oil rig staff if they did not realise the cause of the variation.

4.2.2 Algorithmic Issues

The above sections present non-numeric factors that influence the content of a forecast, such as qualitative overview, impact of user, data reliability, and forecaster variations. But what about the numbers themselves, what type of time-series analysis is best for producing summaries?

The comparison with the initial algorithm suggested by the forecasters themselves was particularly useful here. This algorithm essentially used a threshold model, where wind speed and direction were mentioned at the beginning of a forecast period and then whenever they changed by a threshold amount (typically 5 kt for speed and 22.5 degrees for direction, although the actual threshold amount depended on the wind speed). Corpus analysis and observation of forecasters as they worked suggested that

- A linear segmentation model [5,7] might be a better fit to what forecasters wrote than a threshold one.

- If wind speed or direction is changing slowly but consistently, this will often be reported even if the overall change is small.

- Human forecasters like to report wind direction and speed as changing at the same time, even if the model suggests that in fact the speed change happens a bit before or after the direction change.

The above behaviour would emerge from an algorithm, which was based on linear segmentation and tried to optimise a combination of the accuracy of the segmentation and the length of the text. The length optimisation would bias the algorithm towards reporting speed and direction changes as occurring at the same time.

4.2.3 Non-event Reporting

In the domain of gas turbines, the main task is reporting unexpected behaviour. One interesting observation here was that summaries are required to report a non-event – an event that should have occurred based on the state of affairs inferred from the input data, but never actually occurred. For example, if a controller attempts to increase fuel flow, but fuel flow does not change. This clearly indicates that the summarising system must be in a position to compute the state of the gas turbine based on the input data, and reason with that state to make predictions about the data. This once again points indirectly towards the need of an overview explained in 4.1.1.

5. Evaluation and Implementation

Although KA will continue, the focus of the project now includes testing the hypotheses about summarising time-series data, which emerged from our KA activities and which were (partially) described above. In particular, we are currently implementing a test-bed, which includes a core system, into which new modules can easily be inserted, and a testing framework that automatically runs the system with the new modules on corpus input data and compares the result against the corresponding manually written texts in the corpus. Since we are primarily interested in content issues, the comparison to corpus texts will be made on a conceptual level (using a conceptual mark-up scheme we have developed) as well as on a text level.

5.1 SUMTIME-MOUSAM

SUMTIME-MOUSAM (Figure 2) is a framework system that makes it easy to implement and evaluate new ideas for summarising weather data (initially) and gas turbine data (at a later stage). The framework consists of

- "Infrastructure" software for accessing data files, automatically comparing software output to human-written texts, regression testing of new software versions.

- An ontology which defines a conceptual level of representation of weather forecasts

- A corpus of human-written forecasts with their corresponding conceptual representations

- An initial system based on observations from KA, for generating conceptual representations and then forecast texts from data.

5.1.1 Data/Corpus

This component manages input data/corpus for the entire system. SUMTIME has collected a large corpus of weather data and its corresponding forecast texts from WNI Oceanroutes. Currently the size of the corpus is 500 (data set - forecast text pairs) and is growing as we receive data and its corresponding forecast text twice daily from WNI Oceanroutes. In the gas turbine domain, we have collected continuous one-month data with 250 (approx.) analog channels and 700 (approx.) digital channels sampled every second. SUMTIME-MOUSAM views the corpus data

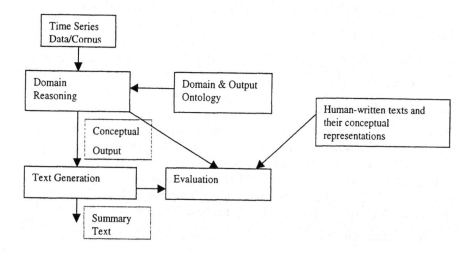

Figure 2. Architecture of SUMTIME-MOUSAM

as a set of 'projects', each project consisting of a set of input data sets and an output forecast text. Project stores the configuration information for a unique experiment carried out on SUMTIME-MOUSAM. An experiment here means the generation of a summary text (or conceptual representation of the summary) from a definite input data set by using one of the models we want to test.

5.1.2 Conceptual Representation

The output of the domain reasoning component is a conceptual representation, not text. A later module converts this conceptual representation to text. The conceptual representation will be defined in output ontology (see below), perhaps at a low level. This conceptual representation gives us at least two advantages:

- It allows us to separately evaluate content and linguistic expression. We also derive conceptual representations from our corpus of human generated summary, and we compare computer summaries to human summaries.

- This representation gives us a convenient way of coding the corpus texts, which facilitates machine learning exercises to be carried out on the corpus.

At the moment we have conceptual representation for wind text and weather text. We define a "conceptual level" of a wind forecast to consist of a tuple with the following elements

- Time
- Wind speed lower range
- Wind speed upper range
- Wind direction (in degrees)
- Modifiers (gusts, shower, steady-change, gradual-change)

5.1.2.1 Example

1) Forecast period 1 from 26Dec2000_15.prn

  50M: N 18-23 EASING 12-18 TONIGHT, GUSTS 40 IN SHOWERS

This is represented as 2 tuples

  (1500, 18, 23, 0, nil)

  (2100, 12, 18, 0, gusts+showers)

5.1.3 Domain Reasoning

This component is responsible for handling the domain reasoning to be performed on the data both while abstracting the numerical data into their conceptual representations and also while deriving new concepts from the input data. The domain reasoning referred to above could be a simple numerical computation such as computing total cloud cover from individual components of cloud, or a more complex inference such as determining the stability of an air mass.

5.1.4 Text Generation

This component is responsible for converting the output generated in the conceptual form into English text. Here the major issues are micro planning and lexical selection. As of today, this module is still not implemented. But like the domain reasoning, the SUMTIME-MOUSAM text generation module will be structured so that, new components can easily be inserted, and will have clear APIs.

5.1.5 Domain & Output Ontology

In SUMTIME, studies on corpus analysis and observations from KA sessions both suggest that the domain ontology, that is the specification of underlying concepts, underlying the overview may be quite different from the ontology underlying the actual output texts. The domain ontology includes concepts used by experts when reasoning about a domain (such as air masses or motivation), while the output ontology includes concepts useful for communicating information to the end user (such as wind speed, or longer life expectancy).

5.1.6 Output from the Initial Prototype

Figure 3 shows output from an initial prototype of SUMTIME-MOUSAM. Note that the text is more verbose than the human forecast text shown in Figure 1. We are currently working on improving the machine output based on comparisons with human-written texts.

```
06-24 GMT, 02-Mar 2001:
W 8-13, veering WNW in the mid-afternoon.

00-24 GMT, 03-Mar 2001:
WNW 8-13 soon NW 8-13, backing WSW in the early morning, then
SSW during the morning, becoming 18-23 around midday, veering
SW during the night, becoming 25-30 around midnight.

00-24 GMT, 04-Mar 2001:
SW 25-30, veering WSW in the early morning, then W 18-23
during the morning, becoming 8-13 in the early evening,
backing SSW during the night, then S 20-25 but increasing in
squally showers at times to 35 around midnight.
```

Figure 3. Wind texts from SUMTIME-MOUSAM for Data shown in Table 1

6. Summary and Future

An overall message emerging from the KA activities carried out so far in SUMTIME is that textual summaries are not just descriptions of the visual appearance of time-series data. Instead they are communicative artefacts in which the authors use their knowledge of the domain (overall weather situation, local weather variations, reliability of the data) and the user (especially typical user tasks and procedures) to craft short texts which will help users make decisions or perform tasks. And it is perhaps their incorporation of domain and user knowledge, which makes textual weather forecasts more valuable than a table or graph, as well as the fine control which text allows over exactly what information is and is not communicated. We plan to continue KA activities for eliciting more detailed knowledge about summarisation. SUMTIME-MOUSAM is being used to evaluate the observations from the KA. Subsequent stages of the project will include applying our time-series summarisation ideas to a new domain, and also hopefully performing a user-task evaluation of generated forecasts and gas turbine summaries, to see if they actually help real users perform real tasks.

Acknowledgements

Many thanks to our collaborators at WNI/Oceanroutes and Intelligent Applications, especially Dave Selway, Rob Milne, and Jon Aylett; this work would not be possible without them! This project is supported by the UK Engineering and Physical Sciences Research Council (EPSRC), under grant GR/M76881.

References

1. Boyd S (1998). TREND: a system for generating intelligent descriptions of time-series data. In *Proceedings of the IEEE International Conference on Intelligent Processing Systems (ICIPS-1998)*.

2. Goldberg, E; Driedger, N; and Kittredge, R (1994). Using Natural-Language Processing to Produce Weather Reports. *IEEE Expert* **9**:45-53.

3. Hayes-Roth, F., Waterman, D., and Lenat, D. (Eds) (1983). *Building Expert Systems.* Addison-Wesley.

4. Lidija Iordanskaja, Myunghee Kim, Richard Kitregde, Benoit Lavoie, and Alian Polguere. 1992. Generation of extended bilingual statistical reports. In *Proceedings of the 14th International Conference on Computational Linguistics (COLING-1992)*, Volume 3, pages 1019-1023.

5. Eammon Keogh (1997). A fast and robust method for pattern matching in time-series data. In *Proceedings of WUSS-97.*

6. Karen Kukich. (1983). Design and implementation of a knowledge-based report generator. In *Proceedings of the 21st Annual Meeting of the Association for Computational Linguistics (ACL-1983)*, pages 145-150.

7. Hunter, J and McIntosh, N (1999). Knowledge-Based event detection in complex time series data. *LNAI 1620*, pp. 271-280.

8. Igor Mel'cuk. (1988). *Dependency Syntax: Theory and Practice.* State University of New York Press, Albany, NY.

9. Reiter, E and Dale, R (2000). *Building Natural Language Generation Systems.* Cambridge University Press, 2000.

10. Reiter, E; Robertson, R; and Osman, L (2000). Knowledge Acquisition for Natural Language Generation. *Proceedings of the First International Conference on Natural Language Generation (INLG-2000)*, pages 217-224.

11. Scott,A; Clayton, J; and Gibson, E (1991). *A Practical Guide to Knowledge Acquisition.* Addison-Wesley

12. Shahar, Y and Cheng, C. (1999). Intelligent visualization and exploration of time-oriented clinical data. *Topics in Health Information Management*, 20:15-31.

13. Shahar, Y (1997). Framework for Knowledge-Based Temporal abstraction. *Artificial Intelligence* **90**:79-133.

14. Sripada, S, Reiter, E, Hunter, J and Yu, J. (2001). SUMTIME: Observation from KA for Weather Domain. Technical Report AUCS/TR0102. Dept. of Computing Science, University of Aberdeen.

15. Sripada, S, Reiter, E, Hunter, J and Yu, J. (2001). A Two-stage Model for Content Determination. In *Proceedings of ENLGW-2001 pp3-10.*

SESSION 5:

INTELLIGENT SYSTEMS

The Development of a Ramp Metering Strategy Based on Artificial Neural Networks

Mehdi Fallah Tafti, BSc, MSc, PhD

Transport Systems, WS Atkins Consultants Lt., Caradog House, Cleppa Park, Newport NP10 8UG, UK

Abstract

A microscopic simulation model, representing traffic behaviour in the vicinity of merges on motorways, was applied to produce a set of data representing traffic patterns in the merge area, ramp metering rates, and the corresponding vehicle journey times. The data were used to develop an Artificial Neural Network (ANN) model, which anticipates the average journey time of mainline vehicles that enter an upstream section during a 30s interval.

The ANN model was applied to develop an ANN based ramp metering strategy, which adjusts metering rates to maintain the average journey times of vehicles close to their desired or target value, and to reduce congestion. The mathematical form of the metering model is similar to feedback control strategies. The effectiveness of the ANN based ramp metering strategy is demonstrated using the simulation model to compare performance with that of other local ramp metering strategies. The ANN based metering strategy is shown to reduce the average journey time of the traffic stream, increase the vehicle throughput, and reduce congestion.

1. Introduction

Ramp metering is employed to improve the overall operation of the mainline of a motorway by controlling the entry of the vehicles from one or more ramps. Ramp metering techniques are usually based on signal control systems operating under predetermined algorithms and are assessed by the success in reducing congestion, and flow breakdown in the vicinity of merges.

Ramp metering strategies may be categorised as either local, which applies to a single ramp, or co-ordinated, which set up optimum control for a series of ramps. Local ramp metering strategies have progressed from non-traffic responsive strategies to feedforward traffic responsive, and then feedback traffic responsive strategies ([1], [2], [3], [4], [5],[6], and [7]).

Among these local strategies, the ALINEA strategy [7], which applies feedback philosophy and automatic control theory, has shown the best performance in robustness, and congestion handling, although this strategy still allows some congestion. Linear behaviour, local characteristics, and dependence on only one local traffic parameter, limits the success of feedback control systems such as ALINEA in preventing the onset of congestion, or eliminating that which occurs [8].

Artificial intelligence techniques such as fuzzy logic and Artificial Neural Networks (ANN) have been applied, as innovative approaches, to solve a range of problems in the field of traffic engineering (e.g. [8], [9], [10], [11], [12], [13], [14] [15], [16]) and to develop enhanced ramp metering strategies ([17], [18]). Zhang and Ritchie (1997) showed that the linear behaviour of the feedback control systems can be improved, using the ANNs, to develop non-linear gain factors in the feedback control systems [8].

One of the limitations, which can be attributed to the current feedback control systems, is the use of local traffic parameters such as occupancy or density as the measure of congestion. These parameters, when used as the measures of congestion, will not be available until congestion has reached the measurement section. These measures do not always represent the traffic pattern, in a long section of motorway, starting upstream of the merge, which contributes to the formation of congestion. A potential improvement in ramp metering strategies could follow from using the traffic parameters, which represent traffic patterns for a longer section of the merge area. For example, the average journey time of vehicles in a section starting upstream of the merge and extending downstream of the merge is one criterion, which could be used.

Using the future predicted values of traffic parameters instead of using their current values could also be helpful in predicting congestion. By anticipating potential congestion and reacting appropriately, the performance of a ramp metering strategy would be enhanced. ANNs could be used to provide the future predicted values of the average journey time of mainline traffic in the merge area, according to the current values of traffic parameters in this area. Any improvement in the performance of local ramp metering strategies would benefit the performance of well developed multiple ramp metering strategies such as hierarchical ramp metering strategies in which the strengths of both local and area-wide strategies are combined (e.g. [19] and [20]).

The process used to develop an enhanced ramp metering strategy follows:
-   assemble the data sets required for the development of an ANN model,
-   develop an ANN model which uses the traffic parameters of the motorway and the entry ramp to anticipate the average journey time of vehicles in the merge area,
-   devise an ANN based ramp metering strategy which compares the anticipated average journey time of vehicles to the target or desired value of the system to calculate the required metering rate for the next cycle, and
-   compare the performance of the developed control strategy with that of existing strategies.

Sufficient data for a range of conditions required to develop an appropriate ANN model are not easily available from site measurements under controlled conditions. A microscopic simulation model [21] was used to generate data for the development of the ANN model. The simulation model also provided a tool to evaluate the performance of the ANN model. This paper only deals with the last two steps of this process and a full description of the ANN model development is given elsewhere [22]. A brief description of the ANN model is provided in the following section.

2. An overview of the ANN model

The average journey time of the mainline vehicles that enter an upstream section, shown in Figure 1, along the distance L and during a 30s interval, was chosen as the output of the ANN model. The relationship, which was defined using the ANN technique, can be expressed in the following form:

$$Av\_Journt = f(Up\_Spd, Up\_Flow, Dn\_Spd, Dn\_Ocup, PHGVS, MetR) \qquad (1)$$

Where:

Av_Journt is the average journey time of the mainline vehicles that enter an upstream section along the distance of 2.1km during a 30s interval,

Up_Spd, Up_Flow are the average speed and flow of vehicles measured at an upstream detector location during the last 30s interval

Dn_Spd and Dn_Ocup are the average speed and occupancy of vehicles measured at a downstream detector location during the last 30s interval,

HGVs is the percentage of Heavy Good Vehicles measured at a downstream detector location during the last 30s interval, and

MetR is the metering rate during the last 30s interval.

The structure of the finally selected ANN model, including the model inputs, and the model output and the corresponding transform function are shown in Figure 2. As indicated in this Figure, the ANN structure has one hidden layer, which consists of two PEs.

3. The ANN based ramp metering strategy development

The relationship for calculating the required metering rate for the next cycle period was obtained through the following steps.

1) The average sensitivity ($Sens_c$) of model output (d_{Avjmt}) to each input variable including the metering rate (MetR) is available from the ANN model and represents the partial derivation of model output (d_{Avjmt}) with respect to this particular model input (d_{MetR}) or:

$$\frac{d_{Avjnt}}{d_{MetR}} = Sens_c \qquad (2)$$

2) On the basis that the metering rate for the next cycle should be selected so that the average journey time of vehicles reaches a target value, the left side of the above equation can be expanded to the following form:

$$\frac{(Opt_{Jmt} - Prd_{Jmt})}{(New_{MetR} - Prv_{MetR})} = Sens_c \qquad (3)$$

Where Prv_{MetR} is the metering rate during the last cycle period; New_{MetR} the metering rate for the next cycle period; Prd_{Jmt} the predicted average journey time of vehicles from the ANN model using the last 30s traffic data measurement; Opt_{Jmt} the target average journey time of vehicles along the same section; and $Sens_c$ the sensitivity of the output of the ANN model to the MetR in real world units.

3) Equation 3 can be rewritten for New_{MetR} as below:

$$New_{MetR} = Prv_{MetR} + \frac{1}{Sens_c} \times (Opt_{Jmt} - Prd_{Jmt}) \qquad (4)$$

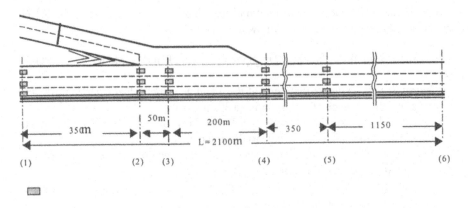

Fig. 1. Layout of merge section.

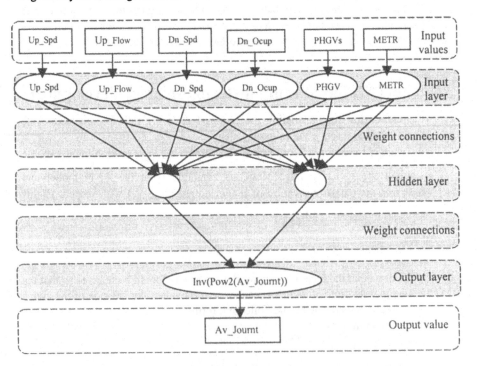

Fig. 2. The structure of the finally selected ANN model.

Equation 4 represents a simplified form of feedback controllers in which only the I-component of a PID (Proportional-Integral-Derivative) controller, is used. This approach is similarly used in the ALINEA strategy [7]. The main advantages of the controller developed in this study over the ALINEA strategy are:

- this strategy uses the future predicted value of the average journey time and therefore provides the opportunity for the system to react earlier, before serious congestion develops,
- the average journey time used in this strategy represents the traffic situation in a relatively long section of the motorway, starting from an upstream location and

extending to a section located downstream of the merge. Unlike the ALINEA strategy, which is only based on a local downstream occupancy, this model reacts to the changes in the traffic pattern in a longer road section, and

- the regulation or gain factor ($1/Sens_c$) in this strategy in contrast to the ALINEA strategy could be variable, as explained later in this section.

The value of Prd_{Jmt} in equation 4 can be calculated from the ANN model using detector data, measured during 30s intervals, as input data. The variation in the average journey time of vehicles predicted by the ANN model in consecutive cycles may lead to a sudden high variation in the metering rate in the consecutive cycles. The effect can be reduced using exponentially smoothed values of Prd_{Jmt}. This approach has been used in some traffic responsive strategies e.g. Demand - Capacity strategy and in the ALINEA strategy. In each cycle, the smoothed value of Prd_{Jmt} ($Smooth(Prd_{Jmt})$) can be obtained using the following equation:

$$Smooth(Prd_{Jmt}) = Smoothf \times Prd_{Jmt} + (1 - Smoothf) \times PrSmooth(Prd_{Jmt}) \qquad (5)$$

Where Smoothf is smoothing factor which is assumed to be 0.25 as is typical in the other strategies, and $PrSmooth(Prd_{Jmt})$ is the smoothed value of Prd_{Jmt} in the previous cycle.

The value of $Sens_c$ in the equation 4 can be calculated using one of the following approaches.

- The average sensitivity of the output of the ANN model to the MetR can be obtained from the ANN and equally used for all situations. The average sensitivity of the model to the MetR, using this approach, was computed to be 0.0038 (sec)/(veh/h).
- The sensitivity of the model output to each input variable can be calculated by the ANN for each individual input data set.

The second approach was considered to be more sensitive to the variation of traffic conditions in the merge area and was therefore adopted for this application. The value of $Sens_c$ is also related to the measurements of traffic data over 30s intervals, which could create high fluctuations in the computed metering rate. Thus the smoothed value of $Sens_c$ was applied in equation 4 using the following equation.

$$Smooth(Sens_c) = Smoothf \times Sens_c + (1 - smoothf) \times PrSmooth(Sens_c) \qquad (6)$$

Where $Smooth(Sens_c)$ is the smoothed value of $Sens_c$ and $PrSmooth(Sens_c)$ is the smoothed value of $Sens_c$ calculated in the previous cycle.

Substituting the parameters Prd_{Jmt} and $Sens_c$ with their smoothed values, equation 4 is rewritten in the following form:

$$New_{MetR} = Prv_{MetR} + \frac{1}{Smooth(Sens_c)} \times (Opt_{Jmt} - Smooth(Prd_{Jmt})) \qquad (7)$$

The parameter Opt_{Jmt} in the above equation is a critical parameter, which is site specific and should be determined for each site. The proposed method to calculate this parameter is described in the next section. The process, which is required to calculate the metering rate for the next cycle period, is summarised in the flowchart of Figure 3.

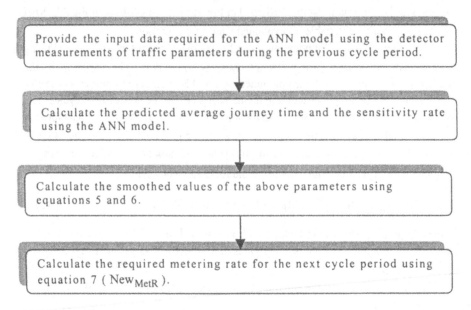

Fig. 3. The computation process to calculate the appropriate metering rate in the ANN based metering strategy.

4. Comparison of the performance of the ANN based metering strategy with other strategies

The performance of the developed ANN based metering strategy and the following strategies were compared against a benchmark for similar conditions in which no ramp metering strategy was in operation. The strategies were:

- *Fixed time strategy*, which is a non-traffic responsive strategy in which the signals operate on a fixed timing [23].
- *Variable fixed time strategy*, which is in an enhanced version of the above strategy. In this strategy, based on typical historical traffic patterns of merge area, variable predetermined timings are used [2].
- *Demand - Capacity strategy*, which is a feedforward traffic responsive strategy and reacts to traffic conditions upstream of the merge [4]. This strategy is based on measuring the demand upstream of the merge and comparing this demand with the capacity of bottleneck downstream of the merge.
- *Wootton-Jeffreys strategy*, which is a feedforward traffic responsive strategy similar to the Demand - Capacity strategy with differences in the method of calculating downstream capacity, signal timing, and use of the mainline speed in the control system [5].
- *ALINEA strategy*, which is a feedback control strategy [7]. This strategy adjusts the metering rate to keep the occupancy of the section downstream of the merge at a pre-specified level, called the desired or target occupancy.

4.1 Set up for the ramp metering strategies

It is essential that the comparison of strategies should be fair. Each ramp metering strategy has a series of parameters, which should be decided before its online implementation. There is at least one critical parameter, which is usually site specific, associated with each strategy. The other parameters necessary for the operation of each strategy tend to be less sensitive and can be applied equitably in different strategies. The simulation model was run several times for each strategy to determine an optimum value for the critical parameter of that strategy. This procedure ensured that as far as possible all strategies were subsequently compared on an equal basis i.e. the ANN strategy did not have an advantage by being judged on the basis of the application of the same simulation model used to develop it. The following approach was used for each strategy.

- In order to decide the boundaries within which the optimal value of the critical parameter should be sought, the results available from the application of each strategy in previously published studies were used.

- The simulation model was run with a sufficient range of critical values around the initial values. A typical demand profile, representing total traffic flow (motorway + ramp) during peak periods on British merge sections was applied. The total traffic flows in different runs were randomly varied by 15% around the mean values with the same random numbers for different strategies. The percentage of HGVs was assumed as 15%, and the proportion of the entry ramp traffic was assumed as 25%. These values are again the typical average values, which were observed in a study conducted by Hounsell et al. (1992) for British merge sections [24]. The merge layout applied in the development of the ANN model was used for the simulation model.

- Starting from a low value, an increase in the value of the critical parameter of each strategy would usually be accompanied by an increase in the downstream throughput of vehicles. Beyond a threshold, further increase in the value of critical parameter would not change the total throughput noticeably. Traffic flow downstream of the merge would become unstable and fluctuations in the downstream throughput would appear. The average downstream throughput resulting from different runs was plotted, against the values assumed for the critical parameter, to identify the desirable or target value for each strategy. As an example, the plots for the ALINEA strategy and ANN based strategy are shown in Figure 4. The value for the critical parameter of each strategy in which the total downstream throughput of vehicles approaches its maximum threshold was selected as the target value for the critical parameter of each strategy. This approach ensured that reduction in congestion and journey time of vehicles has not been achieved at the expense of reducing the total throughput of vehicles.

- In this study a period of 30s was assumed for the cycle time of all of the deployed strategies except the Wootton-Jeffreys strategy in which a fixed cycle time is not applicable. This cycle period is consistent with most of the traffic responsive strategies chosen for comparison. An amber aspect of 3s was assumed between green and red aspects in all of the strategies.

- The queue override system of each ramp metering strategy was deactivated in order to eliminate any bias, which it may have on the representation of the real performance of different strategies.

a- ALINEA strategy

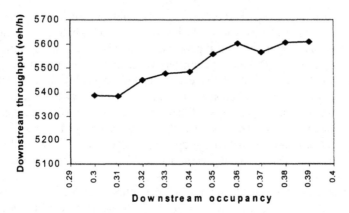

b- ANN based strategy

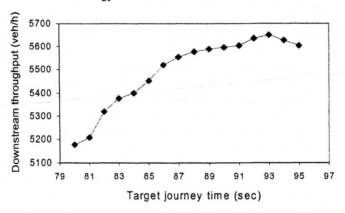

Fig. 4. The variation of the downstream throughput with the assumed values for the critical parameter of the ALINEA strategy and the ANN based strategy.

The following values were assumed for the parameters of each strategy, including the critical parameter.

* Fixed time strategy: Green time (G) = 15s (critical parameter), Amber time (A) = 3s, and Red time (R) = 12s.
* Variable fixed time strategy:
  green time for congestion building up period (critical parameter) = 18s, A = 3s, and R = 9s,
  green time for congestion period (critical parameter) = 12s, A = 3s, and R = 15s, and
  green time for congestion recovery period (critical parameter) = 18s, A = 3s, and R = 9s.
* Wootton–Jeffreys strategy: max. downstream throughput = 6300 veh/h, min. green time = 7s, min. R = 7s, and max. R = 40s, and upstream speed threshold for the outside lane = 45 km/h.

❖ Demand – Capacity strategy: downstream capacity (critical parameter) = 6600 veh/h, lower downstream speed threshold = 35 km/h, upper downstream speed threshold = 50 km/h, and smoothing factor = 0.25.
❖ ALINEA strategy: downstream desired occupancy (critical parameter) = 0.35, gain parameter = 70 veh/h, smoothing factor = 0.25.
❖ ANN based strategy: desired average journey time of vehicles (critical parameter) = 91s, smoothing factor = 0.25.

4.2 Basis for evaluation

The following method was used to provide a comprehensive set of results.
- Three demand flow profiles representing the variation of traffic flow during peak periods, were applied for each strategy.
- Three proportions of the entry ramp traffic were assumed i.e. 15, 22.5, and 30 %.
- Four different seed numbers were generated and applied for each strategy.
- The percentage of HGVs was assumed to be 15% in all runs.

A total of 36 runs (3 different flow profiles × 3 different proportions of the entry ramp traffic × 4 different seed numbers) were performed for each strategy and for similar situation with no ramp metering. The following measures were obtained from these runs and were used to compare the performance of different strategies, including the ANN based metering strategy, with the non-metered operating situation.

• *The average journey time of the entry ramp traffic, the mainline traffic, and the overall traffic.* The average journey time of the entry ramp vehicles was measured from their generation point to cross section 6, shown in Figure 1, over a 2.3km length. The average journey time of the mainline traffic was measured along the section between cross sections 1 and 6 over a 2.1km length. The measured average journey time of vehicles was then divided over the length of the corresponding measurement section in order to be expressed per kilometre unit.
• *The throughput of the mainline traffic, the entry ramp traffic, and the overall traffic,* were all measured at cross section 6 in Figure 1.
• *The duration of congestion,* was defined as the proportion of time in which the speed of the mainline vehicles downstream of the merge had been less than 85 km/h. This threshold was used as the boundary between congested and uncongested situations, and was applied in a similar study [25].
• *The duration of severe congestion,* was defined as the proportion of time for which the speed of the mainline vehicles recorded downstream of the merge dropped below 50 km/h. The location of speed measurement was at the cross section 4 indicated in Figure 1.

The change in the average performance of each strategy in comparison to the non-metering situation, using the above measures, was then calculated. Figures 5 to 7 show the results of the comparison.

4.3 Discussion of the results

4.3.1 *The average journey time of vehicles*

The change in the average journey time of the mainline traffic, the entry ramp traffic, and the overall traffic in comparison to the non-metering situation, for each ramp metering strategy, is shown in Figure 5. The results indicate that all the ramp metering strategies would decrease the average journey time of the mainline (see Figure 5-a) but at the expense of an increase to the average journey time of the entry ramp traffic (see Figure 5-b). All the strategies achieved a net decrease in the journey time of the overall traffic (see Figure 5-c). The ANN based strategy and the ALINEA strategy showed the best performance with the ANN based strategy reducing the journey time of all traffic by 2.5% more than the ALINEA strategy.

4.3.2   *The throughput of traffic*

The change in the throughput, resulting from deploying different strategies, in comparison to the non-metering situation, is shown in Figure 6. All the strategies increased the throughput of the mainline traffic (see Figure 6-a) and decreased the throughput of the entry ramp traffic (see Figure 6-b). However, there was a net gain in the throughput of the overall traffic in all of the situations in which a metering strategy was used (see Figure 6-c). The ANN based strategy provided the highest gain in the throughput of traffic and was better than the ALINEA strategy by 1.8%.

4.3.3   *Congestion duration*

The change in the congestion duration of different strategies in comparison to the non-metering situation, using two different speed thresholds, is shown in Figure 7. All the reviewed strategies showed a reduction in the duration of congestion in comparison to the non-metering situation. The ANN based strategy and the ALINEA strategy provided the most improved performance and the ANN strategy was better than the ALINEA strategy by 19% (see Figure 7-a).

For the speed threshold of 50 km/h, all of the deployed strategies showed an overall reduction in severe congestion duration in comparison with the non-metering situation. As indicated in Figure 7-b, the ANN based strategy demonstrated a better performance than the other strategies and was better than the ALINEA strategy by 43%.

5.   Conclusions

Overall, it can be concluded that the ANN based strategy, developed in this study, provided better performance than the other strategies. The ALINEA strategy was the second best in this comparison. The ALINEA strategy and the ANN based strategy are both simplified versions of linear feedback controllers and have a similar structure. The superior performance of the ANN based strategy could be attributed to the use of the future predicted average journey time of traffic and also a variable gain factor $(1/\text{Sens}_c)$.

The gain factor $(1/\text{Sens}_c)$ used in the ANN based strategy is sensitive to the variation of the average journey time. This parameter should also be sensitive to the degree of error in the operation of the metering system ($\text{Error} = \text{Opt}_{\text{Jrmt}} - \text{Pr d}_{\text{Jrmt}}$). A further improvement in this strategy would be the development of an ANN model, which predicts the required gain factor for the control system in each cycle according to the predicted average journey time of traffic and the degree of error in the operation of the metering system.

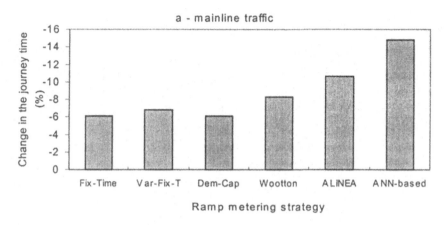

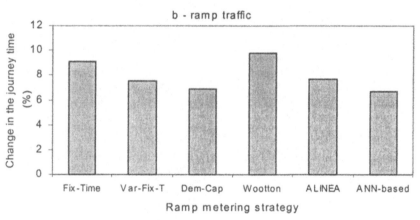

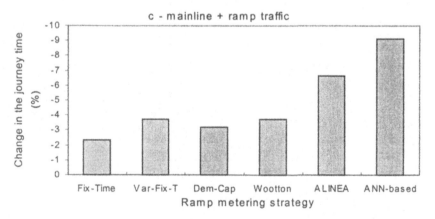

Fig. 5. Change in the average journey time in comparison with the non-metering situation, using different metering strategies.

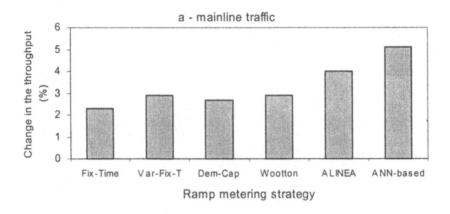

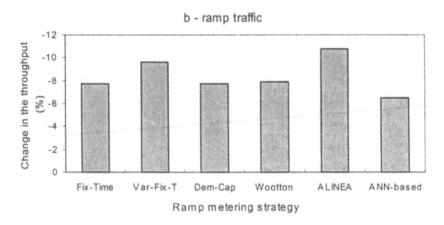

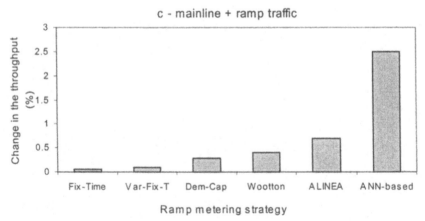

Fig. 6. Change in the throughput in comparison with the non-metering situation, using different metering strategies.

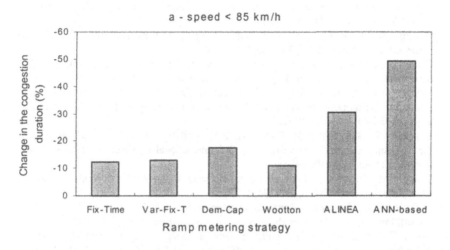

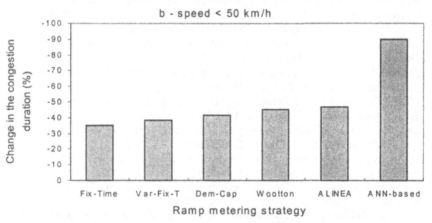

Fig. 7. Change in the congestion duration in comparison with the non-metering situation, using different metering strategies.

Acknowledgements

The author would like to express his gratitude to Dr John G Hunt, his PhD supervisor at the School of Engineering, Cardiff University, the Ministry of Higher Education of Iran for providing the financial support of this study, and the support of his current employer WS Atkins Consultants Ltd.

References

1. Wattleworth JA, Berry DS. Peak period control of a freeway system - Some theoretical investigations. Highway Research Record 89, 1-25, 1965.
2. May AD. Optimization techniques applied to improving freeway operations. Transportation Research Record 495, 75-91, 1974.

3. Koble,T., Adams TA, et al. Control strategies in response to freeway incidents. FHWA, Report No. FHWA/RD-80/005, 1980.
4. Wilshire R, Black R, et al. ITE Traffic Control Systems Handbook. Institute of Transportation Engineers, Washington, D.C. , 1985.
5. Owens D, Schofield MJ. Access control on the M6 motorway: Evaluation of Britain's first ramp metering scheme. Traffic Engineering and Control 29 (12), 616-623, 1988.
6. Papageorgiou M, Blosseville J.M, Haj-Salem H. Modelling and real-time control of Boulevard Peripherique in Paris: Part2: coordinated on-ramp metering. Transportation Research-B 24(5), 361-370, 1990.
7. Haj-Salem H, Blosselville JM, Papageorgiou M. ALINEA- A local feedback control law for on-ramp metering: A real life study. 3rd International Conference on Road Traffic Control, London, 194-198, 1990.
8. Zhang HM, Ritchie SG. Freeway Ramp Metering Using Artificial Neural Networks. Transportation Research C 5, 273-286, 1997.
9. Faghri A, Hua, J. Roadway seasonal classification using Neural Networks. Proc. of Int. Conf. on Artf. Intel. Appl. in Transportation Engineering, San Buenaventura, CA, 1992.
10. Xiong Y, Schneider JB. Transportation network design using a Cumulative Genetic Algorithm and a Neural Network. Transportation Research Record 1364, pp. 37-44, 1992.
11. Dougherty MS, et al. The use of Neural Networks to recognize and predict traffic congestion. Traffic Engineering and Control 34(6), 311-314, 1993.
12. Ritchie SG, Cheu RL. Simulation of freeway incident detection using Artificial Neural Networks. Transportation Research C 1, 203-217, 1993.
13. Hunt JG, Lyons GD. Modelling dual carriageway lane changing using Neural Networks. Transportation Research C 2(4), 231-245, 1994.
14. Chang GL, Su, CC. Predicting intersection queue with neural network models. Transportation Research C 13(3), 175-191, 1995.
15. Ledoux C. An urban traffic control system integrating Neural Networks. IEE Conf. on Road Traffic Monitoring and Control, Conf. Publ. No. 422, 1996.
16. Dia, H, Rose, G. Development and evaluation of Neural Network freeway incident detection models using field data. Transportation Research C 5(5), 313-331, 1997.
17. Chen OJ, May, A., 1990. Freeway ramp control using Fuzzy Set Theory for Inexact Reasoning. Transportation Research A 24 (1), 15-25.
18. Taylor C, Meldrum D. Simulation testing of a Fuzzy Neural Ramp metering algorithm. Washington State Department of Transportation, Olympia, Washington, 1995.
19. Hotz, A, Much T. A distributed hierarchical system architecture for advanced traffic management systems and advanced traffic information systems. Proceedings of the Second Annual Meeting of IVHS America , 1992.
20. Chen OJ, Hotz AF, Ben-Akiva ME. Development and evaluation of a dynamic ramp metering control model. The Proceedings of 8th International Federation of the Automatic Control (IFAC) Symposium on Transportation Systems, Chania, Greece, 1997.
21. Fallah-Tafti, M. The application of simulation and Neural Networks to develop a ramp metering strategy, PhD Dissertation, The University of Wales - Cardiff, UK, 1999.
22. Fallah-Tafti, M. The application of Artificial Neural Networks to anticipate the average journey time of traffic in the vicinity of merges, Journal of Knowledge Based Systems, 14(3-4), pp. 203-212, Elsevier, , 2001.
23. Wattleworth JA, Berry DS. Peak period control of a freeway system - Some theoretical investigations. Highway Research Record 89, 1-25, 1965.
24. Hounsell NB, Barnard SR, McDonald M. An investigation of flow breakdown and merge capacity on motorways. Transport Research Laboratory, Berkshire , 1992.
25. Harwood NH. An assessment of ramp metering strategies using SISTM. Transport Research Laboratory, Project Report 36(12), 1993.

When Eigenfaces are Combined with Wavelets

Bai Li & Yihui Liu
School of Computer Science & Information Technology
The University of Nottingham
Nottingham NG8 1BB
bai@cs.nott.ac.uk, yxl@cs.nott.ac.uk

Abstract. The paper presents a novel and interesting combination of wavelet techniques and eigenfaces to extract features for face recognition. Eigenfaces reduce the dimensions of face vectors whilst wavelets reveal information that is unavailable in the original image. Extensive experiments have been conducted to test the new approach on the ORL face database, using a radial basis function neural network classifier. The results of the experiments are encouraging and the new approach is a step forward in face recognition.

1 Introduction

Face recognition can be applied to a wide variety of problems, ranging from security to virtual reality systems, as such it has attracted the attention of many researchers worldwide. It is extraordinary how quickly, accurately and effortlessly humans can tell one face from another, irrespective of illumination or pose, for a computer to do the same reasonably well a considerable amount of research and development needs to be done.

A face recognition system must be able to deal with many variations due to different lighting conditions, poses, and alien objects present in face images. Feature selection is fundamental to the success of face recognition. In this paper we are concerned with mathematical transform-based feature selection methods, such as the eigenface method and wavelets [1][3][4].

The purpose of the eigenface approach is to reduce the dimensions of face vectors. This is achieved by the using Principal Component Analysis [2] to find a set of new basis vectors (the eigenfaces). Each face vector is then represented by its projection coefficients onto the eigenfaces. As the number of eigenfaces is much smaller than the number of pixels of an image, the dimensions of face vectors are thus reduced. The dimensions can be reduced further by discarding those eigenfaces corresponding to smaller eigen values, as the coefficients computed at these eigenfaces have small variance across the whole training set therefore are not important for discriminating different classes. However experiments show that the eigenface method is not robust in dealing with variations in lighting conditions. To overcome this problem we resort to wavelets decomposition to break images into approximations and details of different levels of scales and work on the approximations images.

2 Wavelets

Wavelets are mathematical basis functions that are used to represent other functions. Wavelets have many advantages over other mathematical transforms such as Fourier transform. Functions with discontinuities and functions with sharp spikes usually take substantially fewer wavelet basis functions than sine-cosine functions to achieve a comparable approximation. This results in a number of useful applications of wavelets such as data compression, noise removal, and detecting features in images.

In wavelet multi-resolution analysis of images, an image is filtered and decomposed into several approximations and details components and each component is then studied separately. Corresponding to these components are scaling functions and wavelets. Scaling functions compute the average of the images whilst wavelets compute the details of the images. The average (smooth) signal plus the details at level j combine into a multi-resolution of the signal at the finer level j+1. Because of repeated scaling that produces them, wavelets decompose a signal into details at all scales. More specifically, the original image is split into approximation A_i and details D_{hi}, D_{vi}, D_{di} at level i, in horizontal, vertical, and diagonal directions. The approximations and details are constructed from their coefficients at each level of the decomposition. The coefficients of the jth level approximation of the image are put through both a low-pass and a high-pass row filter and the results are column downsampled (only even indexed columns are kept). The downsampled results are put through both a low-pass and a high-pass column filter and the results are row downsampled (only even indexed rows are kept). The resulting four matrices are the coefficients of the j+1 level approximation and details of the image in horizontal, vertical and diagonal directions. In Figure 1, the images in the first two rows are 6 approximations images obtained by a 6-level wavelet decomposition and the images in the last row are the details images at level 1.

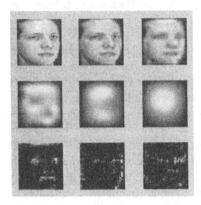

Figure 1. Example approximations and details images

In the experiments described in this paper, a face image is represented by its 3 approximations images. The vector representation of the 3 approximations images are concatenated to produce a new vector and it is this new vector that is used to construct the eigenfaces. Once the eigenfaces are created each face image is projected onto the eigenfaces and the set of coefficients obtained is the final representation of the face image.

3 Radial Basis Function Network

A radial basis function network has two layers of neurons. Each neuron in the hidden layer implements the radial basis transfer function and is created for an input vector. The weight vectors connecting the input to the hidden layer neurons are the transpose of the input matrix. Input to a hidden layer neuron is therefore the distance between the input vector and the weight vector connecting to the hidden layer neuron. If the distance is small the output of the hidden layer neuron is 1 otherwise 0. The second layer neurons implement the liner transfer function and the weight vectors connecting to the second layer neurons are calculated using the input (so radial basis function outputs) and the target matrices.

The output of a neural network normally only indicates the class of the input, but not exactly which object of the class the input is nearest to in distance. This is not a problem as in face recognition what we are only interested is the class of an input image. However it will be a bonus if a neural network can tell us at the same time not only the class of an image but also its nearest image in the training set. This is possible by using a hierarchical radial basis function network, an example of which is shown in Figure 2 below. The first level of the hierarchy classifies the input into a class, once this is done, the second level of the hierarchy finds the nearest object of the input in the training set. Each sub-network again has again two layers, the first layer of which implements the normal radial basis transfer function and the second layer implements the competitive transfer function. The second-layer weights are set to the matrix made of target vectors. 40 such sub-networks are created for the 40 classes. The sub-network is trained using the training faces of the class. For example if there are 5 training faces per class, input to the network could be a 200x5 matrix representing 5 face vectors of 200 dimensions, and the output of the network could be a 5x5matrix assigning each of the 5 training faces to one of the 5 classes.

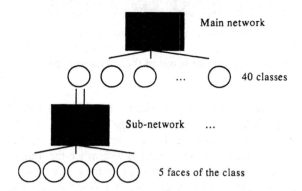

Figure 2. Hierarchical radial basis function network

4 Experiments

In this section we refer to our method of combining eigenfaces and wavelets as the eigen-wavelet method and we this method with the original eigenface method for face recognition. The face database used in the comparison is the ORL face database and the classifier used is a radial basis function network. The database contains 400 face images acquired of 40 individuals (10 images per individual) over many years, with various lighting conditions, facial expressions, and poses. Experiments are conducted using 6, 5, 4, 3 training faces per person respectively. During these experiments the dimensions of the face vectors are reduced gradually in an attempt to find the dimension that gives the best classification performance. The spread parameter of the radial basis function network is also allowed to vary to see how it affects the performance.

6/4 Experiment
In this experiment 6 training faces per class are used as training faces and 4 faces per class are used for testing. There are altogether 240 (6*40) training faces so 240 eigenfaces are constructed. Images are then represented as 240 dimensional vectors after projection onto the eigenfaces. The eigen-wavelet method performs 100% accurately when the dimension is 70 onwards and network spread 7. The best performance of the original eigenface method is 99.38% when the dimension is between 130 and 150 and network spread 3. An interesting example of 6/4 experiment is shown in Figure 3 below. The 6 training faces all wear glasses, but 2 of the 4 test faces wear no glasses still the network correctly identified them.

a) 6 training faces

b) 4 correctly classified test faces

Figure 3. Example result of the 6/4 experiment

5/5 Experiment
In this experiment there are 200 (5x40) training face vectors and 200 test face vectors. Once the eigenfaces are created each image is projected onto the eigenfaces and the 200 projection coefficients are the final representation of the image. The best performance of the eigen-wavelet method is 98% when the dimension is about 140 and network spread 17. The best performance of the original eigenface method is 97.50% when the dimension is between 130 and 150 and network spread 3. The eigen-wavelet method is robust in dealing with variations in poses and alien objects. 5 training faces and 5 test faces of a class are shown in Figure 4 below. The faces in

the last row are the outputs from the radial basis function network to the input faces in the middle row. As can be see that the third test face wears no glasses, but is identified by the network as the second training face wearing glasses.

5 training faces of a class   5 test faces of the class

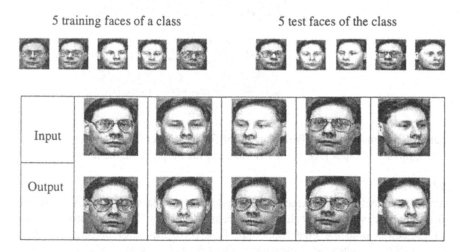

Figure 4. Example result of the 5/5 experiment. Each of the 5 columns contains an input face to the neural network classifier and the output from the network.

With the 5/5 experiment the eigen-wavelet method has three classification errors. It is not surprising that these errors occurred as the faces involved in each error look quite similar as can be seen in Figure 5 below.

5 training faces per person   5 test faces per person

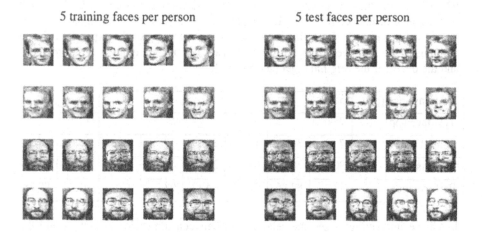

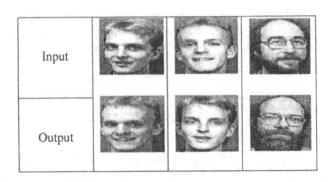

Figure 5. The only mis-classified faces of the 5/5 experiment. Each of the 3 columns contains an input face to the network and the output from the network.

4/6 Experiment

In this experiment 4 training faces and 6 test faces per class are used. As there are 160 training faces in total, each image is represented as a 160 dimensional vector after projection onto the eigenfaces. The best performance of the eigen-wavelet method is 97.08% when the dimension is about 60 and network spread 11. The best performance of the original eigenface method is 94.17% when the dimension is 30 and network spread 3.

3/7 Experiment

In this experiment 3 training faces per class are used for training data and 7 faces per person are used for testing. A total of 120 training and 280 testing vectors of 120 dimensions are obtained. The best performance of the eigen-wavelet method is 92.86% when the dimension is about 90 and network spread 7. The best performance of the original eigenface method is 87.86% when the dimension is 30 and network spread 3. The following table gives a summary of the experiments. The columns of the last three rows are split into two, one for the eigen-wavelet method, and the other for the original eigenface method.

Training face (pp)	3		4		5		6	
Test face (pp)	7		6		5		4	
Spread	7	3	11	3	17	3	8	3
Dimension	90	30	60	30	140	130	70	130
Performance	92.86	87.86	97.08	94.17	98	97.5	100	99.38

It will be interesting to see the relationship between dimension reduction and the performance of the network. The following figure shows the network performance against the number of dimensions. The horizontal axis represents the number of dimensions of feature vectors and the vertical axis represents the number of classification errors.

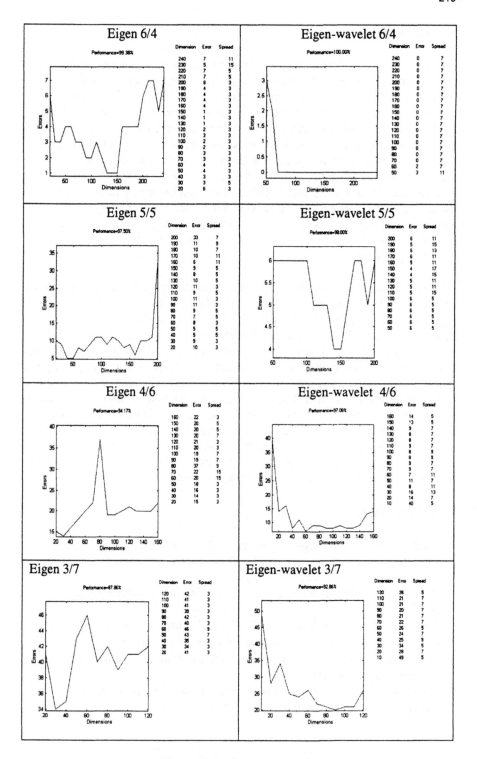

Figure 6. Performance graph

5 Discussion

From the results described in the previous section, it is clear that the eigen-wavelet method is more reliable and consistent in performance than the original eigenface method, able to give a more than 90% performance even when there are only three training faces for each class. The contrast in performance between the eigen-wavelet and the original eigenface method gets bigger as the number of training faces decreases, the eigen-wavelet method deals with smaller number of training faces better. It is interesting to note that in the Eigen 4/6 experiment the number of errors peaks at dimension 80 and goes down afterwards. As the dimensions correspond to the eigenfaces in decreasing order of their corresponding eigen values, it suggests that some eigenfaces, regardless the magnitudes of their corresponding eigen values, have adverse effects on performance. This may be because the projections of different classes onto these eigenfaces coincide, which we should bear in mind in dimension reduction.

Our experiments results compare favorably with those by Tolba et al [5]. They achieved a 99.5% recognition rate on the ORL face database using 5 training faces per person. However, the high accuracy is achieved by combining multi-classifiers, the Learning Vector Quantization and Radial Basis Function network, as well as by multi-training of these classifiers. The classifiers are trained with the original training data as a whole first, then again with two groups of data by splitting the original training set. One group contains previously correctly identified data and one previously wrongly identified. Thereafter, a front-end classifier has to be trained on the outputs of the two classifiers to produce the final classification. Both their two classifiers assign some faces into classes that bear little resemblance to the faces. Tolba also uses the whole image of intensity values as input to the classifiers. The size of the images affects the performance significantly. Images have to be pre-processed to reduce their sizes before training and recognition take place.

6 References

1. Belhumeur P. et al, Eigen Faces vs. Fisherfaces: Recognition Using Class Specific Linear Projection, IEEE Transactions on Pattern Analysis and Machine Intelligence, Vol. 19, July 1997.
2. Jolliffe, I.T., Principal Component Analysis. Springer-Verlag; New York; 1986.
3. Pentland, et al, View-Based and Modular Eigenspaces for Face Recognition Proceedings of Computer Vision and Pattern Recognition, 1994.
4. Turk, M. and Pentland, A., Eigenfaces for Recognition, Journal of Cognitive Neuroscience, 3 (1), 1991.
5. Combined Classifiers for Invariant Face Recognition, Tolba A. S. and Anu-Rezq A. N., 0-7695-0446-9/99, IEEE, 1999.

AUTHOR INDEX